NO MAN IS JUST A NUMBER

NO MAN IS JUST A NUMBER

TWENTY YEARS ON THE FORCE:

A TRUE STORY OF LIFE, DEATH, CHANGE AND TRANSFORMATION.

ROBERT CLARKE

Copyright © 2025 Robert Clarke

The moral right of the author has been asserted.

Apart from any fair dealing for the purposes of research or private study, or criticism or review, as permitted under the Copyright, Designs and Patents Act 1988, this publication may only be reproduced, stored or transmitted, in any form or by any means, with the prior permission in writing of the publishers, or in the case of reprographic reproduction in accordance with the terms of licences issued by the Copyright Licensing Agency. Enquiries concerning reproduction outside those terms should be sent to the publishers.

The manufacturer's authorised representative in the EU for product safety is Authorised Rep Compliance Ltd, 71 Lower Baggot Street, Dublin D02 P593 Ireland (www.arccompliance.com)

Troubador Publishing Ltd
Unit E2 Airfield Business Park,
Harrison Road, Market Harborough,
Leicestershire. LE16 7UL
Tel: 0116 2792299
Email: books@troubador.co.uk
Web: www.troubador.co.uk

ISBN 978 1836282 594

British Library Cataloguing in Publication Data.
A catalogue record for this book is available from the British Library.

Printed and bound in Great Britain by 4edge Limited
Typeset in 12pt Minion Pro by Troubador Publishing Ltd, Leicester, UK

For my children.
May you always know how much I love and cherish you.

AUTHOR'S NOTE

This is a book about true crime and policing, and within its pages are a life's work, all of which I am incredibly proud of. It is also a book simply about humanness, and I hope it will inspire and uplift readers worldwide.

We all have a tale to tell, and I feel incredibly privileged to be able to tell mine. During this process I have been forced to unbox and revisit chapters of my life which I had previously locked away. It has been a truly cathartic experience, and I am relieved. For years I had suppressed my experiences and, once out of uniform, almost denied my policing background entirely. Authenticity is of upmost importance to me, so when I began to write, I knew an approximation of the truth wouldn't suffice; I had to show parts of myself I had never previously considered or dared to explore. For the privacy of my family, my former colleagues, the victims I worked to assist and the criminals I worked to inhibit, all names in this book have been changed. Everything else is completely true, written as I experienced it. The stories within paint only one picture of British policing – it was my life, through my lens.

For twenty years I served, beginning in the early nineties, and it has never been truer that policing is not the job it once was. Over the two decades my career spanned, society changed dramatically, and so did the police force. This book is not designed to glamourise the police, but it is not designed to kick them in the teeth either.

The police provide a vital and necessary role in our society, and the job is unrelenting. The range of work that police officers engage in is *staggering, as you will go on to read. Each day presents its own unique and complex challenges and whilst, personally, I always appreciated the uncertainty of not knowing what lay around the corner, it does reveal the need for a broader political and social discourse regarding the role of our police services, and where they should focus their limited resources. The police are the final line of enquiry and with nobody else to pass on the responsibility to, they are the expected solution to any problem. In contrast, without oversimplifying their roles, other emergency services typically work within well-defined parameters. If something is on fire or upside down, call the fire brigade. If someone isn't breathing or requires more than a simple bandage, call an ambulance. The bulk of other issues fall squarely on the shoulders of the police.*

The difficulty and darkness police officers are exposed to is enough to make anybody lose faith in humanity. Being a police officer feels like constantly swimming against a strong tide. For example, as soon as one drug dealer is put under lock and key, another one pops up. It has the potential to be incredibly disheartening, so having a 'save the world' mentally will ruin any officer, because the reality is that they won't. Eventually I learnt to be satisfied with one small impact at a time. And then the next small ripple, and the one after that. But many going into the police won't know that, and the mental preparation for even one day on the job is insufficient.

Presently there is not much respect for, or trust in the police, which is understandable given the number of high-profile cases which have recently shed a wholly negative light on the institution. The good examples have always been few and far between and the press rarely talk about the heroes – I suppose they are too busy talking about dereliction of duty, corruption, sexual assault, racism, and abuse of power. Police officers who lack professional and personal integrity, and who are themselves criminal in their behaviour, directly endanger the life of those who are sincere in their intentions. Every officer holds the police's reputation in their hands with everything they do, and any negligent or criminal acts committed by a police officer, regardless of geographical location, impacts on them all.

During my training I think any of us would have been hard pushed to be kicked off, which supports recent concerns about the calibre of police recruits. Lax vetting procedures and failures to carry out comprehensive screening has regrettably contributed to a culture of misogyny, homophobia and racism in some, if not all, UK police forces. Whilst I am sure such issues were present during my time in uniform, they were on a much lesser scale, and I was largely blind to them. Most of the officers that I worked with carried out their duty diligently and with respect for everybody they encountered, criminal, or not.

Within the British police force, cases of misconduct are now at an all-time high. As are instances of sexual assault, coercive behaviour and domestic abuse carried out by serving police officers. The picture painted is a harrowing one, and there are hundreds and thousands of victims; mostly women suffering at the hands of men.

Many unfit for the job still wear a uniform that should signify protection and safety.

We need a policing system which is honest, reliable, fair and just. A perfectly reasonable ask, theoretically. But the current system is intricately riddled with problems. Not least, all the bad apples and complete lack of accountability.

The question that is often levelled at me is, 'would you do it again?' My answer has always been the same. Yes. I would go back and do it all again. But if I was twenty years old now, I would not consider it for one minute. The world in which we live in has changed. Society is far more brittle and fractured now than it was in the 1990s and 2000s. Violence appears an immediate option for most in any given situation and people are generally less tolerant. There is little respect for the police, but I cannot say that they really deserve a great deal.

The police are only able to carry out their job only by the consent of the public, but the behaviour of many uniformed officers has led to such mistrust in the institution that in many cases that consent is withdrawn. There is an issue around how current society perceives authority, and it must be questioned whether some police officers should hold the position of authority that they do. The police may be armed with the uniform, a taser, and a baton, but the public are armed now with more knowledge, mobile phones and a justified prejudice. The current state of the system is failing, and I hope that over the coming years we see some much-needed reform. Without adequate funding and support for such an essential component of our societal infrastructure, we risk poor outcomes for the very communities the police force are designed to serve and protect.

1

We came around the corner as the last of the four shots was fired.

As both officers lowered their weapons slowly, my eyes were drawn to the mammoth heap of a man lying on the ground, outside a row of houses on a typical terraced street. The initial call to the police was from the female victim of a domestic dispute. During which, her partner had rampaged through their home in a frenzy, destroying everything he could get his hands on. He had assaulted her, before leaving the property, giving her chance to make the distress call. Without delay, an officer was dispatched and whilst inside taking the victim's statement, the suspect returned to the address. He fired a shotgun through the front window and immediately the stakes were raised.

It had been a notably scorching early summer's day in the early 2000s. The air was filled with the smell of burning charcoal and barbequed meat, and even at eight o'clock in the evening the temperature was still twenty degrees. On nights like that there was a certain energy to the atmosphere. A buzz: created by increased numbers of people outside, enjoying the fine weather, and typically consuming more alcohol than is advised. On nights like that we could expect to be as busy as a chip shop at teatime, and it was the anticipation that something would go off at any minute which fuelled my adrenaline.

Not wanting to miss out on the action, and because the team needed extra hands, I had offered to come in two hours early for my night shift, starting at seven in the evening instead of nine. After pacing around at the front door for a while, I left the house at half-five, to arrive at the Tactical Firearms Unit (TFU) at quarter past six.

Standard police units cover a specific division or borough, whereas the more specialist teams such as the dog handlers, traffic, tactical aid, and firearms are a force-wide resource. We had been bumbling about for an hour or so when the call came over the force-wide radio.

'*Any X-ray Foxtrot available? There is an officer needing assistance at 61 Horseshoe Avenue.*' X-ray Foxtrot was the code for firearms assistance.

'*This is X-ray Foxtrot 9678. We are on our way.*'

We always kept our communications on the radio as succinct as possible, to avoid unnecessarily blocking the airwaves. I then tuned into my other radio which offered a direct line into the operator, to get some further details.

'*The suspect is a white male, six foot nine inches and weighing approximately twenty-five stone. He has fired two shots through the front window of the property and is currently trying to gain entry.*'

For reference, the description of the suspect painted him as being of a similar size and stature to heavyweight boxer Tyson Fury, wielding a shotgun.

The officer inside the property and the already-wounded victim were trying to barricade the smashed window, to prevent the suspect from appearing in the living room. I can't say I was overly concerned at the prospect of dealing with the situation that had been described. Arguably I was quite enthused. It was an opportunity to exercise my abilities and do the job I had trained so intensely for.

We were a few miles away and I expected it would only be matter of minutes before we arrived on the scene. I was confident that if they were able to keep him from entering the property, the situation would soon be over, without anybody getting hurt.

My partner for the evening was Graham, and to put it mildly, I was less than fond of him. The main reason being that it was so glaringly obvious to me he was in the job for the all the wrong reasons. He was a charlatan, only in it for the kit and the kudos without any real desire to want to help people.

Nevertheless, he assured me he knew the area well as he lived locally, so there would be no need for me to navigate. Excellent. Not having to keep my eye on a map allowed me time to get better prepared. Hopping into the back of the car I unlocked the gun box and prepared both machine guns, slinging mine across my body. We were already each carrying a handgun in a holster on our leg that was always ready with a loaded magazine, and a bullet in the breach.

Despite his initial insistence that he knew exactly where he was going, my driver somehow managed to take a few wrong turns. Due to our initial proximity to the incident, we should have been first on the scene, but his incompetence meant we were the third police vehicle to arrive.

The first two crews had arrived and as the suspect stood outside the property, they had positioned themselves in an L-shape around him. It was a configuration we used often to ensure there was never any blue-on-blue, meaning no officer was in the direct firing line of another. They then issued a challenge to the suspect.

'ARMED POLICE! PUT THE WEAPON DOWN!'

He disregarded their instruction and instead turned to point the shotgun directly in the face of one of my colleagues. Showing no sign he was going to comply, in a second he then turned to brandish his weapon in the face of another one of my colleagues. Both officers fired two shots each.

We drove right up to the scene and jumping out of the car, I radioed for an ambulance. As I got my hands on the suspect, he began writhing around on the floor trying to resist me, despite nursing four bullet wounds. After I had cuffed him, I shouted to the others to check they were okay. Graham was still sitting at the wheel of the car, his door not yet open. Once the suspect had stopped trying to fight, I propped him up against the red-brick wall of the house and shouted to Graham to grab our trauma kit, and to get off his arse to come and help administer first aid. As I crouched down next to the suspect, I began to scan the scene, mainly to establish whether he was on his own, and if there was any more potential risk. The area was cordoned off, and nosey neighbours were ushered back inside their homes, where they sat and surveyed from their windows instead. The ambulance arrived but unfortunately not in enough time. Shot and handcuffed, our suspect died right there on the pavement.

Beyond that point it all felt surreal. I watched as the parade of senior officers arrived on the scene, and the body was taken away. It was a momentous thing to have happened, for the police to execute someone in the street, but I could hear the world carrying on in the background, as though it hadn't happened at all. There was chatter in the air, and traffic was still going by on the nearby roads.

In an open area the sound of gunshot can be quite insignificant as it dissipates into the sky, but even the other residents on the street had barely reacted to what they had witnessed. In comparison to those who had issued the fatal shots, I had hardly been involved, but I was still trying to process the events of such a brief moment in time, and just how impactive they were. My colleagues had both just faced down the barrel of a loaded weapon and had decided in that moment to take someone else's life, to preserve their own and that of others.

It was a decision that, as a team, we had to make regularly, and one that had such potential to influence and alter the course of life. It was easy, therefore, for me to imagine the shock they were in, as they processed what had happened before the detectives turned up to take their statements. Their actions were completely justified, and with no subsequent press speculation, and I suspect no form of professional counselling, within a matter of days the officers involved were back on duty.

It was not an unusual day for me, but it sticks out in my mind as a real sliding doors moment. Graham had stalled, I believe purposely taking wrong turns to delay our arrival and therefore avoid being in the thick of the conflict. I have often wondered since, that if we had been the first on scene, would I have issued the fatal shot? Or would the situation have panned out completely differently?

Irrespective of the permission we had to use our weapons, when carrying a gun as a police officer it should always be considered a tool of last resort. Everybody has a tipping point, a line to cross in terms of how they respond to a challenging situation, and throughout my career I did everything I could to remain as far away from that line; to give the person in front of me the opportunity to avoid any harm coming to anybody. Usually, I found that my mouth and quickness of mind were my best weapon, and that most situations *could* be defused.

I would rather have punched someone, run them over, or issued one good hit with a baton, than have had to shoot. A part of me always felt if I had to discharge my weapon, I had partially failed in my role.

Each challenging situation that arose for me as an armed officer presented a threshold of risk. A seesaw of safety: mine, the suspects, and that of any third parties present. Clearly there were some situations that went well beyond the tipping point immediately, but otherwise it was a balance of probability, and if the limit was met, I would have to shoot. Then after shooting, the outcome was in the lap of the Gods. We were taught 'shoot to stop', but in doing that we were instructed to aim for the biggest part of the body, the chest. Given all the vital organs that are found there, being shot in the chest leaves a very high likelihood of death.

It is an incredibly subjective judgement that an individual officer must make. One which they will have to forensically analyse and detail after the fact, for someone else who couldn't possibly comprehend the situation, to try and piece together, or pull apart.

The weight of the decisions taken by armed officers are that of judge, jury, and executioner, but I don't recall anybody ever speaking to me about the severity of that responsibility. *'Rather be tried by twelve than carried by six',* was the saying amongst my peers. I would have always preferred my day in court to explain my actions, than risk not being around at all.

Beyond that job, it was only a matter of weeks before a similar situation unfolded, but it was my turn in the firing line. We had been called to attend a nightclub where the bouncer had reported a dark figure pointing a crossbow at him from across the street, before walking off into the night. We got a description of the suspect and began our manhunt.

I wasn't wholly convinced to begin with that it was a legitimate report, so took it with a pinch of salt. The description of events seemed quite obscure, and it wasn't uncommon for false reports to be made to the police, to try and draw resources away from something else that might have been going on.

We crawled the streets slowly, discussing how we might approach the situation when, and indeed if, we apprehended the individual in question. There wasn't too much to consider as we always worked within standard operating procedures and had a reliance on our training and our teammates. Fortunately, I hadn't been paired up with Graham on this occasion, but with a lad called Dan. Dan was more than competent. A brilliant officer and a brilliant shot.

After the initial communication, a further message came over the radio from the operator.

'X-ray Foxtrot 9678, we have received more information that suggests the suspect has been spotted outside the community centre on Church Street.'

I glanced at Dan who was looking back at me, his eyebrows raised.

'Great,' he sighed.

We couldn't have been heading into a more hostile environment.

The community centre was used mostly as a youth club, in an area notorious for gang violence. It was an area where pretty much everybody was involved one way or another in some sort of criminal activity, and even the youngest of children were taught to hate the police. There was nowhere worse for us to have been.

We arrived outside the venue and as we exited the car, there was uncertainty in the darkness that surrounded us. When one sense is diminished, the others become heightened, so with our vision somewhat impaired I could feel and hear more around me. We had to be incredibly wary and completely alert to the potential of imminent danger at any moment.

An individual matching the vague description we had been given was stood in the doorway. It was dark outside, and the lights were on in the community centre, which meant he appeared to us as nothing more than an ominous, backlit figure, but there was no mistaking the clearly loaded and rather substantial crossbow in his hands. We approached him on foot, and with my handgun drawn I shouted, *'Armed police! Put the weapon on the floor and your hands on your head!'* It was a challenge I issued almost daily at that time of my life.

Ironically, I didn't consider the lad holding the weapon my biggest threat. It was the other dozen young lads who had appeared behind him that posed the greater problem. Being in that area was so dangerous, and the mere fact that we were police officers antagonised them. Even if none of them were in that moment carrying a firearm, they could quickly get on the phone to someone who was. We couldn't afford to hang around. The situation had to be handled quickly, so the decision-making had to be dynamic.

The suspect had taken a step forward which meant we could see him more clearly. His facial expression was vacant, but there was a distinct sense of menace about him. He raised the weapon from his side and aimed it directly at us. Shouting louder, I offered him another opportunity to surrender.

'ARMED POLICE! PUT THE WEAPON ON THE FLOOR AND YOUR HANDS ON YOUR HEAD!'

Failing again to adhere to the instruction I had given, the corners of his mouth had begun to turn up slightly into a smile. It was at that point my training would dictate I put a bullet in him. But, with others stood behind him, there were layers upon layers of considerations beyond whether I just shot him or not. My mind was racing.

I had to consider how much of his body was in my direct line of sight. Where should I aim? The leg? The body? The head? If I shot him, where would he fall? What if I shot him and it went through him into someone else? If I shot him and missed, as unlikely as that would be, then he would certainly shoot me. If I shot him, could I trigger the crossbow to go off? Could anybody end up seriously injured or dead?

We were required to make so many decisions, dozens each second.

Our handguns had something called, 'trigger safety,' which allowed us to apply some pressure to the trigger before the gun would fire, and I had used all the available slack the trigger safety afforded me. Another fraction of a millimetre and the gun would certainly go off. I was convinced I was going to have to shoot him, and my mind was racing as I considered what would happen beyond that point.

If I shot him, I would have to then try and administer first aid. Dan would have to radio it in and secure the crossbow, along with securing our own vehicle which was heavily laden with weapons. The shooting would occur in front of his friends and acquaintances who would then likely try and mob us. My expectation for the situation was not good. The whole scenario had attracted some attention, from those in the club but also from passers-by on the street.

I couldn't take the shot. There were too many people around. Too much risk.

Dan started to pace backwards to the car, not lowering his weapon for a second. He didn't need to say anything, I knew exactly what he was doing. The Range Rover we were in that evening had ballistic plating so I knew the plan was to bring the car forwards so that we could remain on aim, but stand behind the doors to offer ourselves some protection. He drove up to the community centre, as close as he could get, and once he stopped, not lowering my handgun even an inch I ran forward and swung open the passenger door. The ballistic sheet dropped out the bottom which meant as I offered up the threat of my weapon with outstretched arms around the door, the rest of my body was protected from head to toe.

Usually in those situations, due to the extent of the armoury we had, we would start to get compliance through dominance. Some of the suspect's associates had started to back off and he had lowered his weapon slightly, meaning instead of pointing at me it was directed more towards the car. Time seemed to freeze as we waited for a resolve to the situation. He stepped out of the doorway onto the pavement and lowering the crossbow completely to his side, he started to swagger away, as though he hadn't just been engaged in a stand-off with armed police and didn't have a care in the world.

With the crossbow down at his side the risk of it accidentally going off was much less, and there was nobody behind him who could get injured, but I couldn't very well shoot him in the back. We had to change tactic. We jumped back in the car and let him get a few paces under his belt. Mounting a grass verge, Dan revved up behind him as fast as he dared. I waited for the opportune moment before releasing my passenger door and letting it fly open, knocking the suspect to the ground. I jumped straight out to arrest the crossbow-brandishing thug, who unsurprisingly did not want to go quietly.

We couldn't tell at the time, but later learnt that the crossbow in question had been adapted. The weight of the draw had been increased to alter the power at which it fired and the report on the weapon, produced by the ballistics expert, emphasised just how lucky we were. The extent of the modification would have meant that if he had fired at us, it would have easily been able to go through the armour-plated glass of the car, through both of us and out the other side of the vehicle. By all accounts, Dan and I had been incredibly lucky to come away unscathed.

I had the right to shoot him, and there is no doubt in my mind that to have taken that action would have been completely justifiable, but in that area there would have been serious political ramifications had it all gone wrong. I could have taken the shot with complete accuracy, so whilst I stopped to consider it, there is no way I would ever have missed. As it happened, I made the right choice in the right moment, which was always imperative as a police officer, particularly when so much of the job involved making split-second decisions, often based on incomplete sets of data.

2

I was not always an effective decision maker. In my youth I was quite the opposite, in fact. A bit like a butterfly, wherever the wind blew me, that was where I was going. So much so, that I don't remember actively deciding that I even wanted to be a police officer. It seemed more to just happen to me, through alignment in circumstances and chance.

In the year of 1995 I was twenty-one years old, and in the absence of recruitment agencies and job-search websites, was totally reliant on word of mouth or local advertisements to secure paid work. The free paper that came through the door to my parents' house was often a great source of musings. I had been accepted on a six-month placement with Eurocamp in France, but before I was due to depart for a summer of fun, I threw my hat in the ring for a couple of roles that promised a steadier term of employment upon my return. Not thinking too much of it, one of the applications I sent off was for the role of a local police constable.

The train pulled away to take me to Dover, and as though I was some sort of child evacuee, my mum ran down the platform, waving me off with tears in her eyes. I was able to go home up to three times during my placement, but I only made the journey back once, around twelve weeks in.

The timing of my return couldn't have been more convenient as my arrival was only one day after a letter from the local constabulary.

'Dear Mr Clarke,

Regarding your interest in the role of police constable, we are pleased to inform you that your initial application has been successful, and we will be considering you further during our recruitment process.

Enclosed are some forms for your completion. Please return these to us in due course...'

Before returning to my summer fun of organising games of football, and making water slides, I completed the almighty pile of requested documentation and again without a great deal of thought, sent them back in the post.

When I returned home from France mid-September I still had no real clue what my next endeavour would be and I wasn't remotely concerned about it, but waiting for me at home was another letter from the local police force which confirmed my success to the next stage of application. I was requested to send an up-to-date curriculum vitae, two hundred words describing myself, and an explanation as to why I wanted to be a police officer. My answers were clearly good enough and I was subsequently invited to interview.

Given my carefree attitude and lack of real direction, my list of previous positions was quite extensive and included some time working in a men's clothing boutique, along with the odd bit of catalogue modelling. What that meant was, for a man of my age I had quite a bit of decent clobber in my wardrobe, so was safe in the knowledge that I would be suitably well dressed when I attended the local police headquarters for the final stage of consideration. On the day of the interview, I opted to wear a well-fitted two-piece suit, completing my outfit with a woollen trench coat and leather briefcase. I can't imagine what the briefcase would have contained outside of my wallet, complete with bus fare, and maybe some sandwiches for the journey home.

As most people are in their early twenties, I was completely devoid of any real self-awareness, so I paid no attention at all to my surroundings whilst I sat waiting for my name to be called. I am certain that if I had, I would have realised that I was not much like the other hopeful candidates on that day. They were likely all far more streetwise than I was, and probably all thinking the same thing, which was, *'Who is that idiot?'* and *'Why does that idiot have a briefcase?'*

My name was called from the interview room, so I entered and sat down. A stern, clean-shaven, uniformed officer sat across the desk from me. A few feet behind him, sat on a chair in the corner of the room was a thick-set woman with tightly curled brown hair, an obvious battle axe. I had not been in the seat for any longer than three seconds before she stood up to address me.

'Mr Clarke. Kindly take yourself and your salesman's attitude and get out of this room.'

She had spoken with such heartless conviction that I didn't know what to think, or how to respond, so without question I stood up and walked out. Back out in the small corridor I contemplated whether that was it, if I had already been deemed unsuitable. But surely not, I had not even opened my mouth to speak. Instead, I considered it could have been a test, to see how I would respond to direct orders. Thirty seconds or so passed before I heard footsteps from within the room, and then the door swung open. It was the uniformed officer.

'CLARKE!' he bellowed from the doorway, not realising how close in proximity I was.

Once seated again the questions began. As I had spent some time working in a pub, I was able to offer good examples of my experience in managing conflict, or drunks at least. My character references were helpful too as I had previously volunteered on summer sports camps for children with physical and mental disabilities. The interviewing officer seemed impressed by my commitment to such an initiative, and the genuine care I expressed.

Upon leaving I felt it had gone well overall, but beyond the journey home I didn't think any more about it. I had several irons in different fires and was so blasé about everything that I would have gladly turned my hand to something else had the role not materialised. Christmas was approaching and whilst I was out browsing for gifts the week after I decided to get a tattoo. I had checked previously, and as long as it wasn't anything that would be considered offensive, I was quite within my rights to permanently mark myself. In keeping with the fashion of the time, I opted for a tribal band around my bicep, before returning home on the bus with my arm neatly wrapped in clingfilm. Along with the disapproving glare of my father at the sight of my new body art, there was another letter waiting for me. I had been successful at interview and was asked to attend the final stage of the recruitment process, the physical exam.

Just a few days later I arrived at the force training school with hordes of other aspiring recruits to be put through our paces. Sport had always been important to me. I was incredibly fast and lean so expected to find the entire day easy, which I did. Sit-ups and press-ups between running drills were no concern, and a handful of us were tapped on the shoulder before the exercises finished. The instructors were clearly already satisfied that we met the criteria and we were marched away from the hall where the physical assessment was taking place. We lined up outside a small office.

One by one, we were called in to see the force doctor. He cupped my balls and asked me to cough and that was it; the final action before I was formally accepted into the police.

It was the April of 1996 when I arrived at police training college on a Sunday afternoon, ahead of an early start on the Monday morning. We were shown to our accommodation and issued with an induction schedule for the upcoming weeks.

As I stood that evening being measured for my uniform, I was still not entirely convinced that I really wanted the job.

The first week of training saw us learning essential and relevant parts of criminal law. We were introduced to the kit we would receive, such as handcuffs and a baton, and given training on how we were supposed to use them.

The second week saw the beginning of our self-defence lessons.

We were lined up in the gymnasium when we were first confronted by Mickey, our trainer. Weighing at least eighteen stone and built like a rugby player, he first appeared as nothing more than a nasty, aggressive, lump of a man, and if his appearance alone didn't dictate that he was probably incredibly handy in a fight, he also immediately made us aware that he was an integral part of the British Police Wrestling team. The message that we should watch what we said and did whilst in his sessions was received loud and clear.

We were learning how to gain compliance, to enable us to handcuff a difficult detainee, when he asked for a volunteer. The mid-nineties were still very much a time of inequality within the police, so his request was only directed at the male population of our group. I suspect even if a woman had volunteered, he wouldn't have considered them, he wanted a man to fight with.

A broad smile appeared on his face as I began to raise my hand. I may have been slightly taller than he was, but he was not far off twice my weight and was certainly twice my width.

'Fantastic,' he uttered, his eyes gleaming with the excitement of getting to gently brutalise some of the fresh meat.

'What's your name, son?'

'Robert Clarke, Sir.'

'Right, Clarkey boy! Lie face down on that mat!' he spoke enthusiastically as he pointed down to the floor. I obliged his request.

'Now, I want you to tap the mat when you start to feel the pressure, okay?'

'Yes Sir.'

He twisted my arm and began to pull it up my back. I was quite supple, which made it quite an easy thing to withstand, and after a few seconds had passed he was clearly dissatisfied that I had not yet proven his abilities.

'Are you okay, Clarkey?!' he demanded, glancing down at me and up again at the audience of my colleagues who were waiting in anticipation.

With some light humour I responded nervously.

'Yes Sir. Have you started yet?'

I could see some of the onlookers begin to shake their heads slowly.

'It's a good job I like a flexible one!' he laughed.

Just as the words finished leaving his mouth, he applied all the remaining pressure he could to my arm, grabbed the scruff of my neck and slung me headfirst across the floor to the other end of the gym. All that could be heard was the squeaking of my trainers as I made my slow stop to a halt. Brushing myself off as I got up, I then made my way sheepishly back to my place in the line. I felt a little embarrassed but not as embarrassed as he clearly was that I had failed to submit to him, but he laughed it off and recommenced the session.

From that day on he picked on me quite a bit during training, but he was by no means a bully. It became a bit of a standing joke beyond that day that he didn't need anybody to willingly volunteer for any demonstration. He would always just exclaim gladly, *'Come on up here, Clarkey!',* and I would be his guinea pig for the session. I came to learn why he seemed so hacked off with having to teach loads of newbies the basics, and that was because he had been reluctantly taken off active duty after someone had embedded a rake into the back of his head during an arrest.

Around the midway point of our training, we were afforded a week off. Most recruits returned home but another lad, Anthony, and I, agreed we should make the most of the last opportunity we would likely have for absolute freedom. That was, before being actual police officers whose role would be to model good behaviour and uphold the law. Without any plan, we threw a tent in the back of his car and set off driving. Before I knew it, we were heading over the Dartford Bridge on the way to Dover, to board a ferry to France. We arrived at the ferry terminal in the evening to find we had missed the final sailing for the day, so had to wait until the following morning to continue our travels. It wasn't the best start to our adventure but wanting to make the best of every moment we had, we pitched our tent in a nearby field and trotted off into the local town of Folkstone. I cannot account for the sophistication of Folkstone nowadays, but when we arrived in the mid-nineties, it was nothing more than a one-street town. There was a corner shop, a chippy, a small nightclub, and a pub. It was nine o'clock when we began our evening where any self-respecting pair of young men would, in the pub, but I don't think either of us were really prepared for what we walked into.

After collecting our drinks from the bar and sitting for a few minutes at a table, it became apparent there were all sorts of shenanigans going on in the central hub of what we first considered to be a sleepy little town. In the far-right corner from the door, a banquet table had been set out with packets of mouldy sandwiches, and glasses of salt water. The challenge was, anybody who filled a bucket with puke, through eating and drinking what was laid out on display, would win free drinks for the night. You might consider that nobody in their right mind would engage in such a contest. However, in what was a disgusting but equally entertaining sight to behold, a group of men were gathered round the table eating the sandwiches, drinking the saltwater, and then putting their fingers down their throat to try and encourage severe vomiting. Had any of them been successful and filled an entire bucket full of puke, their victory wouldn't have entitled them to top-shelf spirits or decent cask ales. They would have been allowed only to drink from a pre-determined selection of bottled lager and alcopops. It didn't make any sense but was a mildly amusing sight.

On top of the large U-shaped bar was another ongoing game, appropriately dubbed 'Flaming Arse Dance'. People were invited to get up onto the bar, drop their trousers and underwear and put a length of toilet roll between their bum cheeks, with ninety-five per cent of it trailing behind like a tail. The toilet roll was then treated like a fuse and lit at the far end. The aim of the game was to run from one end of the bar to the other, pants around ankles, all while toilet paper burned its way very quickly up towards one's arse crack. Anybody who made it successfully to the far end of the bar, without having their arse cheeks burnt, would be the lucky recipient of a free drink. Whilst I would have preferred to not have been confronted with quite so much male genitalia as I supped my pint, to this day, it was undoubtedly the funniest thing I have ever seen in a pub.

With a few pints down us and enough entertainment to see us through, we agreed to go to the nightclub which was just a few doors down. We entered, two trainee police officers, feeling lean and mean off the back of our training and obviously not from the local area. We were both donning short, military style haircuts and confidently stood out like a pair of sore thumbs. I assume because of our obvious differences to the local bachelors, the likes of whom regularly enjoyed such capers as 'Flaming Arse Dance', a few young ladies took notice of us, and before long we began dancing with them. I noticed a few lads lurking on the outskirts of the dancefloor, clearly disgruntled that some practical foreigners had come along and impeded their chances with the women. Innocently I gestured that they should come and join us.

My gesture was clearly misinterpreted as before I knew it, they flew on to the dancefloor and one of them immediately landed a punch straight on my nose. Before I had any time to compose myself, I turned around to see Anthony rushing my opponent with a dozen windmill punches. The bouncer arrived swiftly, and with my original attacker looking the one far worse for wear, he threw Anthony and I out onto the street. As soon as our feet hit the pavement we began running as fast as we could, back to our tent.

'What the hell happened then?' I panted as we slowed down on the approach to the field.

'You bloody offered him out for a fight!' my friend replied, before clearing his throat of blood and mucus, and spitting it out on the floor, as he bent over still trying to catch his breath.

'I was inviting him to come and join in the dancing!'

'Well, you clearly weren't his type,' he chuckled, looking down at his hands. He was wearing quite a few big rings, all of which had chunks of someone else's skin underneath them. We slept off the excitement of our evening in the tent, before setting off the next morning to France. I don't remember too much more of our trip as all we really did was drink, but I suspect we never made it any further than Calais.

When we returned to training college the week after, I still had a faint bruise on my face to serve as a memento of our experience. I didn't know it at the time, but outside of the highly sanitised version we practised in training, that fight was probably the most realistic exposure I had to what real policing would be like.

There was a parade square on our campus, a similar size to two football pitches, and once weekly throughout training we had to march. This was in part to prepare us for the final parade, but also it taught us discipline, how to work together, and how to respond to the orders of a superior officer without any question.

Our drill sergeant looked like a circus ringmaster; a large, barrel-chested man with an incredibly impressive moustache. He wore a slashed peak on his cap so we could hardly see his eyes and as though we were in the military, when we marched, he shouted the commands of 'left' and 'right' over, and over, in time with our footsteps. Anybody who marched out of time was ordered into a dustbin which he had placed on the perimeter of the square. Every minute or so for the remainder of the session they then had to jump up, lifting open the lid of the dustbin, and shout *'I AM RUBBISH!',* before disappearing back inside the bin.

My training concluded with our passing out parade. I had received my uniform and sworn on the bible to serve the Queen, and the following Monday was due to start my new role as a police constable.

My first day on the job consisted of the usual housekeeping you would expect. There were three of us that had been newly assigned to that station, and we were traipsed across three floors of the old Victorian building, being introduced to the various departments. There had been a tragic incident which occurred locally back in the 1960s, causing at least two dozen deaths which meant rather uniquely, the basement of the station had been fitted out as a morgue, which was where we headed to finish off the tour. As we proceeded to the cold and eerie subterranean level, we were joined by two other officers, at which point I realised that taking probationers down to the morgue was likely somewhat of a team initiation, to give us a bit of the heebie-jeebies. We arrived and were immediately faced with a full wall of fridges for body storage. Big metal doors with large metal trays that slid out from within, ten across and four deep. Then the lights went out, and the three of us froze. Just as the splutters and giggles started from our mentors, they were switched back on again. Hilarious. I assumed that was it in terms of practical jokes.

'*So, who's going in first?*' asked one of the officers, gesturing to the fridges.

It was in that moment I was pleased not to have been the only one from my intake posted to that station, so not the only one who could be subject to mild torment.

We all shuffled nervously but as the silence grew, we started to understand he was being deadly serious. I edged back slightly, as did one other probationer, leaving one very unfortunate new colleague of mine, Shaun, stood front and centre.

Slapping him on the back, they opened one of the doors, slid out the tray and reluctantly he got into position.

'*Don't worry mate. It's just for a minute and we won't shut the door completely...*' one of them said.

Shaun was pushed into the fridges and after just a moment another voice that I didn't recognise came from inside.

'*Cold in here, isn't it?*'

What followed from Shaun was an almighty yelp, and a frantic attempt to get out of the fridge as fast as he possibly could.

We weren't aware at the time, but the morgue was practically disused, only ever serving its intended purpose if the hospital morgue got too full and needed an overflow. The rest of the time it acted as more of an elaborate storage system for the rest of the station. Prior to us arriving down there, another officer, an ally to the prank, had hopped into one of the fridges. Once Shaun was in position, he had reached over and put his hand on his leg as he opened his mouth to speak into the darkness. Understandably, Shaun was a bit shaken and remained practically silent for the remainder of the day. It was not the sort of thing that would likely occur nowadays, and if it did would be dressed up simply as 'banter', but outside the surface humour it certainly felt like an act of bullying. It was an opportunity for the officers to exert their power over newcomers to the team. Peer pressure and bravado saw us laugh along with the joke; despite the fact it was on us. And anyhow, any attempts we could have made to challenge those officers at that time around their conduct I expect would have resulted in us getting a good kicking. Despite any much-needed reform to policing that had occurred up to that point, it was still only the nineties and things were done a lot differently back then.

3

An accidental cop is how I would consider myself. To be a police officer was not something I had ever desired, or indeed considered, until I read the advertisement. Beyond that the process seemed easy. It just happened, so I rolled with it, but was completely naïve to the world that awaited me. Academically I was average but did possess some of the other essential attributes required to be a police officer, such as a desire to drive positive change.

Unfortunately, not all serving police officers I encountered over the next twenty years had that same mentality. Some were in it for the uniform, perhaps due to a long-held childhood fantasy. Others were only in it for the status and powers that go along with the role, which when misused poses a significant threat to others.

Whatever motivation people had for joining the police, if it was not to help and serve then it tended to stick out and be obvious. I fear that is not the case today.

Only now do I recognise that the 'harmless pranks' I witnessed during those early days reflected a deeper-rooted, and troubling culture of bullying. Dismissed as light-hearted antics, they masked a more serious systemic issue. To 'fit in' meant conforming to a prevailing mindset, and those who didn't were often marginalised, ostracised, or compelled to leave.

There were forty on my training intake, a handful of women but mostly men. The police needed numbers and the distinct feeling I got was that as we were all physically able, and mostly white and of

British origin, we would do. But in truth, not everybody is cut out for the job of policing.

Being a police officer is incredibly difficult.

It is not just big trauma events, of which there are plenty, but every moment on any job is wrapped up in negativity. People call the police to state there has been an assault, or an instance of criminal damage, or a road traffic accident. Even a burglary at a sweet factory, where sugar plum fairies worked the machines and candy canes hung from the ceiling, would still be an event centred around an act of dishonesty and malice.

Being a police officer involves always picking up the dirt, and as much as everyone may hope for some sort of positive outcome, a happy ending does not always materialise.

4

My first experience of actual policing saw me working under a team of two police constables. John and Tony were both in their late forties, and in the days of a good old-fashioned bobby on the beat, they were referred to as the 'area men', as they were responsible for the area to which I was first assigned. They knew all the business owners, all the housewives, and all the common criminals on their patch.

In my new role I took absolute pride in how I presented myself, and in a stark contrast to my freshly shaven and rather youthful look, they both sported a face full of stubble and were generally quite scruffy in their overall appearance. John always had a cigarette on the go which had stained his white facial hair orange, just below the right corner of his bottom lip. Tony didn't smoke, but instead constantly gorged himself on whatever food he could get his hands on, without a care in the world for how much of it ended up splattered down his untucked shirt.

In contrast to my enthusiasm and desire to get stuck in to saving the world, the pace at which they worked frustrated me. During my first few weeks with them I was waiting to get out of first gear, but it never happened. I was forced to consider if that was my future in policing: wandering around, an unkempt middle-aged bobby, popping into the local butty shop each day on my way to investigate a shed that had been broken into.

'*Right!*' said Tony briskly, as he slurped the remainder of his third brew of the morning. '*I think it's about time we took you over to see Mrs Ford!*'

I glanced up at him from my desk. *'Who's Mrs Ford?'* I asked, politely feigning interest.

'Don't worry, you'll see... She'll love you. Get your tit on.'

With that he turned on his heel, picked up his own custodian helmet, more commonly referred to as a 'tit hat', and marched out of the office.

We walked everywhere, so we set off walking along the A-road, away from the town centre, and as we walked, he began sharing stories of Mrs Ford. Her husband had not long since passed away but had previously been a senior figure in the local council and therefore had been well in with the chief superintendent, something which she leveraged to her benefit. She had become a regular nuisance, calling the station several times a week, for anything and for nothing; a tap on the window, or an unusual car passing by.

'She practically considers John her own personal policeman!' Tony scoffed.

Forty minutes had passed since we left the station, and the scenery had become noticeably more picturesque as we entered a quainter suburb on the edge of our bounds. Instead of housing estates and retail parks, farmland lined either side of the road. We turned onto a stoney footpath, where he led me to a small row of cottages.

'I'll be leaving you here now then. Your only job...' he grinned, *'is to get out.'* And he pushed me towards her front door.

I assume he saw it as a rite of passage, a challenge I must overcome, but as I had listened to Tony tell me about Mrs Ford, it seemed as though all she wanted was a little bit of comfort and friendship, and it was no hardship at all for me to spend some time providing that. In fact, in my youthful sense of nobility, I was more than pleased to do it. It felt like it was part of my duty in serving the community. She wanted company and reassurance, and I could provide it.

After knocking on the door, I was warmly welcomed in by a spritely lady of around eighty years old, wearing fluffy slippers and clutching her crossword book and pencil. After making a pot of tea we sat down at her kitchen table and began to chat. She was keen to know all about me, where I was from, what I had done before joining the police and how I liked my new role so far.

It was pleasant enough, but after a couple of hours we reached a natural point in the conversation where I felt it was appropriate to make my excuses, so I told Mrs Ford that I had to leave, but that I would certainly be back to visit her again.

'Okay dear, well take these back with you,' she said, thrusting a pack of orange flavour Club biscuits at me.

There is a rule in the police that gifts or gratuities of any sort cannot be accepted, to avoid any situations of favourable treatment. Tony had stressed this to me heavily on our journey over to her house, warning me she would likely try to give me things to take away. It felt like a test of my integrity, to see how honest I was. Would I accept anything Mrs Ford tried to give me? And if I did, would I admit it back at the station?

'I'm sorry, but I am not actually allowed to accept gifts from any members of the public.' I explained to her.

'Nonsense young man! You must take them back to the station. John likes a Club biscuit.'

She had a wicked bright look in her eyes, and I have since found that unassuming little old ladies often possess boundless grit and steely determination. She was not likely to accept that I would not take the biscuits from her.

The conversation went back and forth for a couple more minutes before I told the belligerent old dear one final time that I could not accept her bloody chocolate biscuits and turned to leave the house. With one hand on the latch and the other on the door handle I began to let myself out. With both my hands otherwise engaged, Mrs Ford found her opportune moment and I felt a tug on my police issue trousers, before she shoved the packet of biscuits right down the back of them.

I didn't know what to say, so I said nothing and carried on with my exit. I shut the door behind me and walked away. I walked for at least ten minutes down the main road with them still in the back of my trousers, before daring to remove them. I was so concerned that they were technically a gift, so I really shouldn't touch them. I also didn't put it past Tony to be hiding somewhere nearby, waiting to see what, if anything, I had left her house with.

It transpired in a conversation later that day, that in contradiction with the heavily emphasised gratuities rule, the whole department would often receive and indulge in various sweet treats and baked goods from Mrs Ford, that she often delivered in person to the station. John and Tony explained that she had started to visit a little too frequently, so had effectively been banned from entering the building, but that she was relentless. There was a phone outside the police station which went directly through to the operator switchboard if there was nobody available at the station to speak with. Our office was on the first floor so they could see in advance when she was coming down the road with bags of goodies and when nobody answered the door to her, she would try the phone, and when that didn't work, she just hung the bags of treats on the station door before leaving to go back home. It was a shame, but police stations are not community hubs, and police officers are not social workers, even if the boundaries are blurred and the work does inevitably bleed over into that sphere. I was glad to have spent the time with her that day, and equally glad that despite orders from the top, it seemed some officers were still taking the time to visit her at home for a brew and a natter.

After a month or so, my mentorship with John and Tony ended and I was signed off as competent so began as a fully-fledged police constable. That first year I can only really describe as being the Postman Pat equivalent of policing in that I didn't see much action. The areas I patrolled were relatively decent, middle-class suburbs.

Not yet qualified to drive the police cars I spent my days walking about on my own. With the authority to roam wherever I pleased within the boundaries of my division, I often chose to walk from one police station to another at a time, which was usually a good two hours of plodding.

One winter's day I had just begun the journey back to my home station when it began to snow quite heavily. Snow on the ground tends to dampen any noise, so there was a distinct feeling of peacefulness which I found enjoyable, for the first thirty minutes or so. Beyond that point, without an appropriate coat on and the steel toe caps in my boots beginning to freeze, the novelty soon wore off. Snow also tends to strip people of their ability to operate a vehicle, so as I trudged along, I heard a couple of communications over the radio concerning the weather. It was steadily getting worse, therefore making it increasingly difficult to drive.

'All drivers please come back to the station…' meaning that instead of patrolling around they would only be dispatched to attend an emergency. To me it sounded a lot like, *'Come back, get warm, have a brew and watch some TV.'*

The next communication was, *'All walkers, stay out.'*

The operator may as well have just said, *'Robert, you stay out,'* because I was the only bloody one.

My boots were stiffening, and my nylon socks were doing nothing to prevent the cold eating away at my extremities. My woollen, police issue trousers were getting gradually damper and heavier, but with no other choice I continued plodding along. No gloves, no scarf, just a short bomber jacket and my big tit helmet.

Before too long there was a report of a road traffic accident on the radio.

'PC Clarke, how far away are you?'

I hated doing traffic jobs.

'Just five minutes away from that location, Sir. On my way there now.'

What had started off as a pleasant day of peaceful wandering had truly taken a turn for the worst. Cold, wet, and miserable I was headed to deal with a double-decker bus, full of passengers, which had collided with a parked car. A dozen whiplash claims pending, it felt like a noticeably low point in my new career.

Given the number of passengers, I was mentally preparing myself for the fact that the reporting of the incident could take hours. Fortunately, however, the circumstances of the crash seemed straightforward. The bus had tried to turn a corner on its usual route but the conditions on the road had caused the back end of the vehicle to swing out, hitting a parked car. Out of the fifteen passengers, only three were claiming to be injured.

I set about taking the accident report, reluctantly but diligently. The road was blocked and all those on the bus who were not claiming to be injured wanted to get off and continue with their day, but I had to keep them there to take their details and witness accounts. They were cold, I was cold, and it was safe to say that nobody was enjoying themselves.

Due to the stillness in the atmosphere, I could hear in the distance the tell-tale sign of a vehicle skidding. Taking a step back off the bus onto the pavement I saw another double-decker bus hurtling towards us and before I had time to open my mouth and alert anybody, it ploughed straight into the back of the first bus.

It was therein my luck had changed. Both crashes were compounded into one large event, and as a witness to the second accident, I was no longer able to report on the first. More people on the first bus were then claiming to be injured, along with some on the second bus so I called for the traffic crew to come out and take the report of the accidents, and the statements of then nearly thirty passengers.

What was looking like it would have been a full day of mundane work for me, was whittled down to just an hour. Within fifteen minutes I had gotten back to the station and was drying out with a hot cup of tea.

Whilst only being on foot patrol meant I could rarely attend emergencies, as I could not conceivably get there quickly enough, I mostly enjoyed my time on the beat. I got to see a lot whilst walking around and people got to see me. I offered a reassuring police presence in the community, with people often stopping for a chat with the local bobby on the beat. It was pleasant.

There was a radio DJ on a local station who often ran competitions and executed various pranks as part of his show. One morning, someone had rung into the radio station to give a spoof traffic report, which detailed how there was a newly erected monument on one of the main roundabouts. The monument was described as a six-foot tall, papier mâché penis, complete with equally proportioned bollocks, and, understandably, it seemed to be causing a bit of a distraction on the roads. The congestion around the area was made even worse by the publicity the makeshift sculpture had received on the radio, meaning people were flocking to see it.

'All units. Some joker has put something on the main roundabout near Sainsbury's that is causing a disturbance. Can anybody who is available go and see what it is and bring it back into the property store?'

I was walking that way anyway so communicated that I would go and have a look. From not too far away I could see that there was indeed something on the roundabout and that there were rows and rows of traffic circling it; as though the spectacle they had gone to see was on par with the Arc De Triomphe.

The closer I got the more obvious it became to me what it was, and it was surprisingly lifelike.

'Yeah… it's a massive cock and balls, we definitely need to bring it in as it's carnage over here.'

At then twenty-two years of age, I naïvely assumed someone would be along in a car to help me return it to the station.

'Roger that, PC Clarke. See you when you get back.'

With no other choice, I climbed onto the roundabout, picked up the sculpture and with it over one shoulder I traipsed back to the station. Unsurprisingly I got several beeps from passing cars on my way back. Between the fresh-faced bobby in blue, complete with big tit hat on my head, and the large, phallic sculpture I was clutching on to, one of us truly looked like a massive dick. I arrived at the station and booked it into property, writing at the top of the form under 'Item description': 'Six-foot cock and balls.'

5

Throughout my career I was paired with mentors, who were supposed to guide and support me in navigating the complexities of the role. However, they all shared a common trait, and that is that they were plodders: slow-moving, risk-averse and somewhat uninspiring. They were not as proactive as I had anticipated or would have liked, and if I wanted to achieve and excel, I was completely reliant on my own initiative and determination to push myself forwards. The role of a mentor, which I would then later go on to assume myself, is crucial, as it sets the tone within a team, and expectations for performance. Had I followed the examples that were set for me by any of my mentors, I likely would have achieved very little. Their prevailing attitudes seemed to prioritise staying in their own lane and avoiding involvement in anything outside of their assigned tasks. It was a mentality which surprised me, especially further down the line in roles that are inherently proactive in their nature, such as detective work and firearms operations. In all cases, my mentors embodied everything that I did not want to become.

6

It wasn't too long before I made my first arrest.

One bright, crisp, winter's morning I was carrying out my foot patrol when I decided to cut through a local green space, instead of taking the main road. The birds tweeting from the trees, combined with the good weather gave me an extra spring in my step as I walked along the river's edge. After a few minutes of relishing the freshness of the air, enjoying my surroundings, and feeling a general sense of purpose about my day, I noticed a man in his early twenties appear from one of the many entrances into the park. He was behaving rather suspiciously, walking at pace. And he kept looking behind him as though to check whether he was being followed, so I decided I should oblige his concern. Once I had shouted ahead to him to stop, he decided instead to begin running.

I didn't know that he had committed a crime, but my instinct coupled with his behaviour suggested it was likely that he had. What I did know, however, was that I was fast on my feet, and I would easily be able to catch him and as I started to run myself, it wasn't too long before he was in reaching distance. My mind raced to consider when best to try and apprehend him, and in the moment, there seemed no better course of action other than to rugby tackle him around the waist, forcing us both into the river as I did.

Thankfully, it was only shallow, no more than a couple of feet, but it was freezing cold, and my suspected perpetrator was shocked into submission. Without any further attempts to escape, I handcuffed him and dragged him out of the water.

I hadn't stopped to consider how difficult it might have been to explain my actions had my instincts been wrong, and it is unlikely to imagine that a police officer would simply happen upon someone who was running away from the scene of a crime. But, as we stood on the riverbank, both dripping wet, I turned out his pockets and my initial suspicion was immediately confirmed. From his possession I retrieved several items of fine jewellery which did clearly not belong to him, and I couldn't believe my luck. It was the exact definition of being in the right place at the right time.

In my wet and weighty police issue boots, and my sodden, woollen-blend trousers, I frog-marched my prisoner the thirty-minute walk back to the station and took him straight to the custody suite, where I presented him to the custody sergeant.

I had not yet crossed paths with the custody sergeant on shift that day, but was aware that he had a reputation for being notoriously stringent. Rightly, booking a prisoner into custody is a very formal procedure and despite holding the rank of police sergeant he saw himself as being completely impartial to the police, there instead to preserve prisoner welfare.

His role was the conduit between the police, the prisoner, and any legal representative the prisoner may later have. My role was to relay the circumstances of the arrest, as a way of asking permission from the custody sergeant for the individual to be detained. As I addressed him and introduced myself, he peered down at me from his raised desk, and, ready to take down my account, reached for his carbon paper notepad. It was my first arrest, and I was so eager to get it right.

'Sir, this is one Jonathan Buckley. I arrested and cautioned him on suspicion of burglary at ten forty-seven this morning. The arrest occurred after a short foot pursuit that resulted in me finding several items of stolen jewellery in his possession. He made no reply after caution.'

It was only a short explanation, but I felt as though I had been talking for far too long, so much that my mouth had dried up.

'Thank you, PC Clarke. That is all very well and good, and I will gladly check your prisoner in, but I am afraid you will need to go away *and come back when you are properly dressed.'* Was the response I received.

Panic struck me and I could feel the blood rushing to my face. My appearance as a police constable was something I took very seriously and was mortified to consider that I was in anyway improperly presented. Following the order, I turned around and headed back out of the custody suite, dragging my smirking prisoner with me. Of course I was still damp, but the walk back had managed to drain most the water off both of us, so I wasn't visibly wet. My clip-on tie was on straight, as were both my epaulettes. I wasn't wearing my hat but that shouldn't have mattered as we weren't required to wear them in the custody office. Glancing down I noticed the button on one of my shirt pockets was undone. It seemed a little far-fetched, but I couldn't see anything else that was obviously out of order, so, taking my chances, I fastened it up and walked back in. As I appeared before the custody sergeant for a second time, he nodded at me silently in acknowledgement that I had rectified the issue, and I proceeded again with the details of the arrest.

'Excellent,' he grinned, 'cell four.'

With my prisoner processed I headed to the locker room to ditch my clothes. The only spare garments I had in my locker were a pair of trousers and a shirt, both of which I was glad to put on, but my socks, boots and underpants remained damp for the remaining six hours of my shift.

As I was a new member of the team, I assumed that the custody sergeant's treatment of me had been a test. A test of my respect for him, or just to gauge my reaction to a minor inconvenience whilst trying to do my job. And I latterly became aware that he did tend to make things difficult for some officers, to keep those who needed a reminder on due process in check.

Rightly or wrongly, beyond exchanging pleasantries with people on the street, I didn't consider myself as a community police officer. I saw the main objective of my job as to lock up criminals, so beyond that day I was in and out of the custody suite often. There would have been plenty more chances to get it wrong but that initial experience encouraged me to ensure I was always doing everything completely in line with procedure, and to avoid making any sloppy mistakes.

It was the middle of December and there was a great deal of chatter around the station about the upcoming Christmas party. It was a ticketed event and as I had only recently joined, I was informed that unfortunately there was no availability on the night for me to attend. I acted vaguely disappointed but really, I was quite relieved.

The event itself I expected would be riddled with drunken displays of male bravado, head-to-toe polyester, and enough hairspray to fix a painting to a wall. I didn't let on, but it wasn't really my scene, and I didn't feel as though I would be missing out remotely.

The party was scheduled on a Saturday, and on the Wednesday before one of the dog handlers approached me and explained that the party conflicted with a prior engagement his girlfriend had made, which he had completely forgotten about, so he was happy to let me have his ticket.

I had resigned myself to the fact that I wouldn't be going and was looking forward to some downtime over the weekend, but against my better nature, to show willing, I accepted the ticket with all the enthusiasm I could muster.

The party was being held at a hotel, which was about an hour's drive away from the station. Some of the other lads had arranged to arrive at the hotel during the afternoon, to make use of the facilities before the main event, and I agreed to go along with them. The hotel advertised itself as a health club, but as we shuffled out of the changing rooms, we realised it was nothing more than a disappointing sauna and a less-than-sterile jacuzzi.

For the evening meal we were seated on several long, banquet tables, which was where I chose to remain for most of the night, comfortably surrounded by a few familiar faces. At best, I knew only a dozen of the eighty attendees, and I didn't see fit to make the rounds and force conversation with people I did not know. Unbeknownst to me, at the other end of my table was the front desk clerk, Julie. Given her role in the station, I was reasonably well-acquainted with Julie, and it had not been lost on me that she was incredibly pretty. The news that she had recently split up from her boyfriend had been circulating the station for a couple of weeks, and in his place as her plus-one for the evening she had brought along one of her friends. The DJ had just started playing 'Vienna' by Ultravox when they both appeared at my side.

'*Robert!*' she gushed, glowing with merriment, no doubt caused by the large glass of Sauvignon Blanc she was swilling. '*This is Jane!*'

She went on to explain that Jane had spotted me from the other end of the table and having also recently split up from her boyfriend, asked to be introduced to me.

My first impression of Jane was that she was quite plain-looking, in comparison to Julie at least, and her outfit was quite drab, especially considering it was a Christmas party. So, I wasn't blown away, but I was flattered, and not wanting to be rude I invited her to sit down. She was a little louder than I would have liked, but I was acutely aware that perhaps I was too quiet, so I nodded and smiled as she chattered on to me for what felt like an eternity.

Since the news of her break-up, a few of the officers had been vying for Julie's attention and one seemed to have had more luck than the others. Towards the end of the night, Julie reappeared next to the table where Jane and I were still seated, and explained that a young PC called Tom, would likely be sharing her room. '*But that's okay, you can stay with Robert…*' she said with a suggestive look in her eye.

Despite her thick Northern accent and inability to control her volume, Jane wasn't overly offensive, but I still would have preferred to have retired to my budget hotel room alone. Although it didn't appear I had much choice, so I politely agreed and after a couple more drinks we retreated to my room, staggeringly drunk.

During the night I woke up feeling rather unwell and not wanting to embarrass myself in front of a practical stranger, I made my exit out of the room and into the corridor as quietly as I could to find a communal bathroom. Never having been one to indulge too heavily in alcohol consumption, I was reminded why as my entire dinner resurfaced, on a sea of lager and sambuca.

The following morning Jane and I exchanged pleasantries about hopefully seeing each other again, before going our separate ways. On my way into work on the Monday, Julie stopped me at the front desk and explained how Jane had called her on the Sunday evening and told her how she had really enjoyed her time with me. Then she handed me a piece of paper with Jane's phone number on it. Politely confirming I would be sure to ring her I carried on towards the parade room.

'Oh, and she said she liked your car!' Julie called after me.

It was on the third attempt that I finally passed my driving test at nineteen years old, having been failed twice by the chief instructor; a man so large that he oozed over the passenger seat, meaning that every time I changed gear, I nudged his thunderous thigh. My dad had agreed to buy me my first car, and when we went along to our local garage, he directed me towards a Renault 5, in beige. It was truly awful to look at but also wholly impractical as when I sat in the driver's seat with my feet on the pedals, I had to tilt my neck as my head was stuffed up against the car ceiling. My dad is five foot nine inches, whereas I am six foot two inches, so he was ready to buy it there and then, even though it was clearly a model that had been built with a more petite European market in mind. After expressing my concern that I was just too bloody big for the car, he lost interest. He said he would still pay but had no interest in helping me with any further search.

It was down to me to find something more suitable and annoyingly for him, it didn't take long before I did just that: a Fiat Tipo, 1.9 litre Turbo Diesel, in white. It had a digital dashboard that displayed the engine revs, speakers in the back, a detachable radio, and a golf ball topper on the gear stick. What young man of the nineties could possibly ask for anything more? It was incredibly cool, and

I thoroughly enjoyed driving it around experiencing my increased independence. However, it wasn't quite my perfect ideal motor, and before too long I saw fit to exchange my reliable Fiat, for something that I felt suited me a little better.

An MG Midget. A classic red, two-seater sports car, complete with chrome wheels and bumper. The impression I got from my parents when I returned home with it was as though I had just taken a perfectly good cow out and swapped it for some magic beans. I didn't care, I loved it. It was old and unique and there was nobody else I knew of at the time who had one. And whenever I did pass a fellow MG driver on the road, they would wave at me; acknowledgement that we were part of a special little network. As unique as it was, due to its age, it was riddled with problems and broke down pretty much every other week. Fortunately, I was covered by my dad's AA breakdown cover, until eventually they advised him that they would not turn out to attend my vehicle if it broke down again, and that I just needed to get it properly fixed.

The MG was still taking me about the place when I first started police training, and it saw me through the entire course. I was young and living the dream, but its unreliability was becoming a bit of an issue, and the prospect of ever being late to my new job was crippling me with anxiety each day as I made the journey to work.

The noise coming from my exhaust was deafening and the head gasket had failed, meaning that oil was mixing with water in the engine, which created a large plume of smoke that followed my little red sports car around. It was comedic. I looked like something off *Wacky Races*, but it was certainly a violation of my surrounding environment.

The final straw came one morning as I made my way up the road to the station. One of the station sergeants flashed at me from behind, indicating that I should pull over. He told me under no uncertain circumstances I needed to get my car sorted, or he would personally see to it that I received a ticket for some sort of traffic violation. That was enough for me to finally consider parting ways with my beloved little motor and the following weekend I went to the nearest Kwik Fit garage to have the exhaust fixed. With the repairs complete, I made my way to a local showroom to see what I could possibly exchange it for. On the way there I put the roof down and gave it one final blast up the dual carriageway; the receipt for the works just completed blowing off the dashboard in the wind.

Begrudgingly I wandered the forecourt, looking for something that would be considered more sensible. There was a Ford Mondeo, which had everything my MG didn't: four doors, a radio and was undoubtedly watertight, reliable and safe. The only problem was that I could nowhere near afford it. After a few minutes inspecting the Mondeo, the owner of the garage appeared. He had seen me driving into the car park and it seemed that he had fallen in love with the Midget, in the same way that I first had. In an absolute stroke of luck, he offered me a straight up swap, and I drove away an hour later in a grey Ford Mondeo.

It felt a little dull, so I was surprised to hear that it had acted as an attractive prospect for Jane, but then again, she hadn't come across to me as particularly exceptional herself, so perhaps it was fitting that her interest was piqued by such a mediocre motor. Whilst I hadn't been immediately enamoured with her, a few days after Julie gave me her number I did the proper thing and called, and we arranged to see each other again.

My home station was so small that the station car park was only big enough to accommodate the patrol vehicles, so our personal vehicles were always parked further down the road on a council car park. We only had three station sergeants, and one of them took a great deal of pride over his car: an electric-blue Ford estate which was always completely pristine. As he placed so much value on it, and assumed that everybody else should too, against instruction he never considered parking it anywhere other than the station car park where he could keep his beady eye on it. My experience of him up to that point was that he was a bully, completely intoxicated on the power that the role of police sergeant offered him. He had done nothing at all to make me feel comfortable or welcomed into the team, and rarely ever turned out to help with any actual work. Unfortunately, when it was his shift, he was the most senior ranking officer, and with his superiors based at one of the other stations in the division, there was never anybody there to enforce the rules on him.

It was a bright but cold Sunday morning not long into the new year of 1997, and there was a heavy frost on the ground when I arrived at work at six-thirty. The sergeant headed out to the local Co-op, to get the bacon and eggs needed for us all to have Sunday breakfast, and after reading through the paperwork left by the previous shift, along with another young PC, I headed out to follow up on a complaint that had come in the night before.

The station car park was edged with a small brick wall, and as we warmed up our patrol car, I noticed a cat curled up on top of it. When we arrived back at the station an hour later the cat was still there, and it was at that point that I realised it was most likely dead. Poor bugger. It had curled up asleep and passed away peacefully in the cold, and in doing so presented me with a wonderful opportunity.

In a moment of sheer brilliance coupled with childish immaturity, I picked the cat up and placed it neatly on the bonnet on the sergeant's car, chuckling to myself at the prospect of him leaving the station later that day to find a dead cat curled up on top of his pride and joy.

After breakfast and a quick debrief we set out again for the day, planning to return to the station at half past two in the afternoon, allowing just enough time to get everything in order and make any additional remarks in our pocket notebooks before finishing the shift at three. The sergeant who was due on the afternoon shift had arrived early and instead of waiting to make sure all his team returned safely and were accounted for, our sergeant was making a premature exit. As we turned the corner into the car park he was already in his car, revving the engine and beeping the horn, attempting to rouse the cat and persuade it off his bonnet. His face was turning red with frustration as he yelled at it from the driver's seat. A minute passed before he must have realised that the cat was dead and after carelessly discarding it over the back of the car park wall, he drove off shaking his head.

The following day during our morning parade, he shared with us the story of how the cat had died on his bonnet, how all its insides had started to come out of its mouth, and how due to their acidity, they had left a patch of his paintwork all bubbled. There was no doubt that he would have made my life difficult at every available opportunity if he ever found out it was me who was responsible. Ultimately, I didn't care what he thought of me, but I chose to keep my mouth firmly shut and stifled my laughter.

I was keen to find my place within the institution and toe the line with my other superiors, but all I had experienced of him up to that point was that he was a lazy dictator, and a bully, who wanted far more respect than he was due. He was lucky enough to have a fantastic team around him but he sure as hell didn't deserve it, or the results that we got. In fact, the only thing I ever found him to be remotely good for was cooking a decent fry-up, and that was only because he was a fat, greedy, bastard.

Still behaving like it was the 1970s, there were a couple of real old-school bobbies on our division, of which my chief inspector was the epitome of. Big in presence and big in personality, he absolutely lived for his role in the police.

Occasionally he would turn up to observe our morning parade, during which we had to present details of any appointments for the day, and show our kit belt, truncheon, and handcuffs. Our pocket notebooks were flicked through, checking for any loose pages, doodles, or erasures, and we were assessed on our uniform; whether we were generally well presented, and our shoes were shined. Other than that, I rarely saw him as he spent most of his time in his office in the neighbouring station.

One of my earliest interactions with him was whilst I was taking something into the property store at the other station, which could only be accessed by going through the kitchen.

He was sitting at a table, watching the lunchtime news as he ate.

As I passed, he looked up and caught my eye. Scowling, and before I had time to offer him a formal greeting he stood up, walked over to the bin, and scraped what was still pretty much a full plate of food in.

'*You fucking idiot!*' he barked in his thick Glaswegian accent, before throwing his plate and cutlery into the sink and marching out of the room.

Totally perplexed as to what I had done, when I returned downstairs to the main office, I relayed the strange encounter to one of my more seasoned colleagues.

'Oh yeah,' he chuckled, *'you shouldn't have gone in there. He's got a real thing about other people seeing him eat.'*

He wouldn't eat in front of anybody but wouldn't eat in his office as he liked to watch the television. He was a forceful character who liked what he said and said what he liked. He was completely consumed by the force hierarchy and what his status afforded him, and so the expectation was that everyone else should completely avoid the kitchen whilst he was in there. He rarely came out onto jobs with us, and I can only recall two occasions when I ever saw him outside of the station.

The first of which was on a noticeably beautiful spring day, and after starting my shift in the afternoon I had spent a couple of hours bumbling about with my car windows down, listening to the world buzz around me. Just before rush hour I was flagged down by a member of the public in one of the nicer residential areas on the division. He informed me that he had been mowing his lawn when someone had entered his garage and then left, with something that didn't belong to them.

After giving me quite a detailed physical description he pointed me in the direction the perpetrator had left in. Back in the car I began to crawl around the various cul-de-sacs and ginnels in the area and it didn't take too long before I spotted someone matching the description I had been given. As I pulled over and jumped out of the car, sure enough he started to run. The weather was so pleasant that I had forgone my polyester police jumper, but I was still uncomfortably hot as we ran.

The pursuit went on for half a mile, at which point he must have felt I was getting too close so ducked off somewhere to try and hide. As he ran through an opening in a privet hedge and up a driveway towards someone's house, I lost sight of him. Catching my breath as I slowed down to a walk, I began look around. I knew he couldn't have gone too far as he was only out of my line of sight for a moment, and then I heard a slight noise come from an old outhouse. There he was.

He was a few years younger than me, but we were equally matched in size, so it was nothing more than a true battle of wills. He needed to get away, but I was not going to let him, and what happened next was the sort of altercation you are likely to see only in a movie. It was a real stand-up fight between two men, each trading blows one at a time, and it was at that point a group of residents had gathered to watch.

Drug users often have a strength about them which makes them more immune to hindrances that would otherwise disable a person. His resistance during the fight had led me to conclude that he had most definitely committed an acquisitive crime, and whatever he had stolen would be sold on for money to buy drugs.

I grabbed hold of him, and we ended up rolling around on the concrete. My elbows and forearms were grazed and as we hit the gable end of the house, I hit my head causing me to loosen my grip ever so slightly. He got away from my grasp and ran back towards the main road but within seconds I was on his heels again. Then he disappeared over a six-foot fence and into another garden.

My boots were so heavy, and I was gasping under the additional weight of my body armour, so I knew I wouldn't make it over the fence quickly enough to put a stop to the chase there and then. My only opportunity to catch him was obvious, and as soon as his feet touched the ground on the other side, I smashed through the fence panel, bringing the entire thing down on top of him.

To fully subdue him and cement my victory I got to my feet and like a child on a trampoline I jumped up and down on the fence panel a few times, whilst he lay underneath, defeated. Exhausted and victorious, my tie barely hanging on, I got off and lifted the fence away from him. At some point during the tussle, the emergency panic button on my radio had been pushed so my colleagues were aware of the altercation. We were only a few streets away from a police station, so I walked my perpetrator back down to the main road to await the van. Covered in scratches and scrapes we both sat on the curb and caught our breath. He was calm enough and seemed to acknowledge his fate, and that the best man had won.

Soon enough the station van arrived and to my surprise the chief inspector jumped straight out. The police constable with him opened the van doors and swiftly relieved me of the prisoner, sitting him down on the back step of the van.

Before I had the chance to open my mouth and brief the chief inspector on the incident, he stormed over to the suspect.

'Hey! You! Have you been fucking fighting with my officer?!'

His moustache twitched as he awaited a response.

Rather than simply saying yes, the prisoner gave an evasive retort, and what happened next I am certain I witnessed in perfect slow motion. The chief inspector pulled his right arm as far back as it could go, before releasing it and punching the prisoner square in the face, so hard that it caused him to roll back from his seated position into the cage at the back of the van. Slamming the door behind him, the chief inspector walked off and hopped back in the passenger side, as though he had done nothing more than take a bag of rubbish out and put it in a wheelie bin.

Back at the station it was tea, biscuits, and pats on the back all around, but a week later I was called to see the superintendent for a mild bollocking, where he quizzed me about the three hundred pounds worth of damage I had caused to someone's fence. When he finished speaking, I apologised, and he told me to wait outside his office. A few minutes later he called me back in and issued me with a formal commendation for the very same event, for my dedication and bravery on the job.

During the late 1990s, tensions around the terrorist activities of the IRA were still very much present, and as a police department we were encouraged to be extra cautious around anything that seemed even slightly out of the ordinary.

On what was the only other time I saw the chief inspector come out on a job, we had been called to attend a local post office after a report that a shoebox with wires coming out of it had been left outside.

For all intents and purposes, it was most definitely a bomb.

The post office was evacuated, and we cordoned off the scene. Our only job then was to refuse any access to the area whilst we awaited the army bomb squad. As the most senior officer on the division, the chief inspector had to come out and show his face.

'What the fuck is going on?!' he demanded upon arrival, after pushing his way through a dozen onlookers to the event.

'Well Sir, a member of the public has been in touch and reported an unusual package...' I began to explain.

'Has anybody looked at it or touched it?!'

The five of us on scene stood around looking at one another, none of us able to find the words to explain that no, none of us had been to touch what was suspected to be a bomb. Without a satisfactory response he turned away and marched over to the cordon. After shouting at the officer manning it to *'get out of my fucking way'*, he lifted the police tape and strode over the road.

For no more than thirty seconds he stood looking at the shoebox, whilst we all watched on nervously. He looked over to us and shaking his head he swung his leg back and kicked the shoebox right up into the air. It wasn't a bomb, as we found out as dozens of magazines landed all over the road. He marched back to his car and that was it, job done.

7

One thing I learnt to be of critical importance very early on, was being able to rely on others. Nobody can excel at everything, and it is the unique talents of those around us that can aid our own success. By nature, I am a loner, often uncomfortable trusting others and always instead favouring self-reliance. However, to achieve in such a demanding environment, I had to reframe my understanding of trust and develop collaborative methods that still allowed me to feel a sense of control. I have a strong inclination towards responsibility, and actively seek it out, hesitating to share it with anybody else. Yet the truth is, I would have not accomplished anything significant in my policing career without the support of others.

Every experience in life, whether positive or negative, gives us the opportunity to learn and grow, but it is the challenges we navigate that we often glean the most wisdom from. Reflecting on my time under the command of the sergeant who was the subject of my practical joke, I have gained valuable insights into the traits that define impactful leaders, and have come to conclude that the cat, even in its rigid and lifeless state, possessed more integrity than he did. His behaviour was a stark and constant reminder of what poor leadership looks like. He manipulated the hierarchy and created an environment where junior officers like me felt unable to question his conduct and poor treatment of others.

To the owner of the cat in question – I am sorry. Your pet surely did deserve a more dignified final resting place; however, its final act was one of defiance against an overweight bully, who prioritised himself and his own comfort above anything else. I hope you can share in my solace.

8

In the February of 1997 I attended my first sudden death, after a call to the police had been made by a member of the deceased's family. An elderly gentleman had passed away at home and an officer was required on the scene to complete the necessary paperwork. When I arrived at the large, detached, red-brick house, I was greeted on the front step by the deceased's wife, Mrs Goldmann; an impeccably presented lady in her late seventies.

Once inside the property I was introduced to several other family members, and the first thing that struck me as being rather odd was the noticeable lack of tears and upset. Nobody was pacing around in a fluster or sat sobbing in a corner. They were all incredibly calm, as though they had already gone through the motions of grief and arrived swiftly at acceptance.

'I am terribly sorry to meet you under these circumstances,' I said to Mrs Goldmann as she welcomed me into the lounge, and I continued to explain, *'There are a few things I must do and there may be some questions you need to answer, but we can take as much time as you need.'*

She had such a warm presence about her, and the whole time I spoke she smiled back at me in acknowledgement, with both her hands clasped over mine.

'First of all, I will need to see your husband's body. Do you mind showing me where he is?'

She led me into a large, formal, dining room, and in the centre of the room was a large, eight-seater mahogany dining table. Lying on top of the table, flat on his back, was the deceased. He had a white silk scarf under his chin, and as I rounded the top end of the table, I saw it was tied in a knot, at the top of his head. He looked like he had been bandaged up for toothache.

'Mrs Goldmann,' I paused, trying to keep a straight face, *'can you please tell me why he has this scarf around his head and chin?'*

She explained that his mouth had fallen open when he died and wouldn't stay shut, so she tied him up to make him look less odd. It was ironic, which she recognised and laughed about, which allowed me to relax into a smile and continue with my duties. Once I had completed the few bits of necessary paperwork, I explained that I was going to arrange for the coroner to take him away, so that cause of death could be determined.

'Oh no dear, you needn't take him away. I have the doctor on the phone, and he can confirm whatever you need.'

With that she handed me the phone and I listened as their family general practitioner explained that he was willing to certify the death, based on the circumstances of the deceased's prior health, and the medication he had been taking. Essentially, the death was absolutely expected, and the doctor could say without any further examination, what had killed him.

Still in the infancy of the job, my head was racing with all sorts of conundrums. It was clear that the family had helped move him, because he certainly hadn't died flat on his back on the dining table, and I wondered for a moment if the scarf had been placed on him to cover up the fact he had been strangled. The entire family could have been in cahoots trying to cover up his murder. Was I being incredibly naïve to assume Mrs Goldmann, as lovely as she seemed, was telling me the truth?

The doctor surely sounded convincing, but I had no real way of verifying in that moment who he was. Not to mention it was the legislation that allows for a general practitioner to certify deaths without formal investigation, that Harold Shipman later relied on to get away with his crimes. Swiftly, I put any theories of murder to the back of my mind and decided to take the situation at face value. He was an old fella who had died peacefully at home, surrounded by his family, who had then put him on the dining table and dressed him up like a dog's dinner. Looking back, it was hardly suspicious at all. The circumstances which surrounded the whole incident, as my first sudden death, were especially unique. It was just such an easy situation to navigate, an unusual fluke. A bit like playing football for the first time and scoring a hat trick. After leaving I was satisfied that I had fulfilled my role well.

To do a good job was important to me and I had become increasingly confident in my decision to become a police constable, even if every day had the potential to be incredibly challenging. My youthful innocence and still somewhat limited exposure to the world meant I was still very impressionable, and therefore more susceptible than some of my older colleagues to empathy and general feeling. In the spring of 1997, I visited the home of an elderly lady who had been the victim of a burglary. The perpetrators hadn't gotten away with much in terms of valuables, but the psychological effect of having a stranger in her home had understandably left the victim feeling unsafe. After taking her statement, I assured her that we would investigate, but deep down I knew it was unlikely we would catch whoever had done it. The crime was too unsophisticated. Someone had simply put their foot through the door and broken the lock off.

At the time, the police were offering crime prevention aids such as new locks and burglar alarms, but as the victim didn't live in a high crime area she didn't qualify under the scheme and was not entitled to any additional assistance. It was distressing for me at the time to see a vulnerable individual so scared. I felt completely helpless and wanted so desperately to do more for her.

The following day was scheduled to be my day off, so I told her I would return first thing in the morning and install a proper lock to her front door. I didn't really know what I was doing when it came to ironmongery, but the next morning I made the twenty-mile round trip to purchase a lock, the tools necessary to fit it, and an additional safety chain. I arrived at her home to install the new mechanism and when I left, I was satisfied I had done what I could to make her feel more at ease in her own home. When I returned to work, I felt obliged to share that I had been back to see the victim, and that I had offered some additional support to her on my own time. To my surprise, later that day I was called to see the superintendent, who scolded me for my actions, on the basis that if she was broken into again, the police could somehow be culpable. It seemed ridiculous, but I apologised and went back to work. I wanted to serve, and it was frustrating that there was only so much I could do within the bounds of my role.

Having passed my police driving test I was no longer restricted to foot patrol, and one evening as my night shift was coming to an end, I passed a local milkman doing his rounds. As he pulled away from someone's house, I saw out of the corner of my eye a young boy, crouching down in wait, before approaching the doorstep and hurrying away with the milk and bread that had just been left. It was most unfortunate for him that he had not seen me, so driving ahead a few hundred yards, I parked up and got out of the car to confront him. Looking scared and defeated, he told me his name and age. He was twelve years old, so the correct course of action would have been to arrest him and take him to the station, but that didn't feel remotely the right thing to do. Instead, I took him back to the address he had told me was his home.

He was incredibly sheepish as I tried to converse with him on the short five-minute journey. That could simply have been because I had just caught him in the act of theft, but it seemed there was a little more to it than that and I couldn't shake the feeling that something wasn't right.

We arrived at his house but there was no answer when I knocked at the door. Using a key that he had in his pocket, he unlocked the door, and we entered together. It was half past five in the morning and even after calling out a couple of times, there was a noticeable absence of any adults in the property.

The house was freezing cold and as I entered the lounge, I found there were two other children asleep on the sofa: a girl of around six years old and another boy, no older than two years. The elder boy confirmed they were his siblings.

It was just starting to get light when I called it into the station, and as I was waiting to hear what the next course of action should be, I heard the front door open, and a woman's voice call out.

'Here's some more shopping! I will see you again on Thursday!'

It was a Monday.

Leaping to my feet I stopped her as she was making her way down the front path that led to the house. She had clearly not seen my police car parked close by.

She was their mother, and after a couple of minutes' questioning, I learnt that she had recently separated from their father and was only dropping some provisions off before heading back to her current boyfriend's, where she had been staying for a few weeks. Social services were soon to arrive and took all three children into protective custody. When I eventually got home, I tried to get some rest, but my mind wrestled with how someone could possibly treat their children in such a way and leave them at such risk of harm.

When I started the night shift again later that day, I was informed that social services had been able to temporarily place the children all together with their aunty and uncle, and I was asked to visit them. At the sight of all three children, washed, fed and in clean clothes, I felt reassured I had done everything I could in the way that I thought was best. It had been a brief internal struggle for me to balance proper procedure with what felt like the right thing to do, but stopping to look beyond the initial offence was the best option, to consider the root cause. It was obvious that such a young boy would not choose criminality, unless out of necessity, and I would have hated for him to have had a marker next to his name for the rest of his life, because of an insistence to apply the law as though it was a 'one size fits all' exercise.

Not even a week later I heard that the children had been returned to their mother and it made me feel sick with unease. I couldn't understand why in the first instance she hadn't been arrested and charged with neglect, but then to hear that the system had failed the children again further down the line left me with a bad taste in mouth, and I was completely powerless. She had promised to look after them better and on paper was a respectable professional, with a secure home in a nice enough area. But the job had already proven to me that things are not always as they seem.

At the beginning of my career, I found it incredibly hard to detach myself from a situation, long after my shift had finished, and the crimes which directly affected people had the potential to be quite impactive to my well-being. Particularly in the case of vulnerable margins of society. The need to serve and protect those who needed it the most drove me to always do the best that I could.

Calls to the police regarding concern for welfare were commonplace, and after not taking her milk in for a few days, the local milkman had placed a call expressing his worry about an elderly lady who he delivered to on his rounds. It was nearing half past five in the morning again, and with not long left of my night shift, I headed to the property that belonged to one Mrs Makinson. I pulled up to a 1930s semi-detached house and the lace curtains that hung in the front window were a tell-tale sign that whoever lived there was in their later years.

Section 17 of the Police and Criminal Evidence Act allows an officer to force entry to a property if they suspect someone could be in difficulty inside. Nobody had come to the door when I knocked, and there was indeed several bottles of milk on the doorstep, so I used the powers afforded to me, kicked the door in and gained entry.

A cursory search of the downstairs offered no clue as to where the occupant was, so I headed upstairs and straight into the master bedroom.

The curtains were closed but I could make out the outline of a person in the bed which I assumed was Mrs Makinson. I announced myself as a police officer, before approaching to see if I could rouse her. As I got closer, I saw a cat curled up near her face which I shooed away before reaching out to touch Mrs Makinson's hand. It was stone cold. She had clearly been dead a while.

There was no sign of a disturbance or any suspicious circumstances. It appeared to just be a case an old lady who had passed away in her sleep. Filling out the required paperwork meant that my shift had been extended by at least a few hours, but I didn't mind. I wanted to do a thorough job, especially in the instance of a sudden death. It was my obligation to be diligent, as a last act of service to the deceased.

When I eventually did leave, I returned home for some much-needed rest, and didn't think any more of it. It was just another day on the job.

Whilst the circumstances surrounding her death didn't seem particularly harrowing, Mrs Makinson had not been suffering with any life-threatening illnesses, so was referred for a forensic post-mortem to establish cause of death.

Post-mortems are sometimes carried out after a natural death, but if a death is suspected as being unnatural and therefore potentially criminal, it is referred to the coroner for a forensic post-mortem.

A forensic post-mortem involves a thorough investigation of the inside and outside of the body. Details of any testing done in laboratories, such as toxicology samples, are reviewed, and information of every single bruise, scratch, bullet hole or stab wound is documented. Results and findings are then compiled into a final report for the coroner to review, and then pass judgement on cause of death.

The presence of a police officer is a part of the protocol in the case of a forensic post-mortem and I was asked to attend one before my first six months on the division had ended. It wasn't for the faint hearted, and there was little room for any sentiment or squeamishness either. For some officers observing a post-mortem posed a problem, and they tried to avoid attending them if they could, but not me. Immediately I was fascinated. So much that during my first year, if there were no calls on the radio, I would stay and watch a few back-to-back. As well as being incredibly interested, I also felt it was important that I fully understood the process. The more I knew, the more I could share with grieving relatives, or indeed not share. Some people preferred and could accept detailed information, whilst others required a more watered-down version that would avoid undue distress. I was equipped to offer both.

The report on Mrs Makinson demonstrated that her death was not as straightforward as first assumed. It explained that she had suffered a stroke in bed, which had likely paralysed her. Then, due to her inability to move around the house, she had been unable to put the heating on which meant the house was colder than usual. To keep warm, the cat that I had shooed away, had made its way upstairs to find the only heat source in the house; Mrs Makinson. The conclusion the pathologist drew, was that given the amount of cat hair found in her mouth and throat, her eventual cause of death was suffocation. As she would have been breathing out warm air, the cat followed its natural animal instincts and curled up on her face. Unfortunately, the action of the cat sitting over Mrs Makinson's face wouldn't have created an airtight seal which meant that the innocent act of her feline companion, would have resulted in her slow and distressing demise.

When I had attended the Goldmann house, even though someone had died in the property, there was an immediate feeling of warmth and love in the air. But very quickly I found most other incidents of death usually brought about a wholly different atmosphere, and that was one of distinct cold and sadness.

Not long after I had discovered Mrs Makinson, another concern for welfare came in. This time it was the postman who had notified the police, after noticing through the frosted glass of someone's front door a build-up of letters behind it. When I arrived at the ground-floor flat, I too, saw all the post mounted up in the porch. What I also noticed was a significant number of flies inside the property, both dead and alive. Bracing myself for the smell that a freshly dead body would be omitting, I bent down and shouted through the letterbox.

Interestingly I couldn't smell anything but received no response from within either.

Again with no other choice, I forced entry.

Entering the living room, I had to step over the deceased male who lay on the floor. At first glance I suspected he was in his late fifties. There was no need for me to check for signs of life as it was clear from looking at him that he had been dead for some time. On the right-hand wall was an old electric bar fire which was on, and I assumed had been the entire time since he had died.

When someone first dies, blood ceases to circulate around the body and is then subject to the normal laws of gravity. During this process, which is referred to as hypostasis, all red blood cells eventually sink to the lowest area of the body, where they remain. The subsequent physical part of death is decomposition. There are a few ways the body can decompose, but the most common and the one that applied in this case, was putrefaction. During putrefaction, the body's soft tissues slowly turn to liquid, usually starting in the lower abdomen. The organs which are responsible for digestion, such as the stomach and intestine, are full of bacteria which then spreads through the blood vessels to the rest of the body, where it causes decomposition along the way. Externally, as this is happening, the skin begins to blister with fluid. As the blisters burst, the skin melts away.

Usually, but dependent on ambient temperature, it is a week or so after death that body cavities erupt and tissues turn to liquid.

The deceased in this case had been laying on his side on the floor, meaning everything had settled on one side of his abdomen and ribcage. There was only really one half of him left, with the rest of his body seeming to have melted down into the carpet. It was not a particularly pleasant sight, but I continued with due process.

An hour after I radioed it in, the local undertakers arrived to take the body away. After taking one look at it, they stated they were not equipped or experienced enough to remove it from the property in its current state, and that it would need referring to a specialist team. The further three hours it took for the specialist team to arrive offered me the perfect chance to slow down and make sure I was doing things correctly. My job was to look for suspicious circumstances, and then accurately report and relay my findings. All the while I paced around his home I talked to the deceased, explaining what I was doing, as I would have done had he still been alive.

To put an exact figure on how many dead bodies I saw across my career would be impossible, but I would estimate it to be in the region of two to three hundred.

I worked alongside many officers who struggled in the presence of a dead body, becoming panicked, anxious, or even disgusted. Personally I never found that to be the case, and as such, I always preferred to attend a sudden death alone. It meant that I didn't have to deal with another individual and their feelings and attitude towards the situation. The dead can't hurt you, unlike the living, and to consider treating a dead body as a disgusting object I find largely offensive. The way I viewed it was that there was no material difference between a living victim and dead one, and that someone should not be treated any differently just because their heart has stopped beating. I afforded them as much time and dignity as I would have had they still been breathing. It was my job to be respectful.

After locating the deceased's address book and establishing a few points of contact that should later be notified of his death, I then looked around for a suicide note, which I did not find. Flicking through the unopened post I noted that the oldest letter was dated six months beforehand.

It seemed that he had family, and his flat was on the site of a sheltered housing scheme, which had wardens, yet, tragically, nobody had noticed that he had been dead for potentially, at least five and a half months.

When the team arrived to take the body away, they hopped out of their van in full hazmat suits, with professional breathing apparatus, as though there had been a deadly viral outbreak. Unbeknownst to me at the time, bodies in such a condition as the deceased can harbour seriously nasty bacteria, which I had been completely oblivious to as I walked around his small flat for several hours. Standing in the hallway I watched as they turned the body over, before effectively scooping him up and pouring him into bags to take away. He was really nothing more than an open cavity full of decomposing human tissue. The carpet underneath where his body had been was teeming with maggots.

When I returned to the station I completed a sudden death report, taking my time to ensure I went above and beyond. As it appeared nobody had cared too much for the deceased whilst he was living, I felt that I owed him the highest level of service that I could offer. Death comes to us all, and I hoped that if I ever found myself in the circumstance of such an unfortunate death, that the officer in charge would behave with the same level of professionality as I did.

The body went off to the morgue and my report was filed. Usually, it was at that point my involvement would end, but around two weeks later I was called into the detective inspector's office and quizzed as to whether I had searched the body when I arrived. *'Absolutely not,'* was my short answer. It was so heavily decomposed that whilst I wasn't overly perturbed, I most certainly did not think to touch it.

For a few days after I wondered what the additional questions were in relation to, until I found out that upon admission to the mortuary one of the mortuary staff had taken the bank card and pin number out of his wallet and attempted to use it to withdraw money from a cash machine. They were actions which defied comprehension, and I was enraged at the further indignity caused to the deceased after his lonely death.

The mortuary worker was of course arrested and prosecuted and would never be allowed to ever return to their profession, but the whole experience further cemented in me the importance of the work I was doing; helping those people who were completely helpless.

9

For my efforts in relation to the aforementioned case, I was awarded a Divisional Commander's Award, 'in recognition of outstanding work in connection with the exemplary manner in which he investigated a difficult and unpleasant sudden death and subsequently presented the case to HM Coroner with great care and precision.'

My greatest rewards came from helping others.

Especially those who were particularly vulnerable or grappling with their darkest moments. For many, interacting with a police officer indicates that something has gone awry and in those instances, especially during sudden deaths, I felt a profound responsibility to support those in need. It was my obligation to treat the deceased with the utmost professionalism and respect, to act with integrity, and honour the dignity of the person in front of me.

Being in the presence of dead bodies was not something I had been prepared for. In sombre situations I found the best way to ease my anxiety was to treat the body as though it were still alive. Whether I was checking for signs of injury or carefully removing and bagging their jewellery, I would talk to them about the process, believing that they could hear me. I hoped it would provide them comfort in their transition.

Death is final and can feel especially overwhelming for the bereaved, as it brings about a whirlwind of emotions. I viewed it as my duty to try and alleviate their pain with compassion, whilst also honouring the integrity of due process. Discussions around death are often shrouded in silence, but death should not remain a taboo topic. It is an essential part of life that we must confront openly. It is my opinion that families should engage more in conversations about death, express their wishes and share just how they want to be remembered. After all, we only get one chance to die so we should make sure that, as much as possible, our journey is in alignment with our desires and values. Embracing such discussions in advance could bring an extra layer of clarity and comfort, not only to ourselves but also to our loved ones.

10

The blow constantly dealt by the harshness of reality was softened by working alongside brilliant people. Being a part of a team offered some refuge from the elements of the day job that were less than pleasant.

Sam was another relatively young PC on my team, and he was sometimes referred to as 'Father' around the station, because he was vicar-like in his demeanour. He spoke slowly, in soft, melodic undertones and was nothing short of a lovely guy who had an obvious and genuine care for others. At six foot four inches and nine stone dripping wet, he may not have had the brawn that some of the other proud Alpha team members offered, but he excelled when it came to reassuring or consoling someone in their moment of need. His personality brought a much-needed degree of balance to the team.

Whilst out one day I had detained a young man at the home of his ex-girlfriend, on suspicion of assaulting her. After radioing in for transport to get him back to the station, Sam soon arrived in the station van. My prisoner had failed the attitude test immediately as he spat and kicked at me whilst I restrained him, and he tried to make even the short journey from the house to the van incredibly difficult. Once he was secured and we were on our way, he continued shouting threats and obscenities from the back and lashing out physically in his temporary confinement.

'*Get your seatbelt on, pal…*' Sam said to me from the driver's seat as we pulled away. He continued, with a smile on his face, '*I need to perform a moving brake test…*'

To ensure the safety of a police vehicle, for example to check it hadn't been tampered with, at the beginning of each shift we were advised to have a cursory inspection of the exterior, paying particular attention to the lights and tyres. Then, as soon as practical after setting off, to check that the brakes hadn't been cut and that all four wheels were pulling evenly, a moving brake test was required.

Usually, it would involve nothing more than a light tap on the brakes, but as we increased our speed to just over forty miles per hour, I realised that my somewhat unassuming colleague clearly had a more aggressive version in mind. As the prisoner was still hurling abuse from the back of the van, Sam proceeded to slam his foot down on the brake, so much so that he raised himself up and off the driver's seat and was practically standing up on the pedal.

Within a matter of seconds we had come to a complete stop. From forty to zero, and I heard an almighty crash in the back of the van as the prisoner hit one side, before flying across and hitting the other side with another loud bang.

It seemed to have done the trick in subduing our passenger as for the remainder of the journey we didn't hear another peep, and I enjoyed a brief rest before we had to unpack him again at the other end. We arrived at the station, and I couldn't help but laugh as I opened the van doors. With his hands cuffed behind his back, during the moving brake test he had been unable to stop himself hitting the caged sides of the holding space he was in. He looked like he had been in a waffle machine, with a rather large and prominent mesh print on his face.

Not everybody likes the police. Not everybody respects the job they do and not everybody is grateful for their assistance, which for a while I struggled to come to terms with it, but retrospectively I have come to understand it a bit more. Not everybody is fit for the role and the authority it brings. Some don't possess the character and personality the job requires, others lack discipline, and regrettably, some see the uniform as their right to behave in any way they like, which leads them to completely abusing their powers. However, my experience was that the ones who had clearly become a police officer to obtain a position of power, which they felt they could justifiably abuse in the course of their duty, were very few and far between and therefore easy to spot from a mile away.

One of the PCs on my team had a reputation for being a bit of a bully. Every time he opened his mouth, what came out was either offensive or idiotic, and if anybody was smaller and weaker than he was, he was sure to let them know. We gave him a variety of nicknames one of which was 'Tiny', as he was smaller than most of us. Naturally, he hated it, but it was a gentle way we felt we could keep him in check.

It was a warm evening during early May and the weather was decent, which meant it was a busy shift for us, and the cells in our relatively small station were full.

Tiny was out in the van on his own, likely looking for someone to rub up the wrong way, when he turned up to a call on the radio regarding a fight on a housing estate.

It was not uncommon to turn up to such a call and find that the fight had ended, and the participants dispersed. I found an easy way to make sure that was the case was to put the sirens on as I neared the scene. But when Tiny arrived, he found a heavily intoxicated man, having a merry old time on his own, shouting, and kicking over dustbins. He was clearly causing a disturbance, but if I had been the first officer on scene, my approach would have been different to Tiny's. I likely would have tried to befriend him, before carefully ushering him in the direction of his home or maybe even giving him a lift. To do so wouldn't have been standard protocol, and the bosses wouldn't have approved, but if he had ten more minutes to walk to get home there would have been the potential for ten more minutes of trouble, which could be avoided with some help.

As I was absent at the beginning of the interaction, I can only surmise that Tiny would have been playing King Dick during his first communication with the man, likely shouting from the driver's seat of the van something along the lines of, '*Oi! You! Dickhead! Stop what you are doing and fuck off!*' Whatever he said or did, there is no doubt in my mind that he created a situation where there needn't have been one. The trouble then was, he had to deal with the situation he had created which he wasn't equipped to do alone. Tiny's strongest muscle was his tongue, whereas the other bloke was built like a brick outhouse. Because Tiny's attitude was shitty, the response he received was shitty, which forced him out of the van. It was at that point I expect Tiny realised he had bitten off more than he could chew, and that he had wildly underestimated the size of the problem.

An emergency call was made from Tiny's radio, but nothing could be heard other than muffled shouting so another patrol car and I arrived on scene as quickly as we could. When we did, we found Tiny looking incredibly worse for wear. The big chap was still shouting and flailing his arms, whilst our colleague made feeble and unsuccessful attempts to cuff him. After we assisted in getting the drunken man into the van, Tiny relayed to us the information of the incident, only not entirely as it had occurred. Assisted by a couple of witness statements, we soon drew the correct conclusion that the fight had not exactly been an equal match, as had originally been suggested by our colleague. One woman explained how at one point during the row Tiny had been picked up by the scruff of his neck, and had his face rubbed in a hanging basket. Like a biscuit being dunked in a cup of tea he was then taken along to the next hanging basket for the same treatment. When we arrived back to the custody suite Tiny still had compost in his hair and his shirt pocket to corroborate her story.

The prisoner was still incredibly animated, so we handed him over to the custody staff who went to put him in Cell One whilst he calmed down. The view was we would visit him later to take his statement. Cell One happened to be the only female cell in the station, and it would have been completely fine to put him in there had it been empty, only it wasn't. Thirty minutes later, when the custody clerk returned to the cell, he opened the hatch to see if our man had indeed calmed down, only to be met with the sight of him engaged in intercourse with the female prisoner. Fortunately, she did not dispute her consent and willingness to participate in the act, but that could easily have not been the case. It was a prime example of poor decision-making, which, regrettably, I saw often during times of stress.

'*All units. Is anybody available to attend a domestic at 15 Horseshoe Avenue?*'

'*This is PC Clarke, 9678. Headed there now.*'

'*Good luck, Clarkey. It's fucking Mad Sue again.*'

Calls to attend a domestic disturbance were so common that it was not unusual for me to attend several in a week. Mostly it was a dispute between a man and a woman, but disputes between neighbours were also very common.

Sue was a frequent caller, usually about something totally innocuous but I turned up anyway to listen to her account of what had happened on that particular day, as was my duty.

I stood in Sue's living room and listened whilst she ranted about how her neighbour had repeatedly parked on the road, outside of her house, and how she, Sue, struggled with mobility and therefore expected some more courtesy and consideration.

As she explained to me the scenario, that had been ongoing for months, she was getting increasingly angry. She was becoming so manic in the confines of the front room that for her sake, and indeed for my own, I needed it to stop. The neighbour in question then appeared at the front window, seeming to want to give her account of the story. Sue, at the sight of her nemesis, flew towards the front door in a fit of rage, with no indication that she had an issue with her mobility at all. I knew I needed to stop her causing damage to herself or the neighbour, and the offence I would usually have drawn upon to arrest someone behaving in that way would have been breach of the peace, but in her private dwelling I had no authority whatsoever to do that. Not knowing what I would charge her with, I got out my handcuffs anyway and as I attempted to put them on her, I received a strong slap. She continued to resist my efforts and began trying to scratch and claw at my face, but I got one of her hands in the handcuffs and used the other end to fix her to an old iron radiator which hung on the wall. After a few minutes of screaming at me from her seated position on the floor, she finally settled down and I went outside to talk to the neighbour. Briefly, I listened to her version of events before kindly telling her she was only making the situation worse and that she should just piss off.

Back inside I arrested Sue for assaulting a police officer and a few weeks later she was ordered by the court to pay me compensation; the grand total of forty pounds.

It wasn't the only time that I was assaulted on the job during my first year.

When someone placed a call complaining about a row outside a neighbouring property, I went along to try and de-escalate the situation, only to fail miserably.

Disputes surrounding custody of children amidst a separation were the cause of the aggravation, and it was alleged by the neighbour that a similar row occurred every time the ex-husband picked up or dropped off the children at the family home, where he had formerly resided. I had gone with the view that I would facilitate the handover of the children and prevent a breach of the peace. My experience up to that point dictated that my role would have been to side with the female and take positive action to deal with the male involved, but not on this occasion.

The reason for the separation was due to the former husband seeking companionship outside of his marriage, and it was that day I really understood the quote 'hell hath no fury like a woman scorned.' She was violent, erratic, and verbally abusive; everything I didn't want to deal with on a Sunday morning. He on the other hand was calmness personified and seemed to just want to do the right thing, which aggravated her further.

As I stood between the two of them on the front lawn of the detached house, in a reasonably pleasant cul-de-sac, I tried my best to calm her down. Mistakenly, I assumed she was of no threat to me, and that her grievance was only with her ex-husband. What a teaching moment that turned out to be. In her frustration at me turning up, and in her view, seeming to side with her enemy, she came towards me in a rage. She wasn't quite running but it was at least a mild jog. As she continued to shout, she swung her leg and kicked me straight in the spuds. It took the wind right out of me, and I stooped over for a few seconds before gathering myself together to persevere with my job, despite the severe aching in my testicles and stomach.

Just as she was within spitting distance of him, swearing and gesticulating wildly, I forced my cuffs on her and gladly stuffed her in the back of the van.

She didn't stop her angry crusade the whole ride to the station and I was only too pleased to deposit her in custody, for a much-needed period of reflection.

Turning out to defuse an argument was not a problem for me, and I mostly quite enjoyed the challenge, but the one part of the job I truly detested was town centre patrol. The place was awful, the people were awful, and as much as I tried, I couldn't find one single redeeming factor about being there. I often tried to get involved with something else which would mean I was excused, but was rarely successful, so there I was, on a busy Saturday morning, in Shitsville, Tennessee.

An hour into my shift I was approached by a panicked woman in her early thirties. Her two-year-old daughter had gone missing.

'Someone has taken her!' she shrieked at me, understandably in distress. The father paced up and down behind her, smoking a hand-rolled cigarette.

I was almost certain that the child had not been kidnapped. It was more likely that amidst the panic, the mother and her partner had not really been looking properly, and instead had just been running around flustered, like a pair of headless chickens. I took a description of the child, what she was wearing and where they had last seen her. Then confirming my suspicion, without any form of a plan, the parents dashed off in separate directions to continue the search.

All I had to do was stop and look around.

Pacing slowly, I paid attention to every corner of my surroundings, and it took no longer than two minutes before I found the girl.

She wasn't crying but looked a little bewildered as I scooped her up, explaining we were going to find her mummy and daddy. Back at the spot where the mother had first approached me, I waited, and soon enough, she came back into my view, so I gestured to her and brought her attention to the child. She ran over to me, grabbed her daughter, and without saying a word just walked off. I didn't expect a round of applause but thought she would have at least mustered a thank you.

I had received better receptions from people I had arrested.

In addition to the grim, grey infrastructure, and the feeling of general uncleanliness, the main reason I couldn't stand town centre patrol was because it was shoplifter central, and I expected to deal with the exact same thing each time I was there. In addition to my police radio, I also carried an additional one that was connected to all the security guards, and it was approaching lunchtime on a Saturday when I received a call from one of them to say he had seen a young man find a quiet corner of Marks and Spencer and conceal something down his trousers. Marks and Spencer was always a popular place for shoplifters as it was a large premises that stocked a variety of high-quality goods and had multiple entrances and exits, which made it easy to do a runner.

The information I was given was a standard description of what most working-class young men looked like in the nineties: black tracksuit, trainers, and a shaven head. The security guards often made excessive use of police terminology, so he went on to describe the young man as being actively furtive, which basically meant he was acting suspiciously. As quickly as my enthusiasm would allow, I headed in the direction of Marks and Spencer and when I arrived at the back entrance to the shop, someone who fitted the description was making his exit.

Our eyes locked. He knew who I was, and I had a pretty good idea who he was too.

He was dressed for the chase, whereas I was in my woollen trousers, boots, and big tit hat. Nevertheless, I was fit, and I expect he misjudged his opponent. The chase began, and with every stride I took, I inched closer to him. He made the fatal error of being more concerned with looking behind at me, than looking where he was going. He knew he was going to get caught, as much as I knew I was going to catch him.

He rounded the outside of the building, heading for the pedestrianised part of the town centre and I was no more than six feet behind him when there came a moment where he had to choose which route to go, an actual fork in the road. Had he chosen to go left, we would have been in the large, open-air town square, where his chances of getting away would have been much greater amongst the Saturday morning bustle. He chose instead to go right, back inside a small shopping arcade.

Given my experience of foot chases, I knew when the perfect time to strike was. We were a few feet away from the open shopfront of a Claire's Accessories and the opportunity arrived. It was a real action hero moment, of which there are so few in life, and I launched myself at his waist, torpedoing us both into several stands of hair clips and bobbles and sending them all flying.

An audience had gathered to watch as I cautioned and arrested my runaway thief.

A quick search found that he had a carriage clock down the front of his trousers, which as I tackled him, had left quite an imprint on each of his inner thighs and lower abdomen. When we returned to the station I took him to interview for questioning. He seemed to accept that we both had a role to play so for the remainder of our interaction, we got on relatively well. He was open with the truth and spoke freely; I only wished that all prisoners were as co-operative.

Q: *So, you admit to stealing the item in question, could you explain a little more about your motives for doing do?*

A: *It was supposed to be a present for my girlfriend. I haven't seen her for a while as I just got released this morning from a six-month stretch in prison.*

Sadly, he only got the chance to speak to his girlfriend briefly on the phone and then was detained pending trial. My expectation was that he was headed straight back to prison, to be detained at Her Majesty's pleasure. If only he had stopped to think that his attempts to steal a measly carriage clock would have resulted in him doing more time. Pun largely intended. It was ironic, and a little sad, but I saw it all too often. Some people didn't know anything other than committing crime, and whilst short-term prison sentences act as a deterrent for some, it also hampers any chances of employment upon release and can even bolster criminal connections. The eight of us that had been on shift, coupled with the custody staff, sat down together over some food in the canteen before we all left for home. It gave us an opportunity to share some of our stories from the day. That arrest was easily one of the best moments of my career, and I only wish now that I had a picture to look back on.

I was sat next to the duty sergeant for that shift and he was a man for whom I had a great deal of respect. He was another large, barrel-chested man, who was always dressed in his police tunic; an outfit typically reserved for more formal occasions and not just everyday duty. He was incredibly well spoken but notably unkempt, in the same ilk as Boris Johnson. His hair was mostly grey, and his police tunic was usually covered in ash as he seemed to be constantly wielding a cigarette between his fingers and used dramatic hand gestures every time he spoke.

A large oil portrait of Queen Elizabeth II watched over us all as we sat down and tucked into our meat pie, red cabbage, and mushy peas. Had there been a tablecloth I expect the sergeant would have tucked it down the front of his uniform. As he shovelled food in his mouth at the rate of knots, he commended me on my efforts and chuckled as I explained how the clock had left my suspect with rather uncomfortable injuries. With a mouthful of food, he scoffed to one of my other colleagues, *'More peas, Tony! More peas!'* and sure enough, Tony came along and ladled some more peas onto his already-piled-high plate.

11

While the drama of the arrest of the shoplifter, and the comedic destruction of a shopfront were memorable, what sticks with me the most was the desperation and shortsightedness of the young man involved. He was forthcoming in admitting his guilt, shared his motives, and understood the ramifications of his actions, but the system had already failed him. For acts of petty crime, he would never have been in prison long enough to benefit from any educational programmes or receive support for any underlying issues that were contributing to his criminal behaviour. Short-term sentences rarely achieve anything meaningful and in my opinion are therefore a complete waste of taxpayers' money. In cases such as this one, prison is nothing more than a tool of punishment rather than rehabilitation, which would have served little purpose for the young lad in question. Some offenders are beyond rehabilitation and enjoy a life of crime, but many individuals within the prison system are not active criminals by choice, rather out of necessity. Many are victims of circumstance, poor decisions and challenging situations, and with the right support and guidance most could reintegrate into society and make a positive contribution. A shift in approach from deterrence through punishment, to rehabilitation, is necessary if we are to break the cycle of crime, and help individuals reclaim their lives.

During these early years, I was fortunate to work alongside some incredible individuals. As the newest recruit, and the youngest on my shift, I quickly learnt the value of teamwork. There were five teams at our station, with only one small team of six or seven on shift at any one time. Whilst on duty we were responsible for covering half of a large metropolitan borough. It was a mix of wealthy neighbourhoods, filled with footballers and TV stars, which were situated alongside two of the most deprived council estates in the country. With limited resources we had to be strategic and work smart. We were a tight-knit group, with an almost instinctual ability to anticipate each other's moves. When it came to hunting for suspects in connection with a crime, we seamlessly collaborated, creating an atmosphere of collective intuition that felt almost magical. I had immense respect for my colleagues.

Of course, no group is without its challenges, for example Tiny, who was a constant source of frustration. He was arrogant, and intoxicated by the authority he believed he wielded. Always eager to provoke others, he revelled in the power of knowing he could always play the arrest card if he needed. Nobody ever wanted to partner with him because he was insufferable. Yet he was still a part of our team, and time and time again, when he bit off more than he could chew, it fell to the rest of us to rescue him from the chaos he had created. In the end, his arrogance led to his downfall and he ended up serving a short stretch in prison for perverting the course of justice. Prison, I imagine, was incredibly unforgiving for him. I cannot think of a harsher reality for someone who once wore the badge.

12

Outside of the job, Jane and I had been dating, although I can't say that it was a particularly remarkable romance. The nature of my work meant that the relationship seemed to be mostly in stops and starts, with us never being able to spend more than a couple of days together at a time, and the odd weeknight here and there. Before meeting her, I had been in several relationships, but none of them had lasted longer than a few months, mainly due to my lack of commitment. Jane had shown an interest in pursuing a more serious relationship, and whilst I hadn't been blown away by her when we first met, I was flattered.

My work commitments meant that I didn't have to be overly proactive, and offered the perfect excuse for us not to be in each other's pockets all the time, so I was happy just to go along with it. With neither of us yet living alone, we spent most of our time together at her parents' house. They lived closer to the station than my own parents meaning it was often much easier for me to go there after my shift. Family was everything to Jane, whereas my own experience of 'family' up to that point had been a little indifferent.

I was born in 1974, to very young and inexperienced parents. When my mum found out she was pregnant, my dad had just started his undergraduate degree. Whilst he studied, he wasn't in employment, so when I was born, we lived on financial support provided by the government. For the first seven years of my life, we lived in a ground-floor council flat, which was decorated very much in-keeping with the times. I remember the seventies-style carpet, which was brown with a repeated pattern of yellow circles and twists. The pattern was demarcated with cream lines that were just wide enough for me to use as a track for the handful of toy cars I owned.

Growing up, I wasn't aware that we didn't have any money, and it didn't feel as though it really mattered. It was not an era when the constant pursuit of material artefacts was prevalent, as seems to be the case nowadays.

There was a great sense of community on our estate. Everyone was always willing to lend a hand, or a pint of milk, and one of our neighbours used to let the local kids ride on the back of his motorbike. Parents watched on as he pulled wheelies up and down the street, with small children hanging on to the back and not a helmet in sight. Every Friday afternoon the chippy van came around, bringing with it the smell of minted mushy peas that would waft through our flat. A bag of chips cost just ten pence and every now and again we were just about able to afford them.

The one-and-a-half-mile journey to primary school I walked unescorted, and when the weather warmed up, a lady who lived along the way would bring her budgies out onto her front drive in their cages. We visited my dad's mum on the bus every Saturday, and each week she put on the same spread for lunch: bread and butter, pickled onions, tinned salmon, and a bit of salad. Playing cards together, her bristly top lip when she gave me a kiss, and how she used to walk me to the shop for a couple of pennies' worth of Sports Mixture are what I remember most of her.

My mum's brother was in the army and whilst he was posted to Germany, he left his dog behind in our care, along with his black and white portable television. It had an aerial on top that had to be manipulated to find one of the three available channels. The one thing I remember watching a lot of was Starsky and Hutch. The pace of life back then seemed much slower, meaning the days seemed to last forever. There was quite a large patch of woodland nearby to the estate, and I spent most of my time in there, with my best friend, Stephen, who lived two doors down. We spent our days exploring, walking around with sticks, and skimming stones. It was as though I was a real-life Huckleberry Finn, and for the most part, it was an experience completely devoid of anything dangerous. Apart from one day when we were confronted in the woods by a man in his thirties who asked if we wanted to go and see some puppies. It sounds like a cliché when I recall it now, but that was the offer he made, and it had the potential to develop into quite a serious situation. Stephen was quick to run away, leaving me on my own with the man, who proceeded to expose himself to me before I too ran away and told my mum. She called the police who visited the house to take my statement, but I don't think they took it too seriously. That wasn't the first time the police had been to our house as I had dislocated my shoulder twice in the space of one year, due to my mum being excessively forceful when it came to getting me dressed or pulling my sleeves up. Social services came around too but it never amounted to anything.

Whilst I look back on parts of my carefree childhood with great fondness and attribute a great deal of my independence to my upbringing, I cannot deny there was a part of me that subconsciously longed for parents who had wanted to be more involved with me as I was growing up. My mum always seemed busy and, like lots of children of the seventies, I got the impression she wanted me out from under her feet, so I was just expected to go and play somewhere out of the way.

When my dad finished his undergraduate degree, we still didn't see him a lot as he began his doctorate and accepted a job in in another part of the country, leaving home on a Sunday afternoon only to return Friday night. The most time I ever spent with him was laying on the lounge floor, whilst he sat on the sofa and watched the television on a Saturday evening. If I was quiet, I could stay as long as I liked.

My mum was not afraid to speak her mind and give me an occasional wallop, but my dad was highly intelligent, and very dry. He had a way of making me feel incredibly inferior, and I couldn't challenge him on anything without being intellectually beaten.

Even as a young child he never let me win so much as a game of Tiddlywinks. Whilst he rarely showed his emotions, he often showed his displeasure with things, so I spent a great deal of time seeking his approval, which to this day I never felt I got.

In 1981, my parents welcomed another baby, and we moved house to be closer to my dad's work. Our new home was a three-bedroom, mid-mews property and was quite an obvious upgrade from the council flat I had previously known.

It had a large garden at the front and back, and a detached garage which was large enough to accommodate my dad's canary yellow Volkswagen Golf, but he chose instead to keep that parked on the street where he could see it. Instead, I used the garage space to practise my breakdancing; blasting out hip hop from my cassette boombox to my heart's content. The house move meant that I had joined a new school, which was much bigger than my last, but I swiftly overcame any anxiety around being the new kid by taking a football along with me each day which led me to become popular with the other boys. The school had acres of fields so as much as possible I played football, before too long ending up on the school team.

My class teacher was a middle-aged Iranian woman who was always smoking in class, either with the door open or stood by a window. We would often get our books back after she had marked them with cigarette ash in the pages. One time I had asked her if I could do an experiment, explaining that I was interested in the rate at how different things burned, and she said she was happy for me to do it. For an entire lesson I sat at back of the classroom, behind plastic concertina doors, burning things on my own with a candle she had provided.

My mum had even less time for me than she'd had previously with a baby to look after, but the house on the end of our row was home to a young couple and the husband, Ray, offered to take me along with him fishing. I watched in awe one day as he shot a bird with his air rifle, before tying it up in a tree to hang over the water. We left it there for a couple of weeks, during which time it decayed quite severely, so much that it was baiting the water with the maggots that dropped and therefore making our further fishing attempt far more successful. The first fish I caught was a pike, and it was so aggressive that when it came out of the water it was practically vertical on its tail.

Ray was kind enough to give me an old fishing rod so that I could have a go myself when he wasn't around, and in a stroke of good fortune, I happened upon a dead bird one morning so went to find somewhere to hang it as he had done. In what was quite a dangerous stunt, I shimmied along a high up branch, with a fast-flowing river underneath, and attached my bird. It was the wrong place entirely to do it as the current was so fast that any maggots that fell would have been swiftly swept away.

The firm my dad had been working for eventually went bust, which meant a change in job for him, and another house move for us, again to another part of the country.

We upgraded the property again, from a three-bedroom mid mews to a four-bedroom detached house on one of the nicest estates in the area. I didn't notice at the time but looking back, there was certainly an accumulation of more things. My clothes were no longer hand-me-down, and I had money for magazines and records.

Moving schools yet again wasn't a pleasant experience for me as the move aligned with my transition into senior school, so the school itself was much bigger. It had even more kids and felt incredibly hostile to an outsider. The first few weeks for me were testing. Not only was I the new kid with a different accent, but I was also reasonably good-looking which meant that I got a fair bit of attention from the girls, and then also in turn from the boys. In my first week I got into a fight with one particularly thick-set young lad, who out of nowhere threw a punch at me. I threw a punch back and we wrestled a bit before a teacher intervened. Most of the kids who attended the school were from a part of the town that wasn't as affluent as the area in which I lived, but once I had settled in, I managed to straddle the two camps relatively well. I found that I enjoyed spending my time more with those who were from working-class families, because their upbringing was more like my own had been up to that point.

It was the first time the situation had allowed me the opportunity to make proper friends, as it was guaranteed we were going to stay living in that area at least until my schooling had finished. Before that, all my friendships had been quite shallow because we had not stayed in one place long enough for me to develop them into much more. The fact that we had moved around a bit taught me to become charming and charismatic, as they were the necessary attributes required to quickly develop surface level relationships, and that later proved incredibly useful as a police officer.

There was a difference in the schooling systems between where I had previously been and where I ended up, which meant, in effect, I was repeating a year. My new school had mistaken my familiarity with the curriculum for a real aptitude for academia and I was placed in the top set for everything, but beyond the initial year I started to lag behind the brainier of my peers. Not engaged remotely, I felt like I was just going through the motions, but fortunately was still able to get stuck into sports and survived the remaining years of school on my sporting attributes alone. I was tall, fast, physically bigger than most my age and I didn't mind getting stuck into everything.

Mr Turner taught us both maths and physical education, and had a propensity for throwing board rubbers at anybody who spoke out in his class. The school showers were freezing meaning that nobody liked to use them, but Mr Turner was a stickler for ensuring that we all did. He made us completely undress and whipped each of us with a towel as we ran through the cold trickle of water, barely getting wet.

As I recall it now it seems wildly inappropriate, but it was the eighties so seemed to be considered completely acceptable at the time, and nobody batted an eyelid.

When the weather was too bad to play sports outside, we would play murder ball in the hall. He stood in the middle of the room throwing a medicine ball at us as we ran around the edge. If it hit you, first you were on the floor. Second, you were out of the game.

Midway through 1997 Jane suggested we should take a holiday, and after all the action that the job had so far brought, I was grateful to have a week off and get away. We were young and didn't have too much money, so we settled for what we could get. That turned out to be a cockroach ridden apartment in Pathos, but it was a blissful change in pace and an opportunity for my mind and body to rest.

Jane was a few years older than I was, and when we first met, she had not long since come out of a long-term relationship. I think that is the reason she seemed intent on us being more than just a flash in the pan. As we lay by the pool one afternoon, she mentioned that we should think about moving in together.

I had hardly considered what, if any, real future Jane and I had together, so was completely blindsided by her proposition. It felt a little hasty. However, not wanting to cause any upset or conflict, I agreed we should take the next step in our relationship. I had been looking to move out from my parents' house anyway, so her suggestion was a timely solution. Soon after we returned home, we began renting a mid-terraced, two-up, two-down house, and I returned to work.

When another concern for welfare came in, I was dispatched to a 1930s semi-detached house, where Mrs Smith had not been seen for a few days. Following the usual procedure, I knocked, before shouting through the letterbox.

There was no response, so I kicked the door in, and called out.

'Mrs Smith? It's the police. Are you okay?'

With no answer I forced my way in, and upon entry didn't notice anything remarkable; there was no audible sign of life, but no obvious smell of death either.

After a cursory look around the downstairs of the house I found nothing suspicious and no signs of forced entry. Heading up the stairs I entered the first room on my left, which was the master bedroom. If I hadn't already received a summary description of Mrs Smith, the pink floral duvet and vintage hairbrush and mirror set that lay on her dressing table would have quickly informed me that she was a very typical old lady, living alone. There was no sign of her in the bedroom, but it was evident from the dent in the pillow, and the pulled back duvet, that someone had been in the bed.

Despite it being around three in the afternoon the curtains were closed so I opened them to let in some light, before proceeding to check the other two bedrooms and the bathroom. The toilet was separate to the bathroom and was the last place I checked and sure enough there she was, on the toilet, slumped forward in her nighty and slippers. I shouted for a response, thinking that she could possibly just be deaf and in any moment, she would look up and get the fright of her life. It could have been that she had just fallen asleep on the loo, so I put my hand on her to try and illicit a response, but she was stone cold and as stiff as a board; most definitely dead.

Rigor mortis is one of the most obvious processes that occurs after someone has passed away. Onset is usually a few hours after death and involves the stiffening of all muscles and joints in the body. Crime dramas would have you believe that it is useful in helping to determine the time of death, but that is a common misconception as rigor mortis can be highly variable. It can last only one day in some people and up to four days in others. The time it takes to develop, and the time it takes before it wears off, is largely determined by the temperature of the atmosphere that surrounds the body. Even though I was certain Mrs Smith was no longer in the land of the living, my reaction was to check her pulse. The easiest place to do that was at the side of the neck so I put my hand under her chin to lift her head, and as I did I saw a hole, the diameter of a toilet roll tube, right in the centre of her throat.

The wound was black and burned around the edges, as though it had been cauterised and it caused me immediately to reassess my initial conclusion that Mrs Smith had just died on the toilet in a mishap brought on by old age. I started to consider that there must have been some foul play, and if that was the case, I had just traipsed right through a murder scene, touching nearly everything in sight.

From that point, I had to treat her death very differently. Leaving Mrs Smith in the unfortunate position in which I found her, I went downstairs to place the call to crime support and before too long a detective inspector arrived, along with a doctor.

The house was cordoned off and I briefed my superior on what I had found, before leading them both upstairs to see the body. The doctor was quick to determine that the wound had been made from the inside, so with no signs of forced entry or a struggle, it was likely not a murder. The detective inspector agreed that it seemed to be nothing more than a terrible accident, which relieved me of the concern that I may have just been incredibly careless with what could have been a crime scene.

We had to move the body for the team who were on their way to take her away. The problem wasn't particularly complex, but I found myself confronted with a situation I would have preferred to avoid. As the most junior person, the responsibility naturally fell to me to squeeze into the WC and carry her out.

She stayed in a perfect seated position as I picked her up and fireman lifted her into the master bedroom and placed her on the bed. So that she could be taken to the coroner to exactly determine the cause of death we had to break the rigor mortis, which is an act that doesn't always happen swiftly. It is not like breaking a bone, but instead requires putting a substantial amount of pressure on each joint, which loosens the muscles and allows it to gradually give way. The strength of rigor mortis can be quite surprising, and I never saw a more severe case than I did that day. It took all three of us to straighten her out.

As I left the property, with the image of the charred wound in my head, my brain was in overdrive as to how such a death could have occurred. The only possible scenario I could really think of was that she had an electronic larynx, a voice box device, which must have short circuited and caused the damage. And perhaps as the hole had gotten bigger it had fallen out and I had just failed to see it in the house.

Closure came a week later as I read the coroner's report on her death. He deduced from the location where she was found that she had woken up in the night and needed to use the bathroom. A pretty accurate estimation from the expert. It was then ruled that whilst on the toilet, she had suffered a heart attack, during which she inhaled a cigarette which she must have lit for her middle-of-the-night bathroom break. The cigarette had become lodged in her throat and after her heart had stopped and she passed away, the cigarette continued to burn down, creating the hole I saw in her neck. The butt of the cigarette had been recovered from her throat.

13

A significant aspect of achieving personal success, however that is defined by you, involves becoming comfortable with being uncomfortable. It was being at ease with discomfort that gave me the ability to always carry out my job diligently and professionally, even in the face of obscure or upsetting scenes.

Embracing fears and anxieties as opportunities for growth and learning, rather than obstacles to avoid, is important, particularly in the context of stressful situations. If we can pause and sit with our discomfort before we act, we can shift our perspective on the situation at hand, better manage our stress and maintain high levels of performance under pressure. Cultivating the ability to observe our emotions without acting on them allows for a more thoughtful and strategic response.

To perform at our best, we must learn to manage our initial reactions.

By suppressing the instinctive urge to react, we can deliberately choose how to respond to challenging circumstances. In doing so, we not only enhance our performance, but also foster resilience. Navigating discomfort is therefore a tool for growth and adaptation.

Throughout my life, I've cultivated a habit of stepping into discomfort, viewing it as a valuable opportunity for growth and development. This exhilarating feeling of being outside my comfort zone is where I've learnt the most about myself and my capabilities. The real challenge lies in finding that balance between venturing into the unknown, but also knowing when to retreat to our comfort zones to recharge after pushing our limits.

If you aspire to achieve anything in life, embracing discomfort is not just a necessity; it is essential.

14

I was located on the South division, but it was not uncommon for us to share resources with other divisions when it was required. One morning in the early autumn of 1997, when the North division required extra manpower, I had my first experience of an armed siege. In comparison to ninety per cent of the other officers on the scene I was still a complete novice, so wasn't aware of all the intricacies of such an operation and was mostly an onlooker until given any direction to act.

The particulars of the incident were that a dispute had arisen between a same-sex male couple inside their home, and during the altercation one of them had pulled a kitchen knife and threatened to stab the other to death. By all accounts, the suspect was holding his partner hostage. The police had surrounded the property, and it was very much a *'COME OUT WITH YOUR HANDS ABOVE YOUR HEAD!'* type of affair. A cordon had been put around the perimeter of the house, and there was an ongoing negotiation to try and encourage the culprit out of the property so that he could be arrested. Impatience seemed to have gotten the better of the officer in charge, so a decision was made that the Tactical Aid Group (TAG), would be sent inside the property. When they all piled out of the van, they looked like a rugby team on tour, and I don't think any one of them weighed less than eighteen stone. There were thick in the arm, and a little bit thick in the head too; a specific sort of individual, ideal for the necessary job they carried out, which required plenty of brawn but not too much brains.

Within five minutes of them arriving on the scene, they bashed the door in and stormed the property, likely overwhelming the already distressed man who was being held at knife point, but just seconds after entering they reemerged outside victorious. Two of them had carried the suspect out under their arms as though he was a piece of timber and after they deposited him with our team, he was arrested. The TAG team then went back into the property to do a cursory sweep, to make sure there were no other victims or casualties we had not previously been aware of.

I could hear the proceedings over the radio as they communicated with the team outside.

'Juliet 1. Can you ask that muppet who's just been arrested if there was anything in the tank in the back bedroom? It doesn't have a lid on.'

Sure enough, someone put their head in the back of the police car and quizzed the detainee.

'Juliet to TAG. Yeah, he says it is a tarantula and that the lid should definitely be on.'

The six burley blokes whom I had just seen striding in, as though not fazed by anything in the world, all came running frantically out of the house in a line, each of them shaking themselves off in a weird and wonderful panicked jiggle as they crossed the threshold. It was quite a sight to behold, like something from a *Benny Hill* sketch. Fortunately, the situation had been remedied. Everybody had done the job to the best of their abilities, and nobody had gotten hurt. For me it had been an easy and entertaining day on the beat, but days like that were the exception and not the rule.

'All units, please be aware that a white male, five foot eight and around fifty years old has escaped from the mental health facility on Beech Lane. He is wearing hospital clothing and has exited by smashing through a glass door so is likely bleeding profusely.'

Gone five in the afternoon on any given weekday, mental health teams and social services are all off the clock, leaving only blue light services to pick up the pieces of any incident that might occur. We were trained to do many things, but not necessarily to assist individuals who had very specific needs, especially without any context surrounding their history or current situation. The individual who escaped the hospital was located the morning after we received the call, unfortunately dead.

It had only been a couple of months after Jane and I had received the keys to our new home when the station received a call about a patient who had escaped the nearby psychiatric ward. There are varying levels of security for psychiatric patients – determined by their level of sectioning under the Mental Health Act 1983. For their own safety, some patients are contained without any liberties, but for others, they can exist quite happily under a less restrictive regime which may allow them for example, to be about the hospital grounds unsupervised.

It was not uncommon back then for people to escape the ward and take their own lives. The psychiatric ward in the hospital located on our division, had doors that opened pretty much directly onto a railway track, with only a feeble wire fence on the boundary; a situation I like to think was a catastrophic oversight, rather than being by design.

The escapee in question was a woman in her late thirties. She was usually subject to high security conditions but had somehow managed to get off the ward and proceeded to set fire to herself. Fortunately, she had not made it any further than the hospital grounds so received medical attention immediately. I arrived just as she was being wheeled towards theatre. The burns were so severe that I could barely make out she was human. Her skin was bubbling from the heat of the flames, but she was still conscious. As I walked at pace alongside her, she reached out and touched my hand, and as she did, she went into cardiac arrest and one minute later, she died.

The police usually arrive after death has occurred, rarely present in the actual moment, and I was in complete and utter shock. It was my first experience of a traumatic death, and I had not expected it at all. She died right in front of me in an instant, and not two years previous I had been working in a clothes shop and bumbling around doing bits of odd-job gardening.

To try and describe now how she looked and smelled, and how it made me feel it is nearly an impossible task. The whole incident, although it only lasted several minutes, was uniquely awful.

There were statements to be taken from hospital staff as well as a great deal of paperwork for me to complete back at the station, and for the remainder of my shift I did it all on autopilot, in a total daze. It was nine in the evening when I pulled up at home, still feeling a sense of complete confusion and bewilderment at the events that had unfolded before me. The woman in question was severely mentally ill, and had years of records to explain why she might take such drastic action to end her own life. But when she reached for my hand, I looked her in the eye and saw fear and sadness, perhaps even an understanding of the consequences of her actions, and regret for what she had done. And then she was gone.

Wearily I reached over and retrieved my coat from the passenger seat and then walked towards my front door. As I stepped into my new home, I was met with the unexpected scene of a dozen people, all drinking and laughing as music blared from the stereo. As I stood in the hall, the front door still wide open, trying to understand who everybody was and what they were doing in my home, Jane promptly appeared in view. She likely knew that I would have been reluctant to participate at the best of times, but in that moment there wasn't anything I would have been less inclined to do, than to slap on a fake smile and share a drink with a bunch of people I had deduced were mostly neighbours from our street.

Refusing to accept the drink Jane had tried to put in my hand I shouted out, *'Can everybody please just fuck off out of my house?!'*

The volume and tone of my request left little room for any confusion about what I was asking, and after a few moments of silence, everybody shuffled off and left, mumbling a few awkward apologies as they passed me in the hall.

Jane didn't say a single word. Not to question my behaviour, not to ask what had happened during my day, or indeed to ask if something was the matter. She just glared at me angrily, before bashing a few bottles around the kitchen and storming up the stairs to bed. I spent the night on the sofa, only to be woken the following morning with her stomping through the living room. She made a sarcastic remark that I needed to loosen up and enjoy myself before embarking on several days of the silent treatment. The silence suited me also. Previously, I had always tried to lighten the mood after any disagreements which was never really appreciated, but on this occasion, I was not remotely inclined to try and smooth things over. Not only was I annoyed that any sort of party had not been discussed with me in the first instance, but I was furious that I had been criticised for being a killjoy, when I had just witnessed a woman burn and die right in front of me. Of course, Jane didn't know that at the time, but she never thought to ask what had happened that could have caused me to be so outwardly distressed, and beyond that day I didn't see fit to tell her.

The following week I attended a domestic disturbance at a residential address, which had been described by the call operator as involving a young man who was receiving treatment for some form of mental health condition. As a young adult he had been spending Monday through to Friday in a care facility and returning home to his parents each weekend. The situation sounded serious, so me, Sam and another officer were dispatched to attend.

We arrived at the back door and immediately caught sight of the young man through the kitchen window. He was clearly mentally unstable, which was given away by the fact he was screaming at his mother as he held a ten-inch carving knife to her throat. He looked to be smaller than six feet but was well-built, and it was obvious that before we would be able to overpower and ultimately stop him, he would be able to cause significant harm. We opened the back door and announced ourselves, before Sam and I stepped over the threshold. Our presence seemed to immediately worsen his already erratic condition. His mother looked petrified and was crying as she pleaded with her son to stop. In that moment, I couldn't see how we would be able to de-escalate the situation and prevent him causing harm to her, so expecting the worst, I whispered to my colleague outside that he should radio to have an ambulance on standby. Sam tried to engage the young man in conversation, but he didn't want to talk. He was just screaming at us to leave, and that he was going to kill his mother.

'I know you don't really want to hurt your mother,' Sam said softly and calmly, the only way he knew how. *'From what I understand, she loves you very much. What can I do or say to make you put the knife down, and just speak to me?'*

'I don't know!' our suspect screamed manically. *'I don't like your uniform! It is scaring me!'*

'Well, what if I take my uniform off? Would that help?' Sam replied.

'Do not take your uniform off,' I urged him quietly.

Paying absolutely no attention to what I was saying, he continued to address the suspect.

'Okay. I will take my epaulettes off, and my tie.'

'NO! JUST GO AWAY!!!' the suspect shouted in response.

'How about I take my body armour off too?'

I couldn't believe what I was hearing… *'Do not take your body armour off. He's got a bloody big knife and is clearly willing to use it,'* I hissed in his ear, my own heart beginning to beat a little faster.

Sam lifted his body armour off and handing it to me, ushered me back outside and shut the door, leaving only the three of them stood in the kitchen. It seemed a truly terrible decision which left me not only fearing for the life of the homeowner, but also then for my friend. Feeling completely helpless I radioed for further back-up, for what good it would do. I couldn't feasibly think of what we could do that wouldn't cause a rapid and severe escalation, so I had to trust that Sam knew what he was doing. All the while he was inside, I kept my hand on the door handle and my ear to the door, listening for any form of disturbance. It seemed like the longest ten minutes of my life but soon enough, I felt movement on the other side of the handle, so I stepped back and to my relief, Sam appeared with the suspect subdued and in cuffs. He was sectioned under the Mental Health Act 1983, which allowed him to be detained in a hospital instead of police custody or ultimately, a prison. The mother was in floods of tears, thanking Sam, and telling her son how much she loved him and how everything would be okay. I felt completely overwhelmed with it all. It was such an awful situation for her to be in, one that I hoped would never happen again.

Whilst it was incredibly risky, Sam's behaviour was truly admirable and one of the greatest displays of policing I ever saw. He exercised his individual discretion and chose to police with kindness and humility, instead of brute force.

As soon as he removed his uniform, the suspect no longer viewed him as a threat, which, coupled with Sam's calming presence and genuine desire to help, completely de-escalated the situation. Sam knew the jeopardy of his actions, yet was willing to take the risk, to help the young man in question and avoid a fatal outcome. What a cracking bloke. He had my entire trust and complete respect.

There was barely any time to stop and think before I had a year's service under my belt, and my second Christmas on the force was busy and eventful. I was working the night shift on 24th December, due to finish at seven in the morning on Christmas Day. The plan beyond that was to get a few hours' rest, before setting out to Jane's parents for noon. My first call of the evening was to an accident on the motorway, where a driver had been reported dead at the wheel. After travelling at the upper end of the speed limit at just over seventy miles per hour, the individual in question had cause to harshly apply the brake, to stop for a line of traffic ahead. When she did, the frozen turkey that had been situated on the back parcel shelf flew forwards and hit her in the back of the head, killing her instantly. It was truly tragic, but there was not much for me to do beyond a bit of traffic management whilst her body and car were recovered, and after filing a brief report back at the station, I set back out in the car on my patrol.

There wasn't much trouble to be found as people were filled with merriment, busying themselves with festive activities and sharing good cheer. Two in the morning came and went and as I waited for my shift to finish so I could get home to bed, I remembered being told the year before that Christmas Eve was a good time to catch a burglar. Houses are full of gifts and often unoccupied for the evening as people go out to eat, drink and visit family and friends, but as I continued driving around there was no sign of any masked men running away with loot bags. Half past six eventually arrived and I set off back for the station, weary and never-more-ready to get home and rest. I wished that it wasn't Christmas Day. That way I could avoid the imminent festivities, for which I had absolutely no energy.

As I sat waiting at a set of traffic lights, I could hear the faint sound of an alarm over the diesel engine of the van. It was coming from a pub on the left-hand side of the junction and as I looked over, I saw a man running away from the pub with a large backpack over his shoulder. Like a deer in the headlights, he froze as he saw the van, before continuing with his escape, trying to quicken his pace but seeming to struggle with the weight of whatever he was carrying.

Pulling the van over to the side of the road, I jumped out and began to pursue him on foot. He entered a side alley that unbeknownst to him, was blocked at the other end with a gate and pelting towards him I grabbed hold of his shoulders. As I did, the bag burst, sending one and two-pound coins flying everywhere. He was compliant in the arrest, and I radioed in to say that I had caught a burglary in process, but there was no need to send a van as I was already in one.

There is a small minority of police officers who see it as their God given right to behave like utter arseholes and treat their prisoners in an abusive and derogatory way, but that approach never aligned with my personality. There was no point behaving in such a way, just because I could. I knew that I had to have a relationship of sorts with the prisoner, even just for a short period of time, so it made sense to make that as easy as possible for the both of us. When I interviewed the man, he explained that he had stolen the money out of several fruit machines in the pub, but that he had only done it so he had something to give his children on Christmas morning.

Night shifts always had the potential to be difficult, as inevitably I would finish them totally exhausted, but to end the shift on Christmas

Day, after having locked up a father who was only trying to do his best made me feel nothing short of depressed.

After stepping through the door at just gone nine in the morning, totally drained, and dreading the day ahead, I decided there was little point trying to get any rest so instead jumped in the shower and once dressed, gave Jane her presents.

As I pushed roast potatoes round my plate later that day, my mind wandered to the woman who had been swiftly extinguished by what would have been her Christmas Day lunch, and those near and dear to her whose world had just come crashing in around them, on what was supposed to be a joyous occasion. It seemed unfair but served as a subtle reminder that accidents do happen, and none of us are immune to the perils of death. Then I thought of the man in the cells, and his children who were spending Christmas Day without their father.

It was clear that he was down on his luck and at the point of desperation, and a part of me wished I had known the circumstances before I got out of the van. Maybe I would have turned the other way and just carried on back to the station.

It is incredibly easy to judge people based on an incomplete set of data, the information which is more immediately presented, without digging beneath the surface. For much of my career that is what I did. It is what I was taught and instructed to do, but there were times when I couldn't disregard my own intuition and had to apply my own personal discretion, sensibly. The law is black and white, but upon closer inspection of most situations there is also a lot of grey area, which should not always be ignored.

One afternoon, I exited a newsagent, stocked up with some sugary sustenance to continue my shift, when I smelled the distinct whiff of cannabis coming from the alley behind the row of shops. Rounding the corner, I saw a man in his late twenties, leaning against the back wall of the newsagents, sure enough, smoking a joint.

My own personal experience with drugs was limited to one occasion, which was when I was around the age of fifteen. I had formed a few relative kinships during the couple of years I had been at my senior school, and a few of us frequented young farmers' parties locally. They offered a wholesome atmosphere, the food was always decent, and it afforded us the chance to meet girls. One chilly October evening we sat on the dry-stone wall of a churchyard, waiting for the community centre across the road where the event was taking place, to open, so that we could go inside.

Naturally there were always a few beers snuck in, the odd can of Newcastle Brown here and there, but on that occasion, one of my friends had brought along a spliff, sourced and rolled by his older brother. It was passed along, with each of us taking a drag, or two. My place was fourth in line, and I was quite looking forward to my first experience of drugs as it seemed a real rock and roll thing to do. When it finally reached me, I put it to my mouth and took a large inhale, over exaggerating my movements quite substantially as I threw my head back to breathe in. As though I was departing a boat, ready to begin a scuba dive, I fell backwards over the wall and into the long-wet grass of the graveyard behind. There was a few seconds of laughing from my friends before I heard the beginnings of a conversation, with someone whose voice I did not recognise.

A local bobby on the beat had just so happened to have been patrolling the area and missed catching sight of our illicit activities by a whisper, due to my misfortune.

My associates thought I must have seen him in advance and chucked myself off the wall on purpose, but that wasn't the case. It was simply a stroke of luck, that meant none of us received any formal cautions or indeed prosecutions for being in possession of illegal drugs.

The young man I had caught looked guilty and defeated having just been confronted by a police officer but offered me an explanation as to why he was using the drugs. He explained that he had Crohn's disease, and that smoking weed provided him some much-needed relief from severe pain. He looked unwell, so much that I didn't ask for any proof, but he emptied his pockets anyway and showed me a couple of packets of different medication, and his driver's licence with the corresponding name. Turning on my heel I wished him all the best, walked away, and got back in the car. The same 'one size fits all' approach that I ignored when I found the young boy stealing milk just didn't seem right. There was no point whatsoever in punishing him for something that in the grand scheme of things, seemed to me to be relatively trivial. A drugs charge could have had a substantial impact on his future chances, and he was clearly unwell, so I couldn't in good conscience bring myself to put him through any more difficulty, just because I could or should. I doubt that many other officers would have made the compassionate exception that I did that day, even presented with all the facts. On that occasion I coloured outside of the lines, when my obligation was very much to colour within them.

15

The job was tough, and the scene I was met with at the hospital was one of unimaginable horror. The look in the patient's eyes as she gripped my hand was one of sheer desperation, and for days I was in complete shock at the tragedy of what I had witnessed.

And this event was just one of countless traumatic moments I experienced, each distinct in its impact, and collectively a chilling aspect of my reality.

As a police officer I often faced an overwhelming sense of trauma and grief and was constantly exposed to the raw emotions of others, but there was never any training on how I should deal with the harrowing experiences I dealt with daily.

Finding little support and understanding in my new relationship, I was unable to share the challenges of my days with anybody, and that created a feeling of isolation. For some reason, Jane didn't seem to acknowledge or appreciate that my job was perhaps a little more intense than a regular profession.

Emergency services need more help to manage psychological strain. Prioritising mental well-being is essential for ensuring their long-term resilience and stability.

16

During the mid-nineties car thefts were rife. Hotwiring was not too difficult and whilst some people still used a wheel lock, many didn't. An estimated half a million cars were being stolen on average each year, and with very little CCTV around it meant it was much easier to disappear off-grid to change number plates.

The police had to begin taking measures to proactively tackle the problem, which offered an opportunity for me to have a change of pace, and some respite from the more usual aspects of the job thus far. It was suspected that in and around our area, it was the same bunch of adolescent males who were committing most of the thefts, so along with another officer, Paul, I was placed on a short secondment to focus solely on the issue. The basic aim was to simply catch as many of the thieves as possible, either in the act of theft itself or driving a car that we knew to be stolen. The latter of the two circumstances meant that we had to effectively let them steal a vehicle to begin with, before pursuing and arresting them. It was the ideal scenario, as the evidence chain would be incredibly difficult to dispute in court.

The project meant we were working permanent night shifts for twelve weeks. This displeased Jane no end, as it meant for a short while we would be seeing even less of each other, but for me it was no problem. Switching shifts, week in and week out, I found it to be quite tiring. The consistency of set shifts for a while offered some reprieve from the constant disruption to my system.

Towards the end of a car chase, the perpetrators in the stolen vehicle would typically try to abandon the car and get away on foot. As I was fast on my feet, my main role in the partnership was to jump out whenever a car pursuit inevitably came to an end, and hot foot it after the suspect. Paul was an ex-interceptor. A brilliant driver and a real asset to our wider team. Between us, we made an ideal pairing for the job, and I was living out my boyhood dreams. He was the Starsky to my Hutch, although, I am sure he likely considered himself more the Turner to my Hooch.

Whilst Paul was doing the driving, my other responsibilities were to monitor the radio channel and maintain communication between the operator, and sometimes the police helicopter, giving a running commentary of events as they played out. There were a total of three radios in the car and at times it felt like I was juggling them all, whilst reading the map, and offering directions to Paul. We were frequently well above the speed limit, navigating tight, built-up areas with little margin for error. Even if sometimes I felt for certain we were going to hit something, I had to place absolute faith in his driving skills and soon learnt to trust his capabilities.

As far as people went, he was quite aloof and reserved, and as I was still incredibly junior, I didn't push him too much into chatting. Still quite early into our partnership we found ourselves one evening in hot pursuit of a stolen car, which was doing speeds of at least one hundred miles per hour. We were bombing down the main road through the local town, and as we approached a large crossroads, Paul instructed me to *'get the light on.'*

We had been entrusted with a heavily modified car, to increase the chances of us catching whoever we were chasing. It was not a marked police car so didn't have the usual blue lights fixed to the roof, but did have blue flashing lights in the grill. The light he was referring to was a detachable, flashing blue light, designed to go on the roof of the car. It had a magnetic bottom and could be stuck on when necessary, the sort that is shown in American cop movies, when the undercover officers pull out after the car full of criminals and stick the flashing light on the roof as they go. Such lights were not commonplace, but as nobody else was on the force was doing anything like what we were doing, Paul had sought special approval to have one for the project.

The sirens were blaring, communications were constant on the radio, and I was clinging to the map book, trying to offer directions, and give a running commentary of what was up ahead. The light itself was a large dome, the size of a dinner plate, and attached to it was a coiled wire which plugged into the car cigarette lighter. Sure enough, as soon as I plugged it in it started flashing, just inches away from my eyes. The whole interior of the car was intermittently illuminated bright blue as I began hand-cranking my window down. As soon as I opened my window, due to the high speeds at which we were travelling, the wind began ripping through the car which only added to the assault on my senses. I had nearly managed to get the light stuck to the roof, but as we passed over the large crossroads we hit a dip in the road. At one hundred miles an hour the dip was a big event for the car and the light flung from the roof, instantly hitting the ground behind us. I turned to face Paul, two frayed ends of the coiled wire in my hand, as hundreds of pounds worth of light bounced down the road, smashing to pieces. He didn't utter a single word to me for the rest of the evening. Even when we caught the perpetrator.

He couldn't stay mad for too long however, as we were getting consistently good results. Over the first couple of months, we had managed to catch around half a dozen car thieves, get them in front of the courts, and recover the cars that had been stolen. We were doing such a good job that we became notorious with the local yobs, and they spray painted our names on the shutters of a local shop, with the challenge *'come and get us'*, underneath.

As soon as we came on duty each evening, we would make our first order of business to drive around one of the larger council estates where there were always groups of our targets hanging around. Sometimes they were cocky and would goad us, shouting to us what they planned on stealing that evening and from where. It was all a big game to them, and it turned into one for us too. The whole time I spent on the project was brilliant and was a glimpse into what I had really joined the force to do. We were arresting people pretty much every single day.

A foot chase following the initial car chase was pretty much a given, and it became a little predictable. If there were two absconding from the vehicle, I would naturally go for the passenger, to avoid running between our two cars. Paul would then head after the driver. Towards the end of our time together there was one of these occasions, when we had both jumped out of the car and chased a suspect each. After a few minutes I had detained mine and returned to our car.

'Got one in custody. Where are you now mate?' I radioed to Paul.

I didn't receive a response but could hear a commotion over the radio as Paul attempted to arrest the driver. Before too long he arrived back, looking a little dishevelled, as did his detainee.

We headed back to the station to complete the paperwork, which annoyingly could keep us off the roads for four or even five hours. Anything which the police plan to submit to the courts in the form of evidence must always be shared in advance with the defendant and their solicitor. Whilst it is not uncommon to introduce undisclosed evidence midway through an interview, to see how the defendant responds, they are then permitted to stop the interview and discuss the newly disclosed evidence with their legal representative. The local police helicopter had followed the chase which meant there was video footage we could use to aid the prosecution. Amazing. The evidence chain was golden.

'Right, well just send over the disc and we will get in there and show it to the smug little bastard…' Paul said, practically rubbing his hands together with glee.

'You might want to watch it first…' cautioned the radio operator.

We headed up to the helipad and into the aerodrome office with the onboard communications officer to watch the footage.

It was great, and perfectly captured the entire chase.

We reached the part when both vehicles stopped, and when more than one suspect jumps out of a car, the helicopter always stays with the driver as the main perpetrator of the offence. I disappeared off camera to chase the passenger and the camera tracked the driver into the front garden of a terraced house, where he lay down to hide behind a small privet hedge of no more than three feet high. We watched as Paul came around the corner and immediately spotting the suspect, went to arrest him, and I saw the scuffle ensue that I had heard over my radio at the time of the event itself. The helicopter crew were experienced, so had panned out slightly and altered the angle of the camera, only leaving visible the top of the hedge and Paul, who could be seen crouched down, obviously pummelling the perpetrator into submission. He hadn't caused him any real harm, but we were sure glad we had watched the video first. As the offence was one of an organised series of crimes, the Criminal Investigation Department were responsible for the interviews and we submitted the video to them to assist with their questions, cutting the last thirty seconds from the footage.

Back from secondment and a report of a domestic disturbance was called in by a member of the public, the neighbour to the individuals in question. The address we had been given was on a quiet, suburban, housing estate. I wasn't too far away but switched the blue lights on anyway, to get there as quickly as possible.

It just so happened that one of our detectives was also driving nearby at the time, so decided he too would stop by, as I continued to make my way to the scene.

He arrived and heard movement from within the property and finding the back door ajar, he entered. Stepping straight into the kitchen, he slipped and fell onto the floor. Looking down to what had caused him to slip, he saw what appeared to someone's large and small intestine. Looking up, he saw a man bearing a samurai sword.

I arrived just a moment after and saw him still on the floor. A woman lay dead nearby and there were blood and guts everywhere, as though someone had emptied a bin of offal all over an otherwise spotless kitchen.

Detectives wear plain clothes, but at the first sight of my uniform, the man put down the weapon he was holding and surrendered immediately, much to our relief.

I didn't need to cross the threshold, and it would have been pointless contamination of what was clearly a crime scene if I had. The male suspect put his hands on top of his head and when I beckoned him to do so, he walked towards me, out into the back garden. My role from thereon was prisoner reception so I handcuffed and cautioned him, but due to his limited English I am not convinced he knew exactly what I was saying.

He had killed his wife in a form of ritualistic disembowelment, traditionally conducted by a samurai and commonly referred to as 'hara-kiri'. Anybody who has watched the *Kill Bill* film franchise, may have some understanding of what is involved in such an act, and it is incredibly gruesome. A few moments of him in my custody and it also became apparent that after he had killed his wife, he had tried to take his own life in the same fashion but had not been able to execute the manoeuvre properly. We set off straight to the hospital and when we arrived he was handcuffed to a bed and taken immediately into surgery, where I waited outside. My instructions were to stay with him, not to engage him in conversation, but to keep a log in my pocket notebook of anything he said upon waking. He returned to the general ward after his surgery and after an hour, began to rouse.

'The woman I killed... is she still alive?' he asked me, and they were the only words of English I ever heard him speak.

It later transpired that the couple had been separated for several years, but the dispute about access to the children was still ongoing and he had finally had enough.

He was a Vietnamese national and had served in the army as a young man during the Vietnam War. I can only conclude that the unthinkable levels of violence he had been exposed to during his service meant it was not too much of a leap for him to act the way he did, in such a way that most would consider completely barbaric. For him, such extreme violence was not an anomaly. It was a behaviour shaped by his past. The brutality he displayed was a familiar and tragic response, which was rooted in his history. It was a situation that demonstrated to me just how deeply our individual experiences inform how we react to situations.

Not long after, I found myself reflecting on my experiences on the job so far, and how I was becoming increasingly confident in my abilities as an officer. When another concern for welfare came in I headed straight in the direction of the address given, ready to get stuck in and give it my all.

The particulars of the case were that a woman had called the police out of concern for her elderly father. She described how she had not heard from him for only one day, but that they usually took it in turns to call each other every evening as she resided in France. It was a practise they had been doing for some years so when he failed to call, and subsequently didn't answer when she tried to call him, she was immediately worried. I arrived at the house to find a folded note pinned to the door:

'*To the officer in charge.*'

Well, that was me. I opened the note and read on.

'*I am upstairs in the bedroom and have taken a large amount of phenobarbital. All being well, by the time you arrive I will be dead. My sincerest apologies. With regards, Mr Willis.*'

Phenobarbital is a medication commonly used as a sedative for those who suffer with insomnia. An overdose not identified swiftly would certainly be fatal.

The door was unlocked so I entered the property without any issue, announcing myself as I did. As soon as I was inside, I could hear classical music coming from upstairs. After a brief look around the downstairs of the property I found nothing unusual so headed upstairs, where I had a pretty good idea of what I would find.

As I drew closer to what I assumed was the master bedroom, I could hear tremendous snoring. An elderly gentleman lay on the bed in his pyjamas, dressing gown and slippers. There was a bottle of whisky on the bedside table, along with another note.

'It is after some consideration that I have consciously attempted to take my own life. Should my efforts not be immediately successful I would like to be taken to the Elmwood hospital, under the care of Doctor Mark Jones. Please inform him that I do not want to receive any medical care at all. Instead, to be left until my body eventually gives in and I pass away.'

Immediately I called for an ambulance and then radioed the station with an update. I attempted to wake him but there were no signs that he would regain consciousness. Whilst I waited for assistance I further checked the upstairs of the house, looking specifically for any more letters from him. In the second bedroom I found a large box which happened to be stacked full of letters.

There were letters to utility companies complete with final payment cheques. Letters to his friends and a letter to his daughter. There were invitations to his funeral, with the date of his death and date of the funeral left blank. Each letter was inside an unsealed, stamped and addressed envelope, ready for someone to simply fill in the gaps, seal the envelopes and put them in the post.

In total there were at least one hundred documents, and they had all been typed using an old-fashioned typewriter. The extent of his preparations was admirable, but distinctly poignant. He had been preparing for his death for what seemed to be a good while, and at no point stopped to reconsider.

A few days after he had taken the overdose he passed away. His daughter had returned from France and had been able to say her goodbyes in person at the hospital, where I met her. She looked completely exhausted as we talked for a while at his bedside, and she shared with me what he had written in his letter to her. He apologised but explained that since the loss of his wife he was too weary to continue living.

Out of all the memories from my time as a police officer, it is this event that I have the clearest recollection of. The classical music that was playing when I entered the house seemed to beckon me up the stairs, where it was then overlapped with distinct and comedic snoring.

The deceased was so dignified on his way out. He was meticulous and neat in organising his affairs. He was apologetic in advance for the trouble his actions would cause. Everything was dotted and crossed, yet bizarrely he had made an error when it came to the dosage and had not taken quite enough to ensure immediate fatality. The whole situation was so out of the ordinary, it felt completely surreal.

For the handling of this case I received another Divisional Commander's Award in exemplary service, and a letter to the station from the deceased's daughter, expressing her deepest thanks for my assistance and dedication.

Being able to help people was what mattered to me the most.

The following day was a Saturday. I had just dragged myself out of bed when the house phone rang. I made no attempt to answer it and after several rings it stopped.

'Rob!' Jane shouted up the stairs, *'It's for you!'*

For fuck's sake…

As I made my way down and approached the handset, which was hung on the wall in the lounge, Jane covered the mouthpiece and explained it was her Aunty So-and-so, and that she needed some help. Aunty So-and-so had barely said two words before, but she vaguely knew me so supposed she could call for advice.

'Hello?'

'Robert! Darrell has been arrested and is being held at the local police station. Can you help?!' she said, forgoing any pleasantries you might usually use when asking for a favour.

I yawned, *'I am not sure I can really… What has he been arrested for?'*

'Nothing at all!' she snapped back at me. *'All he did was go for a bloody bike ride!'*

I suspected there was a little more to it than that, and eventually reached a point of understanding what had really happened. For reasons unknown, Darrell had ordered off the internet an all in one, orange Lycra suit. Upon its arrival he had put it straight on and then, wearing nothing underneath, headed out for a bike ride down the nearby promenade. As he cycled up and down the beach front, he had become in a state of arousal, which was clearly visible through his suit. After what I can assume were several complaints from the public about a twenty-year old man cycling around in a questionable outfit, sporting an erection, the police arrived and arrested him for indecent exposure, as they rightly should have.

'Can you call them and explain that he is just a bit different?!'

'Nahhh, not really. The best thing he can do is just co-operate.'

She put the phone down and I took myself off for a shower, scoffing at the absurdity of the situation. Darrell rather unfortunately had a learning disability, which would have been taken into consideration. But so would the fact that just a few months previously, he had been caught masturbating in the vegetable aisle at Tesco.

17

The notion that our actions are informed by our experiences was something that I became increasingly aware of as I navigated my way through society. A similar example to that of the Vietnamese veteran emerged in later years, in one of the more challenging areas I patrolled. The area had historically been home to a mixture of white and Afro-Caribbean families, but over the course of a few years had welcomed a significant number of Somalian families as well, and this influx drastically altered the neighbourhood's dynamic. The local gangs, well-established and accustomed to wielding power found their territory contested, and with newcomers encroaching on what they considered to be their turf, tensions escalated. The Somali men who had entered this environment had come from one of the most dangerous and hostile settings imaginable, following years of civil war in Somalia. They had witnessed incredibly brutal and violent conflict, and so their tolerance for and understanding of violence was drastically different from that of the established residents. After having fought for their lives almost daily, dealing with local gang intimidation paled in comparison. And then in complete contrast, my own upbringing and experience of violence had only ever involved minor altercations in the schoolyard, or on the football pitch.

Our backgrounds shape our worldviews, and we tend to operate from a place based on experience. The disparity in perspectives highlights the importance of considering and appreciating that we all have our own history and trauma, and that some of that could be worse than we could possibly imagine. What one person may tolerate or accept may be entirely inconceivable to another. As we navigate our way through life we must remain mindful of the diverse range of experiences that our society has, and how that can influence how different individuals react to their environment. We all have our own stories and recognising this spectrum of lived experiences can help foster empathy and understanding within our communities.

18

A young girl of six years old had gone missing from her home.

She lived on one of the larger council estates in the area, of which a great deal of the residents were known to us. It was the sort of area where the residents generally sorted out their own problems, and we were more than happy to let that be the case. We weren't at all respected and therefore not wanted or needed, until the wheels really came off.

A missing child was an exceptional circumstance.

When a person goes missing, there is a process to follow in terms of gathering information, so when I arrived at the girl's home, I began the necessary questions to give us the best chance of finding her. I asked for a physical description of her, what she was wearing, and when her parents last saw her. I asked who she usually played with and whether there were any places locally she spent a lot of time and would therefore be familiar with. I asked if there had been any argument or disagreement before she went missing, and if I could have a look around the house.

It was hard to convey to her clearly anxious parents, who were becoming agitated with my questions, that I couldn't just take a photo of her and take to the streets immediately to begin looking. Of course, I wanted to get out there as quickly as possible to find her; the whole area was unsavoury, let alone for a child.

After having gathered the information I needed, I left the house to go back to the van that I had parked directly outside. In an act that perfectly demonstrated the sort of relationship we had with that community, I found that whilst I had been inside some of the locals had decided to slash three of the four tyres, rendering it completely useless. Whilst the family screamed at me from their driveway to go and find their missing daughter, I had to radio for assistance, completely bemused at the response of someone in that community to a police van that was there to help in a time of real need. There wasn't much I would have been able to do on foot, and even if I had thought to leave the van it would likely have been burnt out, so my involvement in the case ended there. I waited until recovery came to take the van to the police garage and by the time I had returned to the station the little girl had been found, safe and well.

Places like that estate, of which I policed many over the years, came with a distinct feeling that crime was necessary to get by in life. There were endless instances of borderline criminality and general underhandedness, but of course plenty of more serious crime too. They were the sorts of places that were home to multiple generational crime families, and to them life really was a case of survival of the fittest. To really thrive as a criminal in such an environment I found there were two main sorts of individual. Those who were big and strong, or those who were mad and bad. Anybody who was a blend of both was a real contender for trouble.

I once arrested someone who looked like the Milky Bar Kid, and I remember thinking at the time just how wet he looked, yet he had already been on trial three separate times for murder. Despite his outward appearance, his reputation was that of a sadistic lunatic and although he wasn't big or strong, he was completely bonkers, and that is how he survived and succeeded in the criminal underworld.

It could sometimes feel very much a case of 'us' and 'them' whilst policing local communities, but the comradery that I experienced amongst all blue light services was a constant source of reassurance. There was never an incident when we worked jointly with either the ambulance or fire service, where it didn't feel as though we pulled together as one larger team. There was just an innate level of respect and mutual understanding for each other's roles, and our respective responsibilities during an emergency.

It was around early May when a house fire had taken a real grip of a semi-detached property, and we had been dispatched to the scene to cordon it off and prevent the public getting involved. The front door to the property was made from solid wood so the fire brigade had not been able to kick it down to gain entry, and I watched on as one of the officers retrieved a large axe from their fire engine and hacked his way through the door, finally allowing them access. Once inside it had become obvious why the door had initially failed to budge, as slumped behind it on the floor was the male resident of the property, who weighed approximately fifteen stone.

After the fire service had dragged him out of the burning building and onto the front lawn, the paramedics quickly established he was dead. There was a large open fracture wound to the back of his head, which had clearly been caused by the axe, so the question was how had he died? Had he died in the fire, or at the hands of the fireman who was trying to save his life?

The fire was extinguished with no further casualties and the body of the deceased male was sent to the mortuary for a forensic post-mortem. All of us who had been involved held our breath as we awaited the verdict on what had caused his death. The layout of the property was such that the front door was directly at the bottom of the staircase, and it was ultimately ruled that he had died of smoke inhalation at the top of the stairs and subsequently fallen. It was a great relief, none least to the officer who had wielded the axe, to hear that the wound caused had made no difference whatsoever.

It was a long-standing joke between the police and the fire service that the latter didn't do a great deal other than go to the gym, rescue cats, or attend sponsored car washes. It was also often intimated that their lack of real work to do gave them plenty of opportunity to stick their nose into other people's business, whenever they got the chance.

A case was passed to our department after a single man in his fifties had placed a call to report a chip pan fire in his home, which was situated in a small, low-rise block of a dozen apartments. For any report of a fire in a dwelling, the fire service must send at least two fire engines, but the police needn't usually be notified. But on the occasion in question, the fire service had arrived and done their bit to extinguish the fire and then decided to give the rest of the apartment the once over, out of nothing other than sheer nosiness. In doing so they made quite a discovery.

One of the officers happened upon a large industrial waste sack in the wardrobe, fastened at the top with a zip tie. After asking the occupant what was inside, and clearly being dissatisfied with the answer *'camera equipment'*, the officer cut open the bag and found an elderly lady inside, curled up in the foetal position, dead.

It was then we got the call.

We never fully got to the bottom of what had happened. The resident claimed it was just a neighbourly dispute that had gone terribly wrong, but during or after he killed her, in what was a particularly violent act, he had stuffed a kitchen sponge down her throat.

As the summer of 1998 was ending, Jane and I moved out of our rented house and bought our first property together. It was a three-bedroom mews house on a newly developed cul-de-sac, and whilst I barely felt as though I was around long enough to enjoy my new home, Jane seemed happy with it. It had a conservatory at the back which led directly onto a large lawn and we both agreed that we would prefer to have some paving at the entrance, instead of stepping out straight onto grass that would likely get very muddy over winter. Both Jane's dad and brother were very handy when it came to jobs about the house, so the expectation was that I could just lay a patio on my days off.

Not wanting to disappoint I got to it at the first opportunity I had.

Without any direction or real idea what I was doing, I measured out the space we wanted to cover and had the materials delivered. After laying the sand down and managing to get it level, I started laying the stones. My efforts continued for an entire morning, but every time I thought it was going well I looked up to see that several stones had somehow moved and become uneven. By the end of the first day, I was annoyed that it had not come together in the way I had hoped, and ended up having to lift all the stones off the sand, ready to try again the following day. To make it worse, the distinct sense that I got from Jane when she returned from work was that I should just try harder, as it was quite a simple task to complete.

Lunchtime the following day came and without any real success, despite another few hours of effort, I had become so angry about the whole thing. I resented Jane for making such demands of me on my days off work and my inability to complete the task had left me feeling completely useless. There was a shed at the bottom of the garden which is where I headed in search of a lump hammer, before going around the entire plot and individually smashed every single sodding stone that I had laid. Then I went inside, dug out the phone book and called a local tradesman to come and quote for the work, and new materials.

Jane was annoyed when she came home to find us still without a patio, but a few weeks later it was complete, and any remnants of her dissatisfaction towards me for not being able to complete the task at hand had gone. The whole experience cemented in my mind that I would not attempt such jobs around the house again, and risk wasting any more of my days off. The demands on my time were already a regular point of contention.

'We need to actually do something together for a change,' Jane said to me over dinner one evening, *'like a proper activity.'*

I could feel my shoulders start to tense at the notion. I had always struggled with forced fun.

'Why don't we go on a bike ride?' she suggested.

I hadn't ridden a bike since I was a child, when I had ridden one everywhere. My dad was the only one who drove in our household and he was usually working, but even when he wasn't working, the chances of him giving me a lift anywhere were always slim to none.

'I don't have a bike,' was my response, trying to curb any notion of such an activity going ahead.

'*We can get you one from the catalogue,*' was hers.

Jane worked for a catalogue company, which at times was beneficial as we were often able to utilise her discount to pick up bits here and there for the house. But in what was predominantly a woman's clothing catalogue, there were very limited options for men's bikes.

'*If I am going to go to the extent of getting a bike, I would rather make sure it is at least a decent one...*'

'*We do sell decent ones!*' she assured me, somewhat offended.

They most certainly did not, so I had a little look around and showed her a few alternative options which she immediately dismissed as being too costly. She was certain that the bike she could get for half the price, would be just as good. I didn't want a bloody bike in the first place but not wanting to seem as though I was looking a gift horse in the mouth, I agreed that she could order one and a couple of weeks later it arrived. Electric blue with yellow graffiti motifs on the frame, it was my worst nightmare, and I was certain I would look like monumental tosser riding it.

The whole reason behind getting the bike was to spend some relaxing and enjoyable time together, and maybe I should have tried to reframe my approach to the whole event, but even before we had left the house to embark on our bike ride, I was not looking forward to it one bit.

We set off on what should have been a nice and easy ride, on a completely flat, disused railway line, but it quickly became apparent that not only did my bike look cheap and nasty, nothing seemed to work quite the way it was supposed to.

One of the pedals had been screwed in the wrong way meaning it wasn't straight in the crank, the brakes were slow, and the full suspension made for less than a comfortable ride. As we rode along, I grumbled to myself.

'*Stop moaning!*' she shouted back to me, meandering ahead on her fully functioning, not-a-budget-option bike.

She didn't consider that the bike was the problem. How could it have been? It had come from her place of work and therefore I must have been the issue.

Gritting my teeth, I persevered with the ride, until I sat back from a semi-standing position and the seat flipped back and practically entered my arse.

That was enough.

Dismounting immediately, I picked the bike up and launched it over the hawthorn hedge that edged the cycle path, straight into a field, never to be seen by me again.

Hearing the commotion, Jane stopped abruptly and yelled back at me, *'What the hell did you do that for?! There was nothing wrong with it!'*

'How would you know?!' I shouted back at her, *'you weren't the one riding it!'*

In her eyes, my response to the situation was unacceptable and looking back, I could have at least pushed it back home and tried to recoup some money by selling it on. But then again, that would have only resulted in further discussion about the whole episode. As it happened, she cycled home, I walked back and there was no further discussion about it. There was no further conversation at all in fact for the rest of the day, but I was content with that. She was annoyed with my behaviour, and I was equally annoyed that she had failed to acknowledge my legitimate concerns around the quality of the shitty bike in the first place. She seemed to brood over the incident for several days, but I was too busy with work to really notice and eventually we slipped back into our version of normal.

My relationship with Jane was the longest one I had been in. At just twenty-four years old I romanticised about life, which led me to say and do what I perceived to be the right thing. Although there were obvious and many differences between us, due to my working schedule our interactions were limited, and our life together was relatively neutral. As we had been already living together a while there felt a certain level of expectation that I should propose. In the absence of any real close friends to confide in, and without feeling able to discuss it with my parents, I committed to the decision in my own mind and found an opportune moment to ask her dad for his blessing, which he was more than happy to give. I had not considered when or how I would propose, or even bought a ring, but the wheels were in motion.

A few weeks after speaking to her dad we went away with her family for a few nights, and spent the first evening in a pub nearby the hotel. Her brother was plying me with pints of Guinness and after four or five I decided that even in the absence of a ring, with all her family around it felt the right time to pop the question. Without thinking any more about it, I climbed up onto a small, circular, table and at several decibels louder than I needed to, slurred my way through a proposal. It wasn't particularly romantic, but it did the job. She accepted and everybody in the pub erupted into applause. Back home the following weekend we went out and Jane picked a ring she liked. Our engagement was official.

It was late summer and as the evening approached, my partner and I had decided to take a walk of the local area to wrap up our shift. It was the weekend, and we were risking having a truly awful time consisting of drunken abuse and nonsense complaints, but that was the job, and someone had to do it.

We finished patrolling the high street and continued our circular route when we reached a crossing at some traffic lights. On the other side of the road there was a group of young lads who seemed at first to be completely harmless, but then at the sight of us began to act aggressively, shouting abusive comments in our direction.

If their behaviour alone hadn't provided a legitimate reason for us to speak to them, the distinct smell of cannabis in the air meant we had cause to suspect they were in possession of illegal drugs. Once on the other side of the road I advised that we had to do a search of their person, which they refused. It was clear that the situation was going to escalate into a conflict, so I radioed for back-up. My expectation was that help would come in the form of members of my own team, but when the van turned up it was members of the team who had just started the night shift.

Previously, I had found that some of the other teams in the station were the sort to act first then ask questions later, and as though they had just downed their protein shakes on the way over, four of them jumped out of the van and were operating straight away at full tilt. Without stopping to have any form of discussion with myself or my colleague, they swiftly took over the situation, forcing a couple of the lads to the floor and cuffing them.

Despite being detained, one of them decided it was wise to continue with his crusade of verbal abuse. Before I had time to intervene, the driver of the van picked him up under his shoulders. and another officer got his legs. When he was completely horizontal, at about four feet in the air, they dropped him to the ground. He made an almighty thud as he hit the pavement, before curling up and wincing in pain.

We all got in the van, and they dropped us off at the station with the prisoners, before heading back out, I assume to find someone else to rough up.

I was concerned about the prisoner who had been injured as he was technically my detainee, but he didn't say anything about the incident and there were no questions from the custody clerk about how he had incurred his injuries.

Such a method of policing was not at all what I had been used to and it really opened my eyes to how some officers chose to behave.

I couldn't understand how it could be that they policed so differently to me and my team, when we worked in the same building as them, under the same superiors.

Then an instance occurred which demonstrated I didn't have to look too far to understand why that was the case.

Once a year we were sent on a one-day refresher course, to requalify in the use of our cuffs, baton, and gas. Of course, we were there to learn the correct techniques but there was also a large emphasis on team bonding, so when we went to a gym nearby the station, I expected a thoroughly enjoyable few hours spent training with our friends and colleagues.

Batons are much shorter now, but when we were training we used a large baton that had a side stick attached. During the first exercise we took it in turns to hold up a large pad, whilst someone else struck it with their baton. I never played around the edges when it came to training, so hit the pads as hard as I could, to get a genuine feel for what it would be like if I ever had to use it on an individual.

The next exercise saw each officer taking it in turns to stand in the middle of a circle, whilst everybody else stood around the outside. The officers around the outside of the circle then had to, one by one, 'attack' the person in the middle. It was hard work, fending off attacks from all angles, but it was good fun. It was designed to keep us sharp and aware of potential threats.

There were two older officers on our training cohort for the day who were both coming to the end of their careers. They had wound down a little and only worked in the custody office. As good friends of a similar age who worked with each other daily, they paired up for the first exercise after lunch, which was a bit of good old-fashioned, one-on-one combat.

Our instructor for the day was technically a serving police officer, but given his role as a full-time trainer he had hardly done a day on the streets in his life. He spoke and behaved in such a way that gave the impression he thought he was a member of the SAS, and undoubtedly, he was a prick.

Naturally, due to their age, the older men in the group had restricted physical capabilities but the instructor saw fit to pressure them into acting beyond their limits.

'I have seen more life in a tramp's vest,' he goaded one of them, *'now give him a proper push!'*

We were on the first floor of the venue, which was nothing more than a dingy local gym and not really fit for purpose. The instructor had applied so much pressure that the officer had acted without thinking, and following instructions, pushed his colleague so hard that he went straight into a plate glass window.

It was incredibly lucky he didn't go all the way through, in which case he would have ended up in the car park and likely died. But his head had gone through, smashing the glass, and causing a large cut of several inches which soon enough started to piss blood. We were all wearing white T-shirts and within minutes of trying to help we looked like extras from a horror film. The officer who had delivered the push was beside himself at the sight of his friend's injury and as we administered first aid, he sat on the floor at the side of the room, his head in his hands weeping in disbelief at what had just happened. Fortunately, the injury had not been fatal, but had severed a nerve which resulted in the wounded officer losing all feeling to one side of his face.

The whole event would have been completely avoidable, had it not been for the inappropriate behaviour of the trainer. We were all asked to give a statement about what had happened and whilst we didn't train with him or indeed use that venue again, the instructor did not face any disciplinary action.

19

Since the event that saw the tyres on my van being slashed, I have wondered countless times why someone would have done that, and the answers always come flooding in.

Many of the locals harboured a dislike for the police, and in that moment, they were presented with an irresistible opportunity. Perhaps they assumed I was in the middle of arresting someone, and that damage to the van would have caused me to abandon my duties. Perhaps they were just bored and sought some mild titillation. Or perhaps they were simply acting out of complete malice. Regardless of the reason, such behaviour is a troubling commentary on society and reveals a segment of the population who seek to obstruct the very people who are tasked with helping them.

The event where one officer was verbally coerced into a situation that led another to sustain a significant injury, was entirely avoidable. The repercussions on the officers involved were severe, and yet the instructor who fostered an aggressive atmosphere faced no consequences. He had been responsible for the venue, and it was his words that played a direct role in creating the conditions that led to a life-changing incident.

How the system addressed this issue I find concerning, as the hierarchy swept it under the rug, ignoring the facts and failing to hold anybody accountable. I recall the heavy scrutiny I faced whilst providing my statement and being advised to use vague and non-committal language, essentially to avoid apportioning any blame.

Looking back, I deeply regret being swept along with that approach. It underscores a culture that prioritises protecting its own, rather than addressing any genuine issues that arise.

Both events highlight a disturbing reality. Whilst individual officers strive to serve and protect, systemic failures can lead to profound consequences. Trust is a two-way street, and when the system fails to acknowledge its shortcomings, it only deepens the rift of mistrust between law enforcement and the public.

20

During the spring of 1999 I took another short break from the usual ins and outs of policing, to work undercover with the licensing department.

My job was to ensure that pubs and clubs were sticking to the terms of their licensing agreement; whether that be checking that they offered substantial food, or that they stopped serving alcohol at the specified time. I was looking for anything that would put them in breach of their licence and to allow me to carry out my duties, I was issued taxpayers money to basically go out and have a few drinks.

The placement was restricted to two months. Assumedly to preserve the liver of anybody who undertook the role, but also to avoid any familiarity with landlords and club owners, therefore mitigating the risk of any instances of bribery.

In addition to myself, a few other PCs and a sergeant from the wider area were put on the team, but the first evening on the job I was paired up with an inspector, Jack. Our scope for the evening was to attend a few of the gay bars in the city centre, whose licensing agreement dictated that anybody who wanted to buy a drink had to be a member of the club. The initial brief we were given was that quite often, pub landlords and club managers are often quite suspicious of new faces in their establishment. That was considered particularly true of gay bars as there was the added risk that straight men would infiltrate and then cause trouble. It's a sad truth, but there really are people out there who have nothing better to do than be homophobic arseholes.

To not cause any suspicion we had to create a back story. I had a shaven head at the time, as did Jack, so it wasn't inconceivable that he could be my older brother, and so they were the roles we assigned ourselves. We agreed that he would be a homosexual man, who had been open with his sexuality for many years. I on the other hand, had only just revealed to those around me I was gay, and as a result had seen the devastating end of my two-year heterosexual relationship.

In 1999 I was still only twenty-five years old and under the circumstances felt genuinely uncomfortable, so I looked it. Jack was a more seasoned professional so looked at ease, thus giving our back story some credibility.

We arrived at the door of the first venue on our list. There were only around ten people in the place when we first arrived, which only added to my discomfort as it made us the focal point for the more regular visitors. It was unusual in that era to meet a transexual, but as we approached the bar to buy some drinks, Julie (formerly John), the licensee of the club, engaged us in conversation as soon as we sat down.

'Alright lads, have you got your membership cards please?'

Job done. Clearly, she would not have been prepared to serve us as non-members.

Jack responded, *'We're not currently members actually, but were hoping we could join.'*

I said nothing.

'Well, that very much depends on what your story is?' Julie enquired, suspiciously.

Jack leant in to tell her my concocted tale of woe whilst I sat on a bar stool, slowly spinning around and observing my surroundings. The establishment was incredibly impressive on the inside, like nothing I had ever seen in any pub or club before. Downstairs there was a large dancefloor, with several square podiums around the edge. On the left-hand side of the space there was a huge staircase that led up to the second floor, which was essentially a massive dancefloor in the form of a balcony, the whole way around the inner perimeter.

After Jack had finished spinning her our tale she was clearly satisfied as she produced two membership cards from the till and handed us a couple of bottled beers.

'You are more than welcome here, my darling,' she said with a smile, reaching across the bar and putting her hand on top of mine.

Even though we had ticked the box in terms of our work responsibilities, we couldn't leave straight away as that would have raised suspicion, so settled in for a while. My feelings of unease had led me to tune out from what was going on around me, so I was completely focussed only on my drink and talking with Jack about what the rest of the evening entailed.

When I did turn around briefly to glance over my shoulder, in the short time we had been sat there chatting, the place had become packed to the rafters. No more than ten metres away from us on one of the podiums, was a large, muscular man, wearing nothing other than a leather harness, leather hotpants and a pair of trainers. He was a brilliant dancer and interacted with the crowd in such a way that I established he was a paid member of staff. Over the course of the next ten minutes, he caught my eye several times and eventually started to point at me whilst he was dancing.

'That bloke dancing over there keeps looking at me and pointing...' I explained to Jack.

He turned to look and then turned back to me. *'Which one?'* he asked.

I began to explain it was the chap donning a full bottle of baby oil, shaking what his mother had given him, but when I turned to look, he had disappeared from the podium. Jack scoffed as though I was trying to wind him up, but within thirty seconds the man reappeared very much in my sight. He was dancing right behind Jack, rubbing up against him, all the while trying to lock eyes with me. As flattering as it was, we felt that was our cue to leave so shouted our thanks to Julie across the bar, before heading out to the next place under investigation.

There was an air of tension at home regarding my secondment. Jane didn't like the fact that again I was working mostly nights for a continuous period, and that it seemed for the most part I was simply going out drinking and having a good time. That is exactly what I was doing, and I would be lying if I said it wasn't great fun.

On another occasion, along with a colleague, I was sent out to a real salt-of-the-earth working-class pub. Unlike the gay bar, where there wasn't a whiff of anything illegal in sight, the pub had it all going on. Even when we arrived at eleven in the morning people were betting on live horse racing which was being shown on a television in the corner of the room.

We approached the bar to order a couple of drinks and asked if they served food too. It would soon be approaching lunchtime and as part of their licensing agreement they were supposed to serve meals, but the weathered skinhead behind the bar told me bluntly that crisps and nuts were the only things on offer. I took a pack of Scampi Fries with my pint, and we sat down at the corner of the bar.

It was a world away from the middle-class pubs I had worked in during my youth, and wasn't the sort of place I would have ever chosen to go. Mostly out of fear.

At first, I thought it was best not to look around too much or engage with any of the punters, as I fully expected them to have been incredibly hostile, but I couldn't have been more wrong. With a couple of drinks in us we relaxed our attitude and started chatting with a few of the locals. To begin with, I had been concerned our cover would be blown, but I soon forgot about that because nobody would really suspect that the Old Bill would stop by for a few pints before noon.

After an hour and a half, someone approached us at the bar with a bag full of sausages and bacon.

'Alright fellas, do you want to buy any meat?'

A different proposition entirely than if I had been asked the same question in the gay bar.

It was very clearly stolen so absolutely, yes, I did want to buy some meat. It was all good evidence for us. With another pint down the hatch and a tenner's worth of bacon under my chair, I had clearly been spotted as another pedlar's opportunity so proceeded to purchase when offered, a bottle of knock-off aftershave, some DVDs, and a couple of Lacoste T-shirts, which went in the bag with my bacon.

It reached half past one, and in the two and a half hours we had been there, in addition to my innocuous purchases, we'd had four or five pints and a couple of bets on the horses. We were scheduled to be collected at two in the afternoon and as the time drew nearer, I was becoming increasingly conscious that I needed to remember what I had bought, for how much, and a general description of who had sold it to me. The problem being that I was steaming drunk. When the phone rang to say someone was outside to collect us, I stumbled to my feet, grabbed my coat, and left, leaving my bag of goodies under the chair behind me.

As I had failed to retrieve the evidence, I was then unable to expense it back, much to the annoyance of Jane.

When I returned home that evening, she was quick to berate me, *'You wasted our money on some dodgy goods?? Which you have not even brought home?!'*

'Yes. Sorry. It was an honest mistake.'

Her face reddened. *'Because you got so drunk in the middle of the day that you couldn't remember to pick up one single carrier bag?!'*

I was still nursing a headache from my liquid lunch and simply wanted to eat my dinner and go to bed, not engage in any dispute. *'It's my job,'* I sighed.

'It's not your job to piss our money away! We are getting married in a couple of months in case you had forgotten…'

I hadn't forgotten, but I can't say I had paid it much attention either.

Me being on shift work meant that my interactions with Jane were always in fits and starts. It wasn't what I would have characterised as a 'proper relationship'. It was more like a plant growing in the window in that it just happened. Now and again, I would be there to water it, but most of the growing happened whilst I wasn't actually present.

Since the engagement there had been a continuous flurry of activity at home. Of course, I was aware that a date had been set and all plans were moving in the direction of our impending nuptials, but I was mostly domicile in the decision-making. I was more than happy with that, and it was my job that offered the perfect excuse to avoid being greatly involved with any organisation or planning. I wasn't always available to make some of the larger decisions required, and I didn't feel comfortable making them either. The day was monumentally important for Jane as the bride, and I didn't want the pressure of getting anything wrong, and risk any upset to her.

My personality is such that I have never liked parties, particularly if they are my own. I strongly disliked being the centre of attention, whereas my wife-to-be was the complete opposite. She did enjoy big occasions and was happy for the focus to be entirely on her. My being preoccupied with work therefore didn't prove to be an issue for once, as it allowed her free rein to plan everything exactly the way she wanted. My only responsibilities were to go and get my suit (from a pre-approved shop), and to have a haircut a day or two before.

It mattered so little to me, and so much to her, that I was happy she was able to have it the way she wanted, even if it would likely cause me some discomfort on the day itself.

My final job with the licensing team was particularly memorable as it ended with me being forcefully put into the back of a police van, handcuffed, and arrested.

Along with a female officer who was posing as my girlfriend for the evening, I had been sent to a local social club. Unusually for the sort of venue, it was located up a country lane, and we passed over several cattle grids on the way there. Despite its remote location it was rumoured to be a hotbed for drug dealing and consumption. All we were there to do was observe; to identify who was selling drugs and then appear to be open to buying some without making a direct enquiry. Ideally, we wanted to be able to make a test purchase, as coupled with our statements, physical contraband would offer solid evidence for the prosecution.

The atmosphere inside the oddly located establishment was peculiar. It was incredibly busy, yet there didn't seem to be anything going on that would have drawn such a crowd. After a few minutes stood with our drinks we found a small table to sit at and I excused myself to the bathroom. As soon as I stepped into the gents, the reason for everybody being there became clear.

Drugs and money were exchanging hands left, right and centre and in no attempt to be discreet, there were lads sniffing cocaine off the sink units and even a few injecting heroin in the cubicles, not even bothering to close the door. It was the most overtly hedonistic display of drug use I had ever seen.

After using the facilities and taking great care not to trip and fall onto any needles, I returned to the table to confer with my female colleague. She described the exact same thing as happening in the ladies and we agreed at that point there was no need to attempt to collect any evidence, we had seen enough and were ready to leave and report back. We stood up and as I helped her on with her coat the room flooded with blinding, bright white light. It was a police raid.

In the moment I lost complete track of who I was and started to panic. As I made my way to the exit, one of the team working the raid, grabbed me and put me under arrest. Whilst working undercover the protocol was to never disclose my real identity at any time. Not even my name. Not even to the police.

We were taken to the nearest station, which was not my own, and as I was being booked into police custody, I asked to see the duty inspector.

'Stop dicking around now mate. What's your name?' the custody sergeant asked, increasingly annoyed after having asked me several times already.

The other dozen young lads who had also been arrested at the social club were piled up in the back of the custody suite, so I knew I couldn't give anything away as it may have been later requested that I visit the venue again.

'*I just need to speak to the duty inspector…*' I sighed, also becoming impatient.

Begrudgingly someone was sent to go and find him and I was taken to a side room where I waited until he arrived. When he did, I produced my warrant card from inside my sock, where I had been stood on it all evening, and the situation was quickly resolved.

My wedding day arrived, and as to be expected for late July it was beautifully sunny and warm. Jane had stayed overnight at her parents, so my morning consisted of nothing more than me, mooching around the house on my own, and it was bliss. I made the most of the solitude and the peace and quiet, ahead of what promised to be a hectic day. The expectation was that I would have to engage in a great deal of pleasantries and conversation, which I was not remotely looking forward to. As the event had drawn closer, I had become increasingly reluctant to even partake, but I was just glad to be finally getting it over and done with; it seemed it was all Jane and I discussed, and it had all gotten a bit tedious.

My alone time on the morning was disturbed by my parents who arrived to take me to the church. Annoyingly they arrived earlier than agreed, which is a trend they still maintain, but one which led to the absolute highlight of the day for me. My dad was driving a red Alfa Romeo at the time, and it was flash. Jane had taken my car to her parents, which posed the ideal opportunity for me to take my dad's out for a spin. I fabricated an excuse about needing to run a last-minute wedding errand and enjoyed twenty minutes alone doing a small circular, on and off the nearest motorway junctions. He would never have let me drive his car under normal circumstances, but it was my wedding day so he mustn't have felt he could say no.

At the church Jane and I proceeded to say our 'I do's'. My family and friendship circle was so small in comparison to hers that the number of guests on each side was clearly disproportionate, but it didn't matter, I was just glad when we left the church and there were no longer hundreds of eyes fixated on me. We were met outside by bells chiming and our guests throwing confetti. Jane gripped hold of my hand tightly and led me down the path, making sure we stopped for people to take our picture on the way. My grandmother was there, and as though she had been clutching to it throughout the entire ceremony, her confetti had clumped together so that when she finally got the chance to throw it, it was less a shower of delicate pieces and more a solid lump of paper.

We moved to a local function suite for our reception, where we went through the traditional motions of a three-course meal, cutting the cake, our first dance, a bit of a disco and an evening buffet. There was too much hustle and bustle for me, so I barely touched my food. I was just waiting for the whole thing to be over.

As far as weddings go, I would consider it a pleasant affair, with all the bells and whistles you might expect. Jane seemed happy with it and that is all I could have hoped for.

A few days later we embarked on a two-week honeymoon, something else I had contributed very little to in terms of organisation. We started in Mexico, but didn't see much whilst we were there. I mentioned it might have been nice to visit some Mayan ruins, but Jane was not interested in doing that. She suggested instead that she might like to try some scuba-diving, but I had no interest in doing that. We ended up just sat around the resort enjoying the sunshine and making the most of our all-inclusive accommodation. The second week we went on a short cruise, which was not something that personally I would have chosen to do. We didn't have a particularly nice cabin so there was no view to speak of, and the place was packed with larger-than-life Americans. There was always some sort of activity ongoing so above the constant rabble of American drawls, *'TWO MINUTES TO SHUFFLEBOARD!'* and *'BINGO STARTING NOW IN THE MAIN HALL!'* was all that could be heard, coming out of the speakers across the entire ship. Feeling as though we were taking part in some sort of twenty-four-hour gameshow was not high on my list of relaxing activities.

I was relieved to get back home to normality, and to my work.

In keeping with the expected course of action as a newlywed couple, not long after celebrating the millennium we found out that

Jane was pregnant. Unlike the other facets of our life, becoming a father was something I was more enthused about. I was looking forward to it and was committed to being the best I could be for my child.

21

My entire career was about seizing opportunities.

And my advice to anybody presented with an opportunity would be, 'just fucking do it'.

Sometimes we have a difficult relationship with risk; it often makes us second-guess our instincts, weighing the potential fallout against the rewards. Yet embracing risk is essential for growth and discovery. Each decision I took to step outside my comfort zone has led to invaluable experiences and insights, reinforcing the idea that the greatest barriers to our own progress and development, often only exist in our minds. When we shift our perspective and view risk not as a threat but as a pathway, we open ourselves up to a world of possibilities.

Taking calculated risks can ultimately lead to personal and professional fulfilment.

By fostering a proactive attitude and viewing every opportunity and experience as a stepping stone, we not only enhance our own lives, but also inspire others to embrace their own potential, too. Every choice we make shapes our journey and defines who we are.

How do you want to define yourself? Are you willing to take the action required to get there? In spite of risk and fear of change?

22

My time as a PC on the beat had been worthwhile and rewarding, but as I settled into absolute domesticity at home, I needed something more exciting and challenging from my work. After some enquiries I was accepted to do a detective traineeship, beginning in the October of 1999. To avoid any bias or favourable treatment, such positions are not carried out on an officer's home division, so I was posted to another area, much closer to the city.

On day one it was glaringly obvious that I was worlds away from the green, leafy suburbs of middle-class mediocrity that I had been policing up to that point, and I was relieved. I had wanted to be more exposed to the darker side of society and the difficulty that went along with it. Not only did I expect that the faster pace of work would keep me engaged, but the higher crime areas and the more challenging cases are where I saw myself as having a greater impact.

When I walked into my new station I felt as though I had been transported back to the 1970s. The station was old-fashioned, not just in aesthetics but also in attitudes and values. My new team had not looked to move with the times at all, nor did they seem to have the desire to. They were rooted in the old-school ways of being tough-talking alpha males who all kept a bottle of whisky in their desk drawer. It was a literal depiction of the BBC drama *Life on Mars*, and I was Sam Tyler, the character played by John Simm, completely bemused at what was before my eyes.

Most of the public I had interacted with up to that point, even the more hardened criminals on my beat, were not excessively offensive. But the group officers on my new patch were used to dealing with the absolute bottom-of-the-barrel scum, day in, day out, which had left them completely hardened.

The detective chief inspector was formidable. So much so that even his superiors, (who he referred to as 'pencil-neck fuckwits'), kept out of his way. He commanded an entire room upon entry without even having to open his mouth. He always seemed to be leaning in the corner of the office, puffing away on a cigarette, completely abreast of all the comings and goings on. When he did open his mouth, it was never anything other than a direct bark. He was like Philip Glenister's character in *Life on Mars*, DCI Gene Hunt, complete with swagger, and I admired him for it.

During my first week I was sent to the local hospital, to take the statement of a man who had arrived at the accident and emergency department with a large wound to the centre of his chest, and significant burns up the back of both his upper arms.

His claim was that he had been seriously assaulted, which certainly did look to be the case. It didn't take a minute of questioning for me to establish that he was blind drunk, so much that I wondered how on earth he had got himself to the hospital, but when I asked, he slurred the word *'bus'*. I asked how he had sustained his injuries, but he couldn't tell me, because he didn't know.

The only thing he could tell me was where he had been prior to arriving to hospital, so I took down the address and headed to what turned out to be a small block of maisonette apartments. After waiting a few minutes in the communal entrance, I was finally buzzed in and made my way to the apartment where my victim claimed to have been. During the initial conversation with the occupant of the address, it was revealed that the victim had indeed been there for much of the day, and that the two of them had spent the time together drinking. I explained to the occupant that his acquaintance had presented himself at hospital with some serious injuries, and that I was trying to understand how they had occurred.

Upon further inspection of the apartment, I found a tomahawk axe propped up in the corner of the living room, and it didn't take a great deal of further questioning to understand that it was the axe that had caused the wound to the victim's chest. Assuming then that the occupant was also responsible for the other injuries to the victim, I arrested him on suspicion grievous bodily harm.

Back at the station I interviewed the suspect, where he revealed more of what had happened. He explained that both men had been drinking together from approximately eight in the morning, and by two in the afternoon had drunk so much that the alcohol had rendered them both unconscious. The suspect was the first to stir and upon waking he began to look for his wallet. When he couldn't find it, he assumed the victim must have taken it, so tried to wake him up to ask its whereabouts. When the victim would not rouse the suspect tried various things to wake him, including hitting him in the chest with an axe. Yet despite receiving a blow that caused an open flesh wound to his sternum the victim remained unconscious. The suspect, so incensed that his wallet had been stolen, proceeded to use a can of deodorant and lighter to torch the back of the victim's arms, which did eventually cause him to stir. The suspect then explained that some more time passed, during which he found his wallet. When the victim fully regained consciousness, in a true display of humility, the suspect then threw him out of his apartment and told him to go and find a hospital. In my author's note at the beginning, I explained that all the stories in this book are actual accounts of real-life events. Everything is true, and honestly, I couldn't make this stuff up if I tried.

In my new role I was policing a completely different portion of the population.

Not only did they show barely any regard for one another, the rules of engagement between the police and the public on my new turf were vastly different. Nobody outside the station walls had any respect for us, so we couldn't turn our back on anybody. Such a 'watch your back' mindset created a siege mentality. It was gang-like; us against them. Before heading out on some jobs we would 'tool up', which essentially meant to help ourselves to a weapon from a large, floor-to-ceiling locker in the station. There was all sorts inside it; I could have probably even put my hands on a pickaxe if I had wanted too. Then off we would go, trudging to work looking like the Seven Dwarves, with a piece of kit over each of our shoulders.

There was one other large locker in the station, which was supervised by Hector.

Outside of his regular capacity as a police officer, Hector had also taken it upon himself to run the divisional adult movie rental service. I wish I was joking, but Hector's locker was absolutely packed full of adult movies, all on VHS, and he kept a logbook to manage their comings and goings. During my first couple of days there I spotted the clearly well-used book open on his desk, and in my role of keen trainee, I asked what it was.

'*Ah ma boy!*' he spoke in a thick Jamaican accent, '*Why that is for the checking in and checking out!*'

I wish I hadn't asked. '*Checking in and out what?*'

'*Come.*' He got to his feet and gestured, '*Follow me.*'

We reached the end of the corridor outside our office, and he opened the locker, which sure enough was full of porn. It was hard not to notice from that day on that individuals from all around the station would pay Hector brief visits at his desk. Senior detectives would come over and ask if he had a minute, before checking in Big Tits 1, and checking out Big Tits 2.

Only a month into my time as a trainee detective, Jane gave birth to our daughter, Alice. I was afforded a couple of weeks paternity leave, during which I tried as hard as I could to become acquainted and bond with the tiny, screaming infant that had arrived into my world. The monumental weight of responsibility that I felt was only dwarfed by the amount of complete love and adoration I had for my new baby.

After spending a fortnight back in the haven of suburbia, changing nappies and passing the baby around Jane's friends and family, I returned to work, ready to get stuck straight back in. Even amidst newborn bliss, I had been acutely aware that I was missing the action and animosity that every day on my new division brought.

Prior to my time as a detective, I was averaging two or three prisoners a week. My role had meant that I only made arrests in the moment; when I happened upon or was called to a crime, without previous intelligence. During my traineeship, my role was to investigate everything, and to follow up with everybody who may have been a viable lead. In doing so, I became a prolific prisoner taker.

Each morning, I turned up with my packed lunch and all my ducks in a row, ready to work. I had organised my days rigorously, sometimes arresting almost by appointment.

Being a detective required a different mindset to simply being a responder. Investigating was a wholly different craft to driving around with blue lights on, sorting out neighbourly disputes. I had to master how to conduct an interview in such a way to illicit further information from suspects. I had to learn how to use my judgement to weigh up people's character, during sometimes incredibly brief interactions. Not to mention the paperwork was significantly more complex.

The station where I had worked up to that point only had a handful of holding cells, but there were twenty at my disposal whilst I was a detective, and they were all underground in the basement of the large Victorian building that was the station.

The cells had great big steel doors that caused an echo in the damp air each time they were slammed shut, and from behind them the muffled shouting from disgruntled inmates could often be heard. It was a dark and horrible place to be, and rightly it felt like a real punishment for those who were locked up there.

One afternoon I was stood at the custody desk completing some paperwork when the smoke alarm went off. The sound reverberated off the metal doors and the concrete of the walls and floor. It was completely deafening. I caught a whiff of smoke in the air and saw that it was seeping out from underneath the door of a storeroom that housed prisoner clothing. A decision was quickly made that all police staff should leave until the fire had been extinguished, but that we would not be evacuating any prisoners.

We knew, due to the amount of concrete in the place, that the fire would not amount to anything serious, so we left them to sit for a few minutes as the smoke thickened before someone put the fire out. My concern about the prisoners' welfare was dispelled by one of my gnarly old colleagues, who assured me that the fire would not have become severe enough to cause any damage, and the risk of unlocking all the cells was far greater in terms of risk management. It was a valid point, but still seemed like a bit of a power play, to put some fear into them. And it certainly went nowhere to build any bridges, but nobody seemed at all to care about that. It was a completely different sort of establishment, with a wholly different character of police officers, than what I had been used to. They were in places unorthodox, but mostly diligent and always got the job done, whatever the cost.

'What time have you got on your statement?' the DCI asked.

'Two minutes past midnight.'

'It was four minutes past…'

Addressing another junior detective he asked, *'What colour top was he wearing?'*

'Black.'

'It was blue. Fucking blue lad!'

We all made the necessary scribbles before he proceeded.

'Are we all straight on what happened? This little fucker has been causing us problems for years, and I want to make sure this time we proper nail his hat on.'

It was nothing more than the occasional bit of hooky, but I was sure that there was likely more collusion in closed circles.

At the beginning of my traineeship, I had been allocated a mentor, but very quickly felt I had outgrown him. Fortunately, my potential had been spotted by some of the more senior officers and one of the detective sergeants, Chris, took me under his wing as his protégé. He was a small and aggressive man, with a thick cockney accent, and I couldn't have been more grateful for his interest in me. He promised me some proper police work, in his words, *'without any fucking about.'*

Despite my experience up to that point, I was still relatively naïve but wasn't fazed by much and jumped at the chance to get involved with anything. I began to work on the more serious cases that trainees wouldn't usually be allowed anywhere near: offences such as murder, rape, abduction, and serious assaults. My level of involvement in comparison to my place in the station hierarchy was unheard of. There was a process in any investigation of 'trace, interview, eliminate', with trainees only ever being allocated one aspect. I was carrying out full investigations, from start to finish and began to learn much more than I had ever banked on. Chris and I worked together pretty much daily, and fortunately shared a very similar approach to the job. Any chance he got to get his hands on someone who had committed a crime and lock them up he would take it, and I felt the same, even if my manner was slightly more refined than his.

'Good afternoon!' he greeted one defence solicitor. *'I have arrested your scumbag client on suspicion of murder. The victim was found with multiple fatal wounds, and your client did it.'*

That was it. His idea of an initial disclosure to the suspect's legal representative ahead of an interview. It was quite a serious case, with the victim being beaten heavily with a fence post before being run over on the road right outside his home.

It felt like such a big deal to me, but Chris was so relaxed, it was all just a big game to him, and I thoroughly enjoyed watching him work.

If he had disclosed any more to the solicitor it would have weighed things in favour of the defence, allowing for a cock and bull story to be created. We knew the suspect had done it but were still in the process of properly gathering the evidence.

The solicitor went away to consult with his client and two hours later returned, stating his client was suffering severe stress due to the allegations.

'I am sure he is stressed, facing such a lengthy stretch in prison!' Chris scoffed. *'Not to worry… We will just go and call the doctor for the precious little bastard!'*

It didn't matter to us that the solicitor was just playing for time, if anything it worked out in our favour whilst we waited for the evidence to come back. When we finally did get into the interview, we had watertight, irrefutable proof that the suspect was indeed guilty and he was escorted straight to the cells, pending his magistrates' hearing. Following the brief interview and the success we had, we grabbed a bite to eat from the canteen and headed out to another station not too far away. There was a prisoner waiting for us there who had been arrested on a warrant that we had outstanding for a local robbery. As we passed over a canal bridge, Chris caught something in the corner of his eye.

'What the fuck is going on down there?' he grumbled, before pulling the car over to the side of the road and huffing at the inconvenience as he got out.

Swiftly, I followed him.

As detectives, we were not only in an unmarked car, but also worked in plain clothes, so as we both stepped out onto the pavement in our suits, we looked like a mismatched pair of insurance salesman who were about to go door-to-door. I was reasonably tall and slim. Chris was only around five foot seven inches, and his jaw and chin were barely distinguishable from his thick neck.

He shouted down from the bridge, *'Oi! You two! What are you doing down there?'*

The two young lads who were spray painting a bike looked back up at us. The bike had clearly been stolen, and the new paint job they were giving it was designed to hide its identity.

'Alright, boss!' the one holding up the bike shouted back. *'Do ya wanna buy a bike?'*

'Fuckers…' muttered Chris. *'Let's have a look then, what have you got there?'* He shouted to them as he started down the steps in their direction.

'It's fifty quid to you, mate.'

'I'll do better than that. I will take it off you for absolutely nothing because I'm the fucking police,' Chris said, producing his badge.

As soon as the words registered in their ears the lad who had been spraying the bike hotfooted it away, leaving the one who was holding the bike in a real fight-or-flight predicament. In an act of summary justice that Chris seemingly felt was appropriate, he stepped forward and pushed the bike and the lad with it, straight into the canal, before turning around and marching back up the steps towards the car. Following him I stopped for a moment when we got back up onto the bridge, just to watch as the young lad dragged himself onto the bank of the canal, in complete shock at what had just happened.

'That'll do,' Chris said, gesturing me to the car, 'we don't have any more time for this shit.'

My job demanded me not to offer instant judgement on people, which was difficult, considering what I saw a lot of was the impact crime had on the lives of innocent victims and their families. To uphold the opinion that anybody accused of a crime should be presumed innocent until proven otherwise, when giving evidence in court, we were never permitted to disclose to the magistrates, judge and jury, if the accused had any previous convictions. To do so risked tainting their view. But as with every system there was a loophole, one that allowed me to make it known if a prisoner did have previous form, without breaking protocol. As part of my questioning, I would often be called to refer to my pocket notebook, to share notes I had made at the time of the incident in question.

'Mr Clarke,' the judge or magistrate would address me. 'Have you had the opportunity to refresh your memory regarding these events?'

'Yes, your honour, I have.'

'And how have you done this?' they would ask, knowing full well. It was all a part of the process.

'By referring to my pocket notebook.' Would be my reply, before I would then go on to give my account... 'On 15th May, I attended *number six Smith Street at ten past two in the afternoon. Whereupon I saw a man, I now know to be Joe Bloggs, date of birth seventeenth of August 1982, SRN number 8769334.'* And so on and so forth with what I witnessed.

If somebody has an SRN number it means they have previously been arrested, which any judge or magistrate would surely know. Members of the jury would usually query what it was and then receive an explanation.

Whilst I do believe in awarding people the merit they deserve, there are unfortunately some amongst society who are not worthy of such treatment. For example, malicious abusers or relentless common criminals I don't think should ever be considered as having a clean slate during their appeal. It was helpful in situations where people were sat on the fence and saw to it that repeat offenders were rightfully punished.

Car thefts were still very much the crime of the decade, and in the area I policed as a detective it was much more of a problem than it had been when I did my previous secondment with Paul. It seemed to be the equivalent of dropping litter.

Our station was receiving five or six calls a day, and no doubt there were other thefts that were not called in to us.

One lad had made a name for himself locally as a shitpot-joyrider, stealing cars for nothing more than a thrill. He was only seventeen years old by the time I crossed paths with him, but he had already been arrested no less than thirty times for stealing cars. He had been put in front of the court system on numerous occasions, but it had constantly failed the public and let him back out onto the streets, only for him to reoffend.

The final time he was caught driving a stolen car he was put before the magistrates who eventually decided that he should be given one last chance to turn a new leaf. He should not have been afforded such an opportunity and it was truly the worst judgement I had ever seen. Upon leaving the court after nothing more than another slap on the wrist, he immediately stole a car to get himself back home which he drove like an utter maniac; with complete disregard for anybody else, likely on a high from his confirmed future freedom.

As the newly freed, shitpot-car-thief rounded a corner onto a residential street, a small boy of five years old was playing with a football in the small front garden of his grandfather's terraced house. As footballs tend to do, it bounced into the road, surely followed by the child. The driver was going at such great speeds that he failed to see the young boy in the road and ran him over. At five years old he was small enough to get stuck under the car but too big to get under the wheel arch, meaning he was picked up by the front nearside wheel, and dragged down the road for about one hundred metres, before the driver abandoned the car and ran.

By the time we had come to be aware of the incident, the local jungle drums had already started beating. The residents in that area knew not to shit on their own doorstep and the driver knew that as soon as he stepped out onto the streets, he would likely be dead within the hour. I was getting ready to go out and hunt for the perpetrator when the front desk called to say that someone had arrived at the front entrance in the boot of a taxi, but was refusing to get out until a police officer was present.

The cowardice of him had led him to seek refuge at the police station. He didn't deserve our protection, but we had a job to do and a procedure to follow, and that started with locking him away. I hoped he would never see the light of day again.

As the investigating officer I attended the boy's post-mortem.

It was always difficult to see a child laying on the mortuary slab, but as a brand-new parent it disturbed me on a much deeper level. As a dedicated expert cut him open and conducted a thorough examination, before surmising what the fatal injury had been, I watched on intently, with a deep sense of sadness that such a precious young life had come to an end. The conclusion was that he had gone into cardiac arrest due to the shock and blood loss, and ultimately his heart had stopped beating. To say it was tough to watch would be an understatement, but I knew I had to do it. Everybody involved in the case was united in our desire to do everything we could to nail the bastard responsible, in the hopes of getting something close to justice.

Two weeks later during the initial hearing, the legal representative for the defence disputed the findings of the post-mortem, and ordered another one be carried out by a different pathologist. We were all enraged at the audacity of the perpetrator, to sit back and try and stall the case, causing further grief to the family and indignity to the deceased. All with the view being found not guilty, despite knowing exactly what he had done. Never had I struggled so much with complete feelings of detestation. It wouldn't have taken much for me to have jumped over the courtroom seating and beaten him to a pulp.

I went along to the second post-mortem.

There were only three forensic pathologists in the area, and fortunately, the one who had been instructed to carry out the second examination had been trained by the one who had carried out the first. They removed the body from the fridge and to my distinct relief and that of the family, they agreed there was no need to open the deceased up again. They discussed what had been done during the first post-mortem, reviewing the initial report, the photographs and tissue samples, all of which was satisfactory for a new report to be produced. Unsurprisingly, it concurred with the original findings.

Eventually, the defendant saw it in his best interest to plead guilty to death by dangerous driving and in what was a complete and utter disgrace, he was awarded only four years in prison; likely to be released after three with good behaviour. There was nobody who wasn't completely horrified by such lenient sentencing.

The grandfather showed no emotion throughout the trial. He was the epitome of calm and expressed deep gratitude to us for working the case. I knew he blamed himself for the boy's death and after the outcome of the court case was disclosed, I visited him at his home. He explained that as soon as the prosecuted reappeared from prison, he would be waiting, and that he would kill him.

I believed him, and I can't say I blamed him.

Never before, or since, would I ever have advocated the use of violence, but that case got me thinking and feeling differently. The system had failed, justice had not been done, and in the moment, I understood why a life for a life could be considered the only suitable resolve.

23

It is incredibly difficult to articulate just how intrusive a post-mortem is, especially, it seemed, in the case of a child. It is equally challenging to observe such a traumatic event, without becoming emotionally invested in the outcome. It was a uniquely horrifying experience, yet my duty compelled me to endure the process, to ensure that proper procedure was followed and documented for the court. The distress and sadness I felt was only dwarfed by the disgust I felt towards the accused, and his lawyer.

Their actions were callous and caused unnecessary additional suffering.

Underlying this tragedy is another systemic failure. There were multiple opportunities beforehand to incarcerate the offender, yet the justice system repeatedly fell short of its responsibilities. The lives affected by court rulings, in one way or another, are profound and lasting.

Each instance where justice fails to protect the vulnerable not only hurts those immediately involved, but also erodes public trust in such institutions and risks further harm.

24

To finalise my detective training, I was tasked with organising and executing an operation that would seek to solve a high value or high impact crime. As an exercise it was designed to demonstrate investigative skills, research ability and would hopefully result in some prison time for the offender or offenders.

Off the back of the tragic incident which resulted in the death of a young boy, and in line with my previous experience working with Paul, the ex-interceptor, it made sense that I would work to tackle car theft.

Traditional hotwiring had been dying out due to technological advances, which changed the modus operandi of car thieves. The preferred operating method had become to steal car keys from houses, and then simply drive the car away.

It is incredibly hard to catch someone in the act of burglary; over the course of my twenty-year career, I only managed it twice. It is however relatively easy to find stolen cars, if you know what you are looking for and where to look. If I could locate the stolen car, there was a good chance that whoever was driving it was the original burglar, or if not, they could likely offer a connection to those involved and be charged with handling stolen goods.

Up to that point as a trainee I had shone. I knew I had done an impeccable job because I had made sure of it. Even with the two weeks I had off for paternity leave, my average arrest rate was still well above what anybody would have expected, and I was well thought of around the station. It felt integral to my own success that the operation was not a failure, and I wanted to give it everything I had.

To formally get my operation up and running, it had to be allocated a name.

As instructed, I called the switchboard and told them I was running an operation, for which they used the computer to generate a name. The names were generated in alphabetical order.

'Okay detective, you have been allocated the name "Cool".'

'Operation Cool'. It really couldn't have felt anymore suave and sophisticated than that and I laughed to myself at the thought of the officer who had called before me being allocated 'Operation Battenburg', or 'Beachball'.

Anytime a call is made to the police, a Force Wide Incident Number is generated and attached to the complaint. Another number is then generated, dependent on the more specific location, which not only allows for monitoring of crime hotspots, but also it means the call can be pinpointed within a few streets of its origin.

To begin my investigation, I examined the information that had been recorded over the previous three months, looking for calls regarding stolen cars, burglary, or general suspicious activity. It was a monumental task as I read through endless call logs on an old, beige box computer, the rows and rows of numbers and letters in green, contrast against the black monitor screen. I wanted to see what had come in from specific areas in my locality, and I had a map on the wall next to my desk where I had already been charting previous crimes of a similar nature.

The next part of the review process was to note down any descriptions that had been given, which direction the perpetrator was seen to leave in, and if a car had been stolen, what the registration number was. Then, to categorise the cars that had been stolen, I drew a nine-square-grid. If the registration number of the stolen car was A123 WME, I would put it in box number one, as 1 was the first number of the plate. If the registration was D554 GHX, it would have gone in box number 5, as 5 was the first number, and so on and so forth. All the information that fed into the grid allowed me to create a quick reference guide of cars already stolen but not yet recovered, and the locations on my map gave clear indication where I should focus my efforts.

It took weeks and weeks and was painstaking in parts but was certainly a real investigation. I loved every minute of it and was on a complete high.

A good old-fashioned sting was what my investigation culminated in, for which I naturally partnered with Chris. We planned to do a full week of nights to finalise Operation Cool and on the days leading up to it, had become increasingly enthused regarding its success. Neither of us had shared any information about what we were doing with anybody else. The less people knew the better, as there was the potential for leaks from within the station, officers of Her Majesty's finest on the payroll of local criminal enterprises.

As we went to collect the unmarked, modified-for-intense-speed vehicle that Chris's advanced driving licence afforded us, we were buzzing. Chris got in the driver's side, and I sat as the passenger with my grid in hand, our flasks of coffee and butties in the back. I had been adamant throughout that my efforts were going to certainly bring before the courts several offenders who had been making a nuisance of themselves and profiting from crime. Chris could see that it would likely be a triumph for us and was glad to be associated with the success, but we really couldn't have imagined in our wildest dreams just how successful it would be.

After pausing for a moment in the car, waiting to turn out of the gates of the station, we set off left down the main road, heading towards the city centre. I glanced down at my grid, my brain registering some of the information, before glancing up to look out of the windscreen at the road ahead. The registration number on the car in front was one I recognised. It was the very first vehicle detailed on my grid, which had been compiled from weeks and weeks of hard work. Honestly, you couldn't write it…

We could clearly make out there were four young males in the car so without sirens or lights, we followed them for ten minutes or so.

When they pulled into the car park of a pub, we followed them and pulled our car up directly behind them, quickly jumping out to stand at either side of their vehicle.

'Alright lads, you are all under arrest,' I beamed as they opened their doors to get out. They had no idea what was happening until I said the words. They were just stopping for a pint to start the evening, before likely moving onto another job.

In no more than fifteen minutes after leaving the station we had stumbled upon four of the main players of the local burglaries and subsequent car thefts. After the first night full of interviews and paperwork, we spent the rest of the week trying to catch further burglaries happening in the act, keeping an eye on the nine-square grid whilst out and about. From the map I had done on the wall I understood most of the ins and outs of local housing estates and we spent one full evening up in an old fire station tower, watching several ginnels and alleyways with our night vision goggles. No further arrests were made for the week, but it didn't matter.

Operation Cool had been a real victory.

Throughout the entire traineeship I had worked my arse off. Dotted every 'i' and crossed every 't'. The DCI would do regular whip-arounds for updates, with most of the other detectives flicking over a couple of pieces of paper on a clipboard before fudging a response. I was prepared, always with four pages on my computer screen packed full of information, details of ten crimes on each. On one occasion he demanded I flick through them all and then asked me a question on each, to which I knew the answers. It brought me great satisfaction to do the work properly, and the expectation soon became that some of my rustier colleagues should model my behaviour. To wrap up my time, a meeting was scheduled for me with the DCI, and I breathed a sigh of relief when he told me how impressed he had been with what I had achieved in my six months. He asked me to remain as a permanent member of the team.

My detective training had been a real eye-opener: to wider society and to the different elements of policing. I had developed more of a sense of myself and began to seriously consider my role in the wider police. The experience had been so great overall that I did stop to consider his offer. The team was incredibly tight knit. Everybody had each other's back, and we were all united against the common cause of tackling criminality. But the ways of working were unconventional in parts, and the culture at the station was too far stuck in the past. It was because of that fact I made my mind up that I didn't want to remain at that station. It didn't chime with my personal values, so I thanked him for his offer but explained that it wasn't what I wanted for the next step in my career.

There was a faint break in his notorious manner as he showed genuine disappointment and sadness that I wouldn't stay, but he slapped me on the back, shook my hand and thanked me for my time regardless.

Equally, I didn't want the next step in my career to be a backwards one, returning to life as a PC at my local station, so I started to wonder where in the institution I was best placed. On one of the cases I had worked with Chris we had been tracking a tumble dryer that was being imported from Spain. The logistical arrangements had been flagged as suspicious as it seemed a lot of trouble to go to for a tumble dryer, when the recipient could have easily purchased one in England. We intercepted it as it entered the country and found twenty kilograms of heroin stuffed inside, which in today's market could have anywhere up to half a million pounds' street value. We removed the heroin, replaced it with something of a similar weight and then a specialist officer dressed up as a UPS driver to deliver it. When the intended recipient opened the door and signed for the white goods, he was arrested on the spot and ultimately sentenced to quite a stretch in prison, along with several of his known associates. It was a massive win for us, keeping the drugs off the streets and putting a bad guy away; even though he would surely have been replaced by another bad guy the day after.

During the operation we engaged with the police interceptors, who wore plain clothes and drove cool cars. Also, the local firearms unit, as it was expected that a drug dealer handling such large quantities would likely have weapons for his own security.

During my discussion with the DCI, I referenced the operation and explained I had been exposed to both teams, and that was the direction I wanted my career to progress in. It was partially to save face, but I explained that as soon as an opportunity came up in either team I wanted to apply. Without any further inclination as to my direction, for all intents and purposes that was my plan.

I finished my detective training in May 2001 and just a couple of months later I received the fortnightly copy of *Force Order*: a newsletter, which usually included a message from the chief constable, any changes in the law, and job vacancies.

My intention truly was to just apply for whichever of the two roles came up next, with no real clue where either would take me. The first advert I came across was for a firearms officer and without giving too much thought about what doing such a role meant, I applied.

25

With the name 'Operation Cool', success felt essential. It may seem now that the success came about in a stroke of luck, but really the incredible outcome was the inevitable result of dedicated effort, strategic preparation and hard work, through meticulous planning and research. Putting in the hours minimised the chance of failure, whilst maximising opportunities for success. I don't possess any extraordinary or innate talents, rather my accomplishments stem from a strong work ethic, resilience and a relentless competitive spirit.

When faced with challenges I believe on going all in. Fully committing to a task allows you to explore your true potential and see what you can achieve. There's no regret worse than knowing you had more to give, but that you didn't push yourself to find it. Of course, it is crucial to be able to identify when stopping and walking away from something is completely acceptable and even necessary, but it should only be after giving everything you have. Ultimately, the essence of resilience lies in understanding what you bring to the table and committing to your endeavours wholeheartedly. Embracing hard work and failure as part of the process, and maintaining a steadfast commitment to your goals can lead to remarkable achievements. The key to success is simple – do the work.

26

Reassuringly, the process to become a firearms officer was an extremely lengthy one. It consisted of rigorous physical testing, a psychological assessment and several interviews, all of which gauged my overall aptitude for the position. After being considered a suitable fit I was then enrolled onto an eight-week training programme, which proved completely different to any learning environment that I had experienced before. So much that on the first day I questioned in my own mind what atmosphere the instructors were trying to create. All the attendees were male, so it was implicit throughout every exercise that it was a dick-swinging competition. Yet on the other hand, it felt completely collegiate, with everyone showing genuine support for each other. I assume that was aided by the fact that there was no quota to meet, and apart from in the case of an obvious failure, everybody on the course was guaranteed a job. The instructors were a handful of men in their late forties who were nothing short of direct in their approach to teaching and learning. They were all current or former firearms officers themselves and absolute subject matter experts. They had a lived example for everything, and it all sounded incredibly dangerous and completely exciting.

Even after just my first day of training, I felt as though a fresh breeze had blown its way into my life, refreshing me entirely. Being a firearms officer felt more aligned to what I wanted to do and should have been doing.

During my final year of senior school, whilst I would have been happy playing sport all day, every day, I did have to pay some attention to academia. I was a competent all-rounder with no clue at all what I wanted to do, but during a career's advice session with the school librarian, it was suggested I could join the army. It gave me food for thought and I decided it warranted further consideration, so took myself to visit the local army careers centre, where my natural athleticism and relative intelligence was magnified greatly. As I was obviously different to the other hopeful recruits I was marked down in that first meeting as a Potential Officer Cadet (POC). The plan was that I would complete my A levels and then receive sponsorship to attend university, before beginning officer training.

It sounded great, and at the time it was very much what I wanted to do. I signed a piece of paper that day at the careers centre and walked out, thinking nothing more of it. Four weeks later, as I sat in my form room during morning registration, an officer in full army attire entered the room and called out my name. When I raised my hand, he walked over and thrust a brown envelope at me, before walking right back out. A few of my classmates gathered round as I opened it, to find within an army travel warrant and some typed instructions.

When I had been asked to state my force preference during the initial meeting I had ticked the box for the Royal Marines, so had been allocated a training experience aboard the *TS Ardent*. Without much discussion with my parents about my plans, having just turned sixteen years old, I finished school two weeks before the summer holidays were due to begin, packed my bag and headed down to London. On the first evening I was introduced to a group of young lads who would be my shipmates for the duration of the experience. There were twelve of us in total and in comparison to the rest, who seemed to me like the Bash Street Kids, I was acutely aware that I did not fit in. There was only one other recruit on POC track with me and that was Bobby. He was of Caribbean descent, and we quickly established between us that in one way or another we were different to the rest.

The following morning, we set sail out of the Thames.

Sure enough, over the duration, Bobby and I were continuously singled out by the instructors for harsher treatment. The hopeful naïvety I had at the age of sixteen assumed they were just testing our metal, but looking back it was most certainly an act of bullying in my case, and fucking racism in his.

We practised navigation, cooking, and in case there was ever a fire on board, firefighting. To practise firefighting everybody used the hose and hydrant, except for me. I was made to wear a fire-retardant suit that at ten stone dripping wet, I could barely move in due to its excessive weight. Coupled with the suit, I was instructed also to put a large mask over my face. It had a tube attached to where my mouth was, and at the other end there was set of foot-operated bellows.

The bellows were old, and the suit was made of fibreglass. As I stood holding the hose, actioning the fire drill, someone stood pumping the bellow, feeding dusty air into the mask. It was terrifying. I could hardly breathe.

We were taught how to manage the ship's engine, which could be done by monitoring the temperature, and for the entire week, Bobby and I were instructed to watch the temperature gauge between two and four in the morning, whilst some of our peers never had to do it once.

Our ship was situated just on the edge of the Channel, practically in the open ocean. The seas were rough due to high winds, which had meant all shipping vessels in the vicinity had stopped and as we waited for the weather to pass before setting sail again, we practised drills for man overboard, using a straw dummy. The straw soaked up the water, so the dummy became as heavy as a real human, requiring some effort to haul it back out. After a few rounds of throwing the dummy in and retrieving it out again the instructing officer turned to me…

'Right, Clarke, in you go!'

I was sure for a minute he was joking, but his stern expression led me to conclude he wasn't. With nothing other than a tatty old life vest and a rope tied around my waist, I plunged into the icy water. I wasn't a particularly strong swimmer, but I knew if I hadn't jumped, I would have been pushed. There were at least thirty seconds of coughing, spluttering, and trying to stay afloat before I felt the rescue attempt begin. Sadly, I didn't have a single positive thing to take away from the entire experience, and was glad to get my ticket home and leave.

Beyond that week there were periodic check ins, to understand what grades I had received at GCSE, and how my college education was going, and then the following summer I was invited again to a training experience. Scarred from my near drowning, I was reluctant, but the offer was two weeks spent in Exmouth with the Royal Marines, and thankfully I went. Unlike my first exposure to the military, it was completely brilliant. We played war games, with extensive planning on how to capture the other team during the night. We ziplined, climbed, abseiled, built covert dens in woodland, and even practised getting out of a helicopter that had been submerged in a large tank of water. It was a live army camp so there were people coming and going the whole time, leaving in their wake an atmosphere of ultimate leadership.

Despite having the best time of my life, I was a rudderless teen, and after returning home I never followed it through. Many times, I have considered why I didn't see fit to push forwards in that direction and I still don't fully understand. I imagine it was likely low confidence in myself and my abilities, whereas the ultimate expression of confidence would have been to be a Royal Marine, the best of the best. There was also the notable absence of any direction or support at home, and I think that had my parents shown any interest or sought to offer any guidance I likely would have seriously pursued it as a career. As it happens, I did not.

The start of my firearms training was the next best thing. It felt militarised, and more akin to what I should have been doing all along.

The learning was a mix of practical and theoretical, and we were schooled and ultimately assessed on the use of two different firearms. I felt as though we were constantly being observed, and we likely were. We had to learn how to strip, reassemble and load our weapons, but also understand how things such as ricochet worked. We were taken to an open-air shooting range and watched as one of the instructors fired bullets at walls, car bonnets and windscreens, to see how different bullets react when they hit different materials, such as brick, metal, or glass.

The first of our weapons was the handgun, a Glock 17, which we practised shooting up to the distance of twenty metres. The second was a Heckler and Koch MP5, a semi-automatic machine gun, which we shot up to fifty metres. Both fired nine-millimetre rounds, which were short, round-nosed bullets designed in such a way that meant if and when they entered a physical target, they would alter their shape upon impact to something resembling a mushroom, making it unlikely they would reappear out the other side.

The general rule of thumb with guns is the shorter the barrel, the less accurate the weapon, and during the first couple of weeks I struggled with accuracy when shooting the Glock. It was problematic, given that handguns were the primary weapon I would be using as a qualified firearms officer. The handgun assessment came at the midway point of the programme, and everybody was nervous as the instructors were rightly unforgiving. More than once, I had resigned myself to the fact that I wouldn't pass but thankfully I did, and my confidence felt a certain uplift. For the next practical assessment, the MP5 was so easy to use that it virtually shot itself. It had a holographic sight, a circle with a dot in the centre that could be lined up on the object of focus, and that was backed up by iron sights should it ever fail. Throughout practise with the MP5 I had consistently scored highly, so there was no doubt in my mind that when the time came to qualify on the final Friday of the programme, I would be successful. Nothing short of brilliant is how it felt when I received the news. I had passed with flying colours and earnt my rite of passage.

In the October of 2001 I was enrolled onto the unit and on the first week of my new job I was allocated the night shift. It was dark outside when I arrived just before nine in the evening and all the lights in the station that was my new base, were dimmed, apart from the light above the front desk which was fully lit. After finding the locker rooms I changed into my new uniform, a navy-blue polo shirt and cargo pants.

I looked good and I felt good. My clip-on tie was a thing of the past.

The first thing on the agenda was an introduction to my colleagues, and as I headed up to the parade room, I was incredibly conscious that I would be walking into an already-established, high-performing team. During training it had been made clear that as a firearms team, we would only ever be as strong as our weakest link, so it was useful to identify who that link might be. If you have not spotted the idiot in the room by day two, it is because it's you.

As I entered the room, I couldn't help but feel intimidated. There were at least eighteen, rather large men, all packed into the small space. In comparison to most of them, I was still relatively young and physically, very slight. The expectation was, having been granted a place on the team, that I would walk straight in and operate on the exact same level as others who had been doing the job for years. If I didn't get up to pace within the first few days it could ultimately be a risk to someone's life, and it would highlight that I did not belong in that environment. I felt that I *did* belong in that environment, and I was adamant to prove that to everyone, not least myself.

I anticipated my first few months would consist of plenty of unwritten tests. Tests of my ability, stoicism, and resilience, and I wanted to rise to the challenge and perform. As I stood inside the doorway of the parade room, I scanned the room, trying to work out who was who, in terms of the hierarchy. Someone I discerned to be a sergeant due to his epaulettes, caught my entrance out of the corner of his eye and shouted across to me, in a voice so loud that everybody stopped what they were doing.

'*Here he is! One of our new boy wonders!*' Fortunately, I was not the only new joiner to the team.

He proceeded, *'We have heard that you used to work on a cruise ship...'* Well I have no idea what had given them that idea. *'As a dancer!'* he continued. He must have had me mistaken for someone else, but there was no time for me to utter a single word before he bellowed, *'SO GET ON THAT TABLE AND GIVE US A DANCE!'*

Within seconds, as though another member of the unit was poised ready, there was something suitably upbeat on the radio. Seeing no other option than to follow the instruction, I got up on a table and gave the best possible performance I could, as the group of big burly men whooped and cheered around me. It was less *Magic Mike* and more The Village People, but it certainly broke the ice and quickly rid me of any nerves or uncertainty I had. That was it, my dose of newbie torment, and I was glad to get it out of the way. As I jumped back down off the table each officer was quick to shake my hand and introduce themselves. It was a relief to feel so welcomed.

Gary was the other newly qualified officer from my training cohort who had been placed within the same team as myself, but he had not been as quick as I in finding the station and getting ready, which meant he was late arriving to the parade room.

His penance for being new was not to perform a table dance but instead to manage the brew fund, which was a totally shite, inconvenience of a job. I had gotten off lightly.

Each team in the station had a metal locker where they kept their tea, coffee, sugar, milk, and snacks. Everybody chucked in a couple of quid each month to keep the supplies cupboard fully stocked and Gary's new role was to collect the money and then purchase the provisions. What a responsibility. It was a poisoned chalice, as it was impossible to please everybody at the same time.

Even in the first week he struggled and was met with *'where are the fucking Hobnobs?',* before having a hot spoon, just used to remove a tea bag from a cuppa, placed on the back of his neck as he walked with a brew in each hand.

With me to my new team I had taken the reputation for being a bit of a sportsman. Wherever possible during my time in the police up to that point I had played football, sometimes for my division and on occasion the wider force team.

Playing for the wider force meant playing in a relatively decent Saturday league, against other regular football teams. For them, playing against the police was the equivalent of their cup final. There was always a degree of hostility towards us, and whilst it never escalated beyond dirty manoeuvres on the pitch, many players on the other teams took the opportunity to dish out low-level aggression to police officers, without concern for ramification. Although I can't say it was always much better playing against other police divisions either. One match I played right midfield when someone had become so disgruntled with my ability, in comparison to his own, that he clearly had enough of playing fairly and punched me square in the face. Before I even had time to register the blow, my teammates were quick to get involved and it descended into an eleven-on-eleven fight. It was swiftly brought to a halt, but despite us having FA referees, nobody was sent off the pitch and we carried back on with the game. Our team secured the victory on that occasion.

Like most boys of my era, I had gotten into football young. Inspired by Glenn Hoddle and Paul Gascoigne, I was happy to be outside with nothing more than a football and a friend or two. I have always been fast, and keen to get stuck in. I mostly played in defence as a child and took every opportunity to execute a sliding tackle, always returning home covered in cuts and grazes to show for my enthusiasm.

During the late eighties, I was training with Luton Town. I had obvious talent and was on track to do quite well within the team, but not long after that, we moved. There was no real attempt from my parents to support me in finding a new club to train with, but eventually I did find a small, local team. In what was a complete and utter fluke, after six months with them, we were invited to play in the Northern Ireland Milk Cup of 1990. Our position in the hierarchy would not have permitted entry under normal circumstances, but another team were unable to attend, and we were a last-minute filler, likely viewed by the other teams as easy pickings.

One of the parents of our players was a psychologist, who ensured our kits for the tournament were white, as he said it would make us appear larger in size and thus more intimidating. As a local Saturday football team, we were excellent, but there was no way we were expected to do well at what was quite a prestigious tournament in the world of youth football. There were international teams attending, along with Liverpool and Manchester United, with a young Ryan Giggs playing in the event. Big crowds were forecast, and it was due to be aired on television. I don't know if I have ever been quite as excited for anything else in my life.

Nicky Barmby was playing for Tottenham, who were drawn as our opposition. Our usual striker was out with an injury, so I was put up front against Spurs and it was a dream come true. My game was always about speed and making a nuisance of myself as much as possible. All usually within the rules, but I was just so eager to play that after scoring in the first match I got a little carried away with myself and was booked. We didn't get far in the tournament, but it hardly mattered.

Just the second week into my new role, the chief inspector shouted down a corridor after me as I was headed to the bathroom.

'Clarke! What are you doing tomorrow?'

Surely, he knew what I was to be doing...

'I'm working, Sir... with you.'

'Oh yes. Right. Well, bring your boots. We have a match against the F division. I will give you a lift.'

Sure enough, he was waiting for me in the car park when I arrived for my shift the following morning and I couldn't believe my luck. Off for a couple of hours to enjoy a game of footy during my first month on the job. Brilliant.

We set off along the motorway in his beat-up, F-reg, Peugeot 205, in beige.

'Be careful on that mat,' he tentatively warned me, gesturing to the passenger footwell.

'How come?' I queried.

'It's covering up a bit of damage,' he explained, 'have a look if you must but be careful.'

The football-sized hole in the bottom of the car meant that when I peeled back one side of the rubber mat, I could see the tarmac of the road moving beneath us. I kept my feet firmly to either side of the footwell for the rest of the journey.

As firearms officers, we were paid for the work that we could do, not necessarily for the work that we did. We didn't get paid any more than regular officers but took on the responsibility of carrying a weapon and placing ourselves more directly in harm's way. There were only ever around a dozen firearms officers on shift at any one time, so it was essential that we were ready and able to carry out the jobs that required us specifically. Checking in a prisoner and completing an arrest report was a few hours of paperwork, and we couldn't afford to be hanging around doing it. Whilst it was for a good reason, it made us slightly unpopular with the other officers and divisional teams who would then have to pick up the slack. I imagine to them it often looked as though we only ever turned up to take the glory of the arrest, all kitted out like G.I. Joe, before hopping back in our cars and leaving the rest of it to others.

We were a specialist team with a particular set of skills, which gave us licence to do all the best bits of policing and not too much of the tedious, more process-driven elements. It was also the nature of our day job that meant we were allowed time to train in the gym on every shift, so we were evidently bigger, stronger, and faster than other teams. What that meant was there was always an extra helping of resentment from our opponents, which added an additional element of combat and edge to the game, and I revelled in it. During that match, in a complete fluke, I scored the best goal of my entire life, which contributed to our victory. It left me on a real high and made me feel further accepted into the department.

For my first six months with firearms, I had been assigned a mentor, Mike. Another old-school bobby, he was set in ways of prehistoric policing and sported an impressive moustache. He was not a man of great intellect but was the single most intimidating person I had ever seen. When we were first introduced, my first thought was whether I would even be able to fit in the car alongside him.

On one of my first shifts as his mentee, he drove me up onto the hills on a particularly bleak night. I had no idea where we were when he eventually stopped the car and switched off the engine, and I struggled to see the lights of the nearest town in the distance. We were still trying to get to know each other to establish a working relationship, but what I understood about him up to that point was that he was interested in food, cups of tea, and the gym. He used our time parked up in the pitch-black darkness to probe into who I was and what I was all about. I explained to him that I was interested in the psychology of human beings, particularly what makes them commit crime, and that I was keen to understand what it meant to be a real leader. Pausing for a moment he looked over his glasses at me and expressly told me that I shouldn't talk about such things, not in his car and not in the parade room. None of my interests were typical of the department, but he made it out as though I were discussing voodoo.

'Anyway,' he grinned, *'we don't have to worry about any of that nonsense... you're my puppy now,'* he said, gripping my thigh with one of his gigantic, frying pan hands.

I wasn't entirely sure what he meant, and I was not confident or comfortable enough to query it with him, so I said nothing in response. He slumped back into the driver's seat and nodded off, whilst I sat waiting for a call to come over the radio so we could return to civilisation and hopefully get stuck into some action.

My assumption was that in my new capacity as a firearms officer I would be saving the world, but the first few weeks I spent with Mike we did nothing of any real value. In fact, it seemed as though we really did nothing more than bumble around his local area in the car. He liked tinkering with cars and machinery, so we made several visits to nearby scrapyards, where he picked up various pieces of junk.

'Is this free?' he would ask, as he loaded whatever it was into the back of a patrol car, using his uniform as a way of obtaining discount.

We visited quite a few nursing homes too, and when I queried why Mike said it was community engagement. Rather, he liked to visit because there was always the offer of a brew, and a plethora of biscuits to choose from. It was bollocks, and not remotely why I had signed up. Often, I refused the cup of tea, politely, which he always scoffed at. His advice to me was that I should never turn down the offer of a drink, as I couldn't possibly know where the next one was coming from. I understood the sentiment, but really, I knew exactly where the next offer of a brew would come from, and that was the next nursing home down the road.

27

Signing up to join the firearms team was a pivotal turning point in my life, which occurred when I was otherwise directionless. Up to that point I had seen and done a lot, but needed to find something that further met my deeply engrained need to perform at the highest level.

Of course, absolute perfection is not always attainable, and that was a hard lesson it took me decades to finally learn. So much time I spent beating myself up internally for any mistakes I ever made whilst at work.

To strive for perfection stemmed from my childhood, as it was only through meeting his incredibly high standards, would my dad ever offer me any recognition or validation.

Any victory against him was always hard-earned. Even when I was very young, he never gave me an easy win and always pushed me to fight.

It's not all bad, of course, as this helped me develop my resilience. Yet rather than his approach being supportive in nature and providing an opportunity for us to foster a connection, he left me feeling inadequate in nearly everything I did.

The pressure for me to attend university was immense, even if it was mostly unspoken. When I did not pursue that path, it further led to an environment of overwhelming tension and a profound lack of connection within the paternal relationship. Beyond my school years he showed little interest in my life and in all the time I ever spent with him growing up, I cannot recall one meaningful conversation.

Throughout my time in the police, he never once enquired about my comings or goings, and I always took it as a complete lack of interest. Now I realise it was because I worked in a realm in which he knew he could not remotely compete.

Choosing to carry a firearm comes with an extraordinary burden, one that includes the possibility of taking a life, not to mention the intense scrutiny that follows such a decision.

It is easy to view firearms officers as abstract figures – just people all in black, with balaclavas on, aiming a weapon. Really, they are just ordinary men and women, who carry an unparalleled weight of responsibility; prepared to confront those who wish to do harm, navigating perilous situations that others never have to face. In such a line of work, the stakes are high, and so are the demands on officers' character and resolve.

We were not paid any more than regular PCs, but money is a poor incentive for someone to carry a gun anyway; it must be about something else. Driven by a desire to protect our communities from the danger that lies around any corner, firearms officers step in to shield the public and are often prepared to pay the ultimate sacrifice.

It is not just a job. It is a deep commitment to serving and safeguarding the community, even at great personal risk.

28

Every four months or so, all firearms officers were required to do a refresher qualification in both weapons, to ensure high standards were maintained. It didn't matter that I had just successfully passed the programme, as the new year of 2002 began, I fell into a natural qualification period within our team and had to be assessed again. The handgun assessment was an area of concern for me, but fortunately I passed with ease, before moving on to be assessed on the MP5, which in the last chapter I described as being 'so easy to use that it virtually shot itself'. At the end of the shooting range I lay in the prone position, flat on my stomach with my legs spread apart, and eyed up my target at fifty metres away. There was a small margin for error, in that we were allowed a percentage of failed shots. On that occasion it was ten per cent of ten rounds, so I could only afford to miss one.

After discharging all the rounds from my weapon, I walked down the range with the instructor to see my target, and there was not a single bullet hole. I had missed every one. In what was a classic rookie error, with the holographic sight of the weapon turned off, I had failed to look through the rear of the two iron sights to cement an accurate view of the target before firing.

Instantly the floor fell out of my world. Anybody who failed was allowed one redo, but if that was unsuccessful, I would be off the team. Anxiety around what I would do if I failed again and lost my place on the unit flooded my senses. I was in disbelief and so angry with myself that I had made such a massive mistake.

On the run up to my reclassification shoot which was just a few days after, I became crippled by the pressure. On the day itself, as I assumed the prone position again, my instructor stood behind me.

'Alright son, I am just going to put my foot here,' he said, standing on the underneath of my bollocks, uncomfortably forcing them to the ground, *'as a gentle reminder to not fuck this up.'*

The relief when I hit the target with every single shot was unrivalled. Within a whisper, that was how close I had gotten to blowing my entire opportunity. Back at the depot I was swiftly encompassed by the support of my peers and I tried as best I could to let the experience blow right over me, to not allow any feelings of inadequacy seep in as I continued along the path I had carved out for myself.

The local robbery squad had executed a warrant on a residential property and during the search had found a shotgun behind one of the kicker boards in the kitchen. As it was a live firearm, we were called to the scene to make sure it was forensically safe, and then subsequently deactivated. Mike and I arrived at the house and were greeted by the suspect's wife. Her husband had already been arrested and removed from the premises, leaving her ballooning off outside, as the police search continued within. There was clearly some tension around the situation because as soon as we were out of the car, she hurtled towards us, screaming *'FUCK OFF, YOU PIGS!'*.

Despite her enthusiasm she wasn't of any real threat to us, and a uniformed officer stepped in to usher her away from the front door where we were headed. We listened as the officer in charge explained why they had been there in the first instance, before he directed us into the lounge. It was a long, rectangular room that had floor-to-ceiling windows at the far end which looked out on the back garden, the bottom three and a half feet of which were frosted glass. The residents of the property owned a Staffordshire Bull Terrier which had been shut outside during the search but could be seen pacing up and down on the other side of the window, clearly interested in the goings on.

Mike was chatting to the detective sergeant and as I stood putting my mask and gloves on ready to inspect the firearm, I watched the dog hop up onto a large trampoline which was in the centre of the lawn. After several seconds it had started to gather some momentum, and before I knew it, it had begun to bounce up and down. It seemed to know that having a jump on the trampoline was a way it could get a good look inside.

As I watched on, it also became apparent that the dog used the trampoline not only as a viewing platform, but also as a toilet, as every time it landed back down a dozen dog poos flew up into the air, before falling back down again as the dog reappeared at the window. Fortunately, the weather was cold, which meant the dog poos were solid, lending themselves favourably to a pure example of physics in action. It was by far the highlight of my week.

We trained on the use of tactics and weapons regularly. Up first on the schedule one morning was a scenario-based exercise in the main station car park. My role was that of the criminal, with the other members of my team playing firearms officers who had received some intelligence that I was in possession of a firearm. Their aim was to approach and detain me as I walked from point A to point B. It was stipulated that I was in no way permitted to get physical with my 'arresting officers', but just that I should ignore their directions and keep travelling, to escape them. The aim being for the instructors to assess how the officers would handle the situation. They tried and failed various approaches, as I was too quick to be apprehended on foot. Playing the stooge was a role that suited my nature, and I enjoyed darting about as some of my heavier colleagues lumbered after me. Eventually they decided they would have greater success approaching me in a vehicle; a method for which, of course, we had specific tactics. As the car approached me from behind, I could sense they were travelling at reasonable speed.

Their plan would have been to pull right in front of me, and for the officer in the passenger seat to jump out and seize me very quickly. Unfortunately for me, the driver misjudged how fast he should have been going and the passenger misjudged when he should have opened his door. They were travelling at thirty miles per hour when the door swung open prematurely and hit me square in the back. I took off from ground and as I flung through the air, I cleared the entire bonnet of the chief inspector's car which was parked nearby.

Instead of recognising the need to call a timeout, when I landed on the tarmac the passenger rushed to handcuff me and used his grip on the cuffs to pull me to my feet. How to properly handcuff a prisoner is basic stuff which is taught very early on in police training. My own 'arresting officer', in his haste to disable me had handcuffed me incorrectly, in such a way which meant my hands were twisted. If he had continued it would have surely caused serious damage to my shoulder, but fortunately one of the instructors intervened and I got away with only a soft tissue injury, opposed to any broken bones. What had broken, however, was a metal element in the handcuffs which meant they couldn't then be unlocked. Unable to be released from the cuffs I was annoyed, and sore. In the armoury the armourer released my shackles using an electric saw, which as much as I trusted his abilities, made me quite uncomfortable. Heading for lunch my mood was low.

Back in training later that afternoon we went straight into a timed exercise during which we had to strip our MP5s down to the bare components, remove all the bullets out of the magazine, and lay it all out neatly on the floor of the firing range. Once all the pieces were on the floor, we had to carry out three minutes of shuttle runs, back and forth on the fifty-metre range, before returning to our weapons to reassemble and reload them. The final element of the exercise was to fire all rounds from the gun at our targets, not missing one. I had redeemed myself since my earlier blunder of just a month or so previously, but the pressure was still on to be one hundred per cent accurate with my shots. Before even getting the opportunity to fire any rounds, I found reassembling the weapon incredibly difficult. It involved pushing a spring onto a pin, which was then inserted into a small metal block, which had to then be inserted into the weapon at a very specific angle. The spring-pin-block element then required a three-quarter turn, which I kept overdoing.

Compared to my peers, I was still incredibly inexperienced, and I wondered how on earth, with their massive hands, they all managed such a fiddly little task.

The timer ran out before I had chance to discharge a single round, meaning I had failed the shoot. Naturally I was devastated.

Failing the drill with the MP5 meant I was not permitted to take any weapons out, and I was taken off active duty until I had successfully completed the exercise. An opportunity to right my wrong was assigned to me for the following week, but for the interim period my role from within the confines of the station became the Weapons Issuing Officer. The armoury was an annex off the parade room, where I pitched up for my desk duty, ready to man the radio and distribute weapons to my colleagues whenever required.

Every single minute that passed sat in that tiny room, inputting data, and monitoring my teammates whereabouts, I was annoyed with myself. It is likely that they were only out doing run-of-the-mill jobs, but it felt as though I was missing out.

Towards the end of my week of self-deprecation, during which I had been working the night shift, two in the morning was approaching and there were still a couple of hours before I was due to finish my shift. My eyelids had become so heavy that I could barely stand to look at the computer monitor as its glare was too bright. There was a noise in the corridor outside which lifted me abruptly out of my slumped position, then the armoury door swung open, and my chief inspector strode in.

'*Good evening, Sir.*' I said, as I jumped to my feet.

'*Good evening, PC Clarke,*' he replied, thumbs in his belt loops as he stood. '*Get your radio and come with me.*'

Assuming I had made another monumental cock-up and was surely off to be reprimanded, I nodded and followed him out of the door and towards our offices on the top floor of the station. As it was the early hours of the morning the place was practically deserted, with only the odd coat on the back of a chair. And apart from a couple of desk lamps and the glow from the fire exit signs, it was mostly pitch black. After he led me through a set of double doors, and into a corridor that went the whole way around the perimeter of the rectangle building, it became clear what I was there to do. There was an MP5 disassembled on the floor, a magazine and a pile of dummy rounds.

'*It seems as though you need a little practise,*' he suggested, then explained '*I want you to assemble this weapon, run a lap of the floor, come back and do it again.*'

'*Okay…*' I responded. Anxiety was creeping in that it was nothing more than an exercise to demoralise me, and that if I failed what seemed to be an unofficial test, he would surely order me off the team. '*How many times?*' I asked.

'*Until I say stop,*' he replied coldly.

With no choice other than to comply, I began. I assembled the weapon, as quickly as I could before doing my first lap. When I returned to the weapon, he had disassembled it again, ready for me to piece back together. The fatigue I had been feeling soon dispersed as adrenalin began to kick in as I ran. Each drill took no longer than a minute and I would hazard a guess to say that I completed it no less than thirty times. I was grateful when eventually I returned to see that he had not taken the weapon apart for yet another time, and he finally instructed me to stop.

There was a moment, whilst I was running, I considered that he was exerting his dominance, simply because he could. But it didn't take me long to realise that I couldn't have been more wrong. He was doing me a favour. So much so that I am confident I could still assemble an MP5 now, with my eyes closed.

With my errors behind me, it didn't take long before I properly acclimatised to my new environment, and the individuals I shared it with. The atmosphere and the team dynamics suited me. Everything was a game and a competition, which I loved. It made me sharp and always on guard. My confidence was up, and I felt more able to be myself around my colleagues.

During a discussion with Mike one afternoon, my mouth kicked in before my brain, and I took the piss out of him in such a way that using words alone, he was not able to respond adequately.

'That's enough now.' he told me firmly, commanding a distinct shift in the atmosphere.

The intimation was that he would deal with me after the shift had finished, and as our lockers were directly opposite one another, I knew that at the end of the day I needed to get my stuff packed away and get out of the station as fast as possible.

To my relief when I arrived in the changing room there was no sign of Mike. Ready to throw on my jacket and go, I opened the door of my locker and got the fright of my life when I saw that he had somehow managed to get himself inside it.

It was as though I had just opened a cupboard to find a gorilla, and I let out an audible yell. It was surprising just how supple he was, that he had managed to get his enormous body into such a small space.

I ran like a child into the toilets, locking the cubicle door behind me.

There was a gap of no more than six inches at the bottom, and a foot and a half at the top. Not enough room for him to squeeze through, and I was certain he wouldn't bash the door down. Feeling safe I breathed a sigh of relief, and then prepared to wait it out until he got fed up and decided to go home. As I revelled in my apparent safety, I looked up and saw his hands on top of the cubicle door.

One thing I had not learnt about Mike was that he had previously been a semi-professional gymnast; the sort that can do a backflip from standing with no effort at all. And as easily as someone would jump over a small garden wall, before I could do anything, he appeared in the cubicle with me. There was barely enough room for one man in there, never mind one normal-sized man and the mammoth that Mike was.

Before I had time to process that he had somehow managed to get in the cubicle, in what was his version of a witty retort, he had pulled one arm up my back and thrust his other hand down the back of my trousers, pulling out what felt like an entire fistful of hair off my arse. What followed was another audible yell from me.

The best, and possibly only good thing about working with Mike, was his knowledge of local police gyms. Particularly the whereabouts of the best ones.

We needed to be fit and able to allow us to effectively do our job and were tested on physical fitness regularly, so hitting the gym was a mandatory part of our normal working day. As long as we took our radio with us, we could go at any point during our shift, for as long as we liked. Mike and I were out doing the rounds one day when he took me to a gym he visited often. As he had been there many times before, he knew where he was going and what he was doing which meant that after getting changed, he was in the main gym before I was. I entered just a couple of minutes afterwards and could already hear the treadmill going. As I rounded the corner I was confronted by Mike, a man of six foot and eight inches, pounding the treadmill, running impressively fast for a man of his size. For reasons unknown, he had chosen to keep his police issue boots on but was wearing nothing else other than his white y-front underpants and a full respirator mask.

He was such a physically intimidating person that I didn't stop to ask what the hell he was doing, I just began my own workout. He did a full cardio and weights routine in the unusual get up, before we set off back out on the job.

The respirator I could understand, if he was trying to increase his lung capacity perhaps, but as for the boots and underpants… maybe he had just forgotten his kit.

My time with Mike should have lasted six months, but after three I requested to be placed under the mentorship of someone else. My justification being that I hadn't worked a single armed response job during my time with him and that I hadn't learnt a great deal about what it really meant to be a firearms officer.

Someone relatively senior must have felt that I had demonstrated some relative competence, as I wasn't allocated another mentor, but instead became the spare ride along and was passed around like a dirty rag. I didn't mind at all. I was enjoying being a more active member of the team, getting better acquainted with my teammates and most importantly, learning the ropes of the job.

It didn't take too long before I fully understood my responsibilities.

It seemed that before I had been skirting around the edges, whereas being a firearms officer felt like a proper job, with real consequences. All the pleasantries were far in the past. My job was one that others couldn't and wouldn't do. If a woman stabbed a man in their home, even the ambulance wouldn't go in before us. We were the last line of defence, dedicated to dealing with the most dangerous portions of society.

Every day that I went to work was an absolute pleasure, and it was all because I worked within a team of truly brilliant people. There was still the odd one clearly only doing it for the uniform and the status. But most were committed to enjoying every young boy's dream of being a real-life action man, doing good and taking down the baddies. That was the camp I was firmly positioned in. Proudly, I identified myself as being one of the more tactically minded members of the team. There was only ever one standard when it came to tactical awareness, and that was complete perfection. White socks are more visible in the dark, and anybody with a pocket full of change could risk an operation by alerting perpetrators to our presence. To assess who was a potential risk to the team, we would be asked randomly to jump up and down on the spot during morning parade, and anybody who jingled would be reprimanded with an informal warning.

The job warranted constant diligence as any error on the job could be fatal.

We completed a great deal of our regular tactical training on the night shift, using the top floor of the station whilst it was quiet to practise room entries and corridor clearances. One of my sergeants would occasionally ring our phones during training, to see if any rang audibly because we had not switched them to silent. If anybody's phone ever did go off, he was sure to let them know how they were a fucking moron, and how he would not allow such a fucking moron to get him or anybody else on our team killed. He was doing what he needed to do to make sure we were always hyper-vigilant, and that could ultimately save our lives.

'YOU ARE NOW SURROUNDED BY ARMED POLICE! COME OUT WITH YOUR HANDS ABOVE YOUR HEAD!'

Armed sieges were a common reason for us to be out of the station. The usual state of play being that there was an armed suspect inside a premises, and we surrounded the perimeter and dealt with the situation; whatever it required.

The first such instance I attended in the capacity as an armed officer had been taking much longer to negotiate than anybody would have liked. So much so, that when we were put on the scene, it was to take over from the day shift who had already been pitched up at the property for several hours.

The circumstances were that a particularly volatile man, armed with a knife, was inside his house making threats to kill his wife.

Whenever we established an armed cordon, each side of the house was given the name of a colour as a form of code. Front of the house, white. Back of the house, black. Right side, red. Left side, green. Another armed officer and I were allocated the black aspect, so got into position laying amongst the hedges in the back garden, with a view of each window on the back of the house. Between the two of us we were to take it in turns to be on aim, ready to shoot, for one hour at a time.

Negotiations had been going on a total of almost eight hours with our team having done three of those, and it was getting a bit tedious.

Our instructing sergeant wanted us to be able to enter the house through either the front door or the front window, as going in at the front was considered less risk for us than going in at the back. The team at the front had been able to gain a good view of inside the house through the front windows, meaning an enhanced understanding of the layout from that aspect. To be able to enter, the suspect's attention needed to be drawn away from the front of the house, so that several members of the team could break down the door and overwhelm him in a matter of seconds.

'*Right,*' the sergeant said as he approached us. '*Loose plan. I am going to provide a distraction at the back here to get this idiot's attention, so the lads can go in at the front... Just flash your torch on and off at that top window for a minute,*' he directed to me.

Following instruction, I pushed the button on my rifle several times, flashing the torch on and off. The figure inside started to move towards the back window, and as soon as he came into view my sergeant shouted, '*Oi! Fucko!*', before lobbing a house brick that he had found discarded at the side of the garden, straight through the back bedroom window. At the sound of the glass smashing, the team burst in the front, and we watched on as the suspect's look of bemusement turned to one of despair as his crusade had come to an end.

29

Throughout my career I witnessed countless different leaders with various leadership styles. It was the approach within my early firearms team that stands out as the most effective. It wasn't always politically correct, but it was authentic and deeply supportive.

I made mistakes, regularly, but was not once made to feel foolish. Instead, I was encouraged to view my errors as opportunities to learn and improve. The activities that I first considered as possible ridicule, were in fact expressions of support. My peers demonstrated such strong expressions of teamwork and camaraderie, and there was a solid foundation of trust amongst us all. They provided me a tremendous safety net, and I am grateful to them all.

Effective training and leadership are about creating conditions where individuals feel safe to engage with pressure, to learn from errors and to emerge stronger as a result. Nowadays, such an atmosphere is referred to as one of 'psychological safety'. It fostered an environment of accountability, in which we all worked towards shared goals.

By working in such a psychologically safe environment, we were prepared not just to handle the physical challenges of our duties, but also to manage the emotional and psychological pressures that accompany them. When the stakes are high it was imperative that our reactions were grounded in thoughtful response, rather than impulsive actions.

There are occasions when it is essential to not allow emotions, or natural chemical responses within our bodies, dictate our actions under pressure. When faced with stress, neurochemical reactions can lead to distorted perceptions and hindered cognitive functioning. The hormones that flood our system during high-stress situations can narrow our focus and promote impulsive reactions rather than thoughtful responses.

The distinction is crucial. Reacting typically leads to negative outcomes, whereas thoughtfully responding opens avenues for better decision-making.

During the exercise which saw me improperly handcuffed, the arresting officer experienced what is sometimes referred to as 'red mist'; a state of heightened emotional response that impacted his judgement and led him to act recklessly. In his frustration or embarrassment over his inability to complete the exercise correctly, he acted impulsively resulting in my injury. This scenario raised the important question, how would such reactions play out in real life?

When I was handcuffed incorrectly, I narrowly avoided a serious injury, yet when I dare watch real-life police shows nowadays, I see the same problematic action happening again and again. There seems to be a great number of officers out there who are wholly inefficient when it comes to gaining compliance. The obvious lack of efficiency in police combat is a risk to the wider public as well as to prisoner welfare. It is a concern that I believe runs consistently throughout police training, from the very beginning.

30

Summer was approaching and I had started the night shift with Tim. Tim was ex-army; a large, handy fella, with a decent brain in his head. He seemed to share the same enthusiasm I did for actively seeking out jobs to do, so as soon as parade finished, we headed straight towards one of the more problematic areas. It wasn't too long before we heard a call over the wider divisional radio, directing any available units to a large pub on the corner of a main road just a few minutes from where we were. There had been a road traffic accident, and a pedestrian had been hit.

An ambulance was already on its way, but as we carried a trauma kit with oxygen and were able to perform advanced first aid, I set us in that direction to offer some immediate assistance. As unfortunate the circumstances were for the injured party, I was glad of the opportunity to practise my first aid skills on a living person. It was an invaluable opportunity to make sure I was as experienced as I could be, to assist any of my colleagues, or a member of the public should they ever need help. And if I ever had to go to the extent of shooting someone, unless it was immediately fatal and irrespective of their criminal propensity, my role as a police officer meant that I had a duty of care for their long-term well-being.

The victim was a lady in her mid-forties. A sex worker, dressed rather stereotypically in a crop top, short skirt, stockings and suspenders. Before beginning her night, she had started in the pub for a few drinks and upon leaving had stumbled into the road and been hit by a passing car. We arrived to see her lying on the tarmac. She was conscious but not complaining of any pain, which led me to think she must also have been high on drugs in addition to the alcohol. Her positioning on the road reminded me of a crime scene chalk outline, as her arms and legs were spread out in differing directions. The driver of the car was still sat behind the wheel, shaking. We were the first on scene and it was clear that she had sustained a compound fracture to her left femur, meaning that the bone had gone completely through her skin, and through the front of her stockings.

As I have already alluded, Tim was a great partner to have along for the ride. That was, until there was a spot of blood, and the injuries the woman in question had sustained caused far more than that. A large arc of blood continuously pulsed out of the wound, going across the entire carriageway of the road. A big bloody rainbow contrast against the warm orange of the setting sun. How poetic.

It was well beyond my capabilities to take any steps to remedy her injuries so all I could do was keep her calm and her head still whilst we waited for the ambulance. My six-foot-six colleague watching on from the side of the road.

'Look at the b...' he began, 'look at the b... look at the b...' He couldn't bring himself to say the word bone, and if he had, he most definitely would have puked his guts up.

Assisting the paramedics in getting her onto a stretcher so she could be transferred into the ambulance, I held her leg in place. Back at the station I was glad to shower and change out of my clothes, which had all been soaked in bloody downpour. Tim, all the while, sat in the corridor, braced against a wall sipping water from a nearby dispenser. I offered him my hand and once he was back on his feet, we set off out again.

Before long three in the morning arrived and we headed back to the station to wind down for the final hour of the shift; local crime permitting. As I shared our story with the others on shift, Tim was still unable to say the word 'bone'.

The transition between a crime scene and home was not always an easy one to make. After my first couple of years I learnt that it was beneficial for me to change out of my uniform whilst still at the station, and always used the journey from work as time alone to decompress and compartmentalise my thoughts; packing them neatly away in the back of my mind, not to be reviewed again.

One early evening I was taking a particularly pleasant drive home, listening to the radio and enjoying the glorious sunshine as I trundled along one of the more scenic roads on my route. Only fifteen minutes or so from home there was a part of the road which was narrower than the rest, which often caused people usually to slow down. The car in front of me had gotten gradually slower and slower before it stopped entirely, and when it started to roll back towards me, I realised there must have been a problem. Within the car I could see the silhouette of a man in the driver's seat, and in the passenger seat there was a woman who was looking behind towards me and waving her arms frantically. Applying the handbrake, I got out of my car to see what the problem was. The driver was in his mid-fifties and judging by the blood-stained foam coming from his mouth and the deep guttural grunting, I ascertained he was having a seizure. So as not lean across him I told the woman to put the handbrake on and unclip his seatbelt, before I dragged him out onto the tarmac. When someone is in a state of seizure, they become quite rigid and strong, and his hands had been gripped so tightly onto the steering wheel that even after he was out of the car they were still clawed.

It was rush hour and cars had begun to pile up behind us. Plenty of people observed as I tried to help him, but nobody exited their car to offer any assistance. He began to convulse as he went into cardiac arrest.

In nothing short of an incredibly fortunate coincidence I had completed a first aid refresher course just the week previously, so autopilot kicked in. After wiping his mouth on my T-shirt I gave a rescue breath and began CPR. It didn't take too long for me to resuscitate him and after two or three cycles he began to fit again.

Eventually, I was able to put him in the recovery position whilst we waited for the ambulance that his wife had called. She went with him in the ambulance, and I moved their car to a nearby layby, before taking the keys and posting them through the door of their home address, which was not too far from my own. I expected that some people in that same situation may have held on to the keys, only to return them in person when the opportunity arose and lap up the gratitude and glory, but that wasn't what I wanted. Driving home was my protected and safe space, but that had been breached and I had been forced into work mode. I just wanted to forget the incident had ever happened. I wanted to get home, have a shower, and lock myself away in the spare room to play some video games, and detach from reality for a while.

'Where the hell have you been?' Jane demanded as I crossed the threshold. *'You said you would be home by six.'*

There was no question as to why my T-shirt was covered in blood, or indeed if I was okay. I offered a brief explanation as to why I had been delayed.

'Well could you have not let me know?!' she demanded.

'Well, no, not really… it would have been pretty difficult for me to pick up the phone whilst I was giving mouth-to-mouth.' I responded dryly.

Top and centre of my mind as I tried to save someone's life was not to ring home and explain that I may be a little later home than expected.

'Well, who was it? Did you give them your details?'

'No, why would I?' I replied, before turning my back on her and heading upstairs.

Upon my return back downstairs to reheat my dinner there was no hint of concern as to how I might be doing and no chance for me to unload any emotion that might have been attached to the whole event. I had held his hand and reassured him that he would be okay, but really I had no idea if he would make it, despite my best efforts.

The man turned out to be the friend of a friend, and after someone had done some digging, his wife had managed to track me down and put a card through our door. It was then that my movements that day suddenly became of interest to my wife. She tried to take a picture of the card to share details of my heroics with her friends and family, but I put an end to any notion of that immediately which antagonised her no end. I didn't care one bit what she thought. The fella had survived the incident and that was all that mattered.

That wasn't the only time I had been forced to intervene in an incident whilst not on shift. When you join the police, you feel as if you are on duty all the time, whether you are wearing your uniform or not. The job exists out of duty hours, and I doubt there are many police officers who would be able to turn a blind eye to someone in need of assistance, even on their day off. The other instance was as Jane and I were driving home with Alice, after seeing an afternoon performance of some truly terrible musical with her parents. We were heading away from town when we approached a large crossroads. There was a white Ford Transit van ahead of us and I could see by the way it was moving that the driver was not in complete control of the vehicle. Soon enough it veered towards the edge of the road and as soon as the wheels met the curb it flipped over. It went straight into a glass bus shelter, before ending up back in the middle of the carriageway on its roof.

This event wasn't an intrusion as much as the other one had been, as it occurred on my beat; a road I drove every day, so it was a very comfortable space for me to operate in. Obviously, I stopped the car immediately and got out to help. There were only three seats in the front of the van, but another four passengers appeared out of the back. The scene was one of massive devastation but after a quick assessment it seemed that everyone was okay. Other civilians had started to ring around the emergency services and I detained the driver through deception, by sitting him down to make sure he was okay. He smelt like a day-old drip tray and with his car keys in my possession, I waited until the police arrived.

There were a dozen considerations going through my head, such as whether the driver was fleeing from something, whether someone else could be following or whether any of his passengers were going to try and attack me for holding onto their acquaintance. Layered on top was the consideration of priorities, in terms of who needed speaking to and in what order.

The whole incident took no more than fifteen minutes to manage, so really wasn't a big deal, but when I returned to the car Jane was furious at me for getting involved. She showed no concern for any of the passengers and didn't consider for a minute that it may have been somewhat challenging for me. I had managed an entire accident situation, surrounded by dozens of people who were all asking questions of me, because I had put myself in charge.

Another day, another job: escorting Billy Shitpot, a Category A prisoner to court. He was just a common gangster, but Category A meant he was either high risk, high value, or both. The worst-case scenario was that during his movement, outside the confines of a secure prison, his buddies might try to spring him from police custody.

The 'gangsters' we typically dealt with were not much like gangsters depicted in Guy Ritchie films. They were never anything more than bullies with guns; young men with a propensity to use violence. Due to the relative inexperience and unsophisticated fashion in which they operated, I can only conclude that they must have picked up most of their tips on how to be a gangster from watching television. Nine times out of ten when a character in a film or television programme picks up a gun, they rack it before shooting. To rack a weapon means to swiftly pull back the top slide, which loads the bullet into the breech, ready for shooting. There is absolutely no need for anybody to do this, apart from in the case of a misfired round, because as soon as a loaded magazine is inserted into a weapon a bullet is already in place ready to shoot. Whilst it is a stupid and unnecessary action, it meant that after a shooting, amongst the spent cartridges there was usually at least one live round which was gold dust for the forensics team.

Such 'gangsters' also often kept their weapon in the waistband of their trousers. It was a means of intimidation, as they could easily lift their shirts to show others that they were carrying a weapon, but anybody who carries a weapon in such a way has no clue what they are doing, and absolutely no sense of firearm safety.

On more than one occasion I saw this method of concealing a weapon go very wrong and one afternoon was dispatched to a report of a young man who had been shot in the foot. He did indeed have a hole in his foot, but also a scorch mark down his inner leg; a clear indicator that the injury had been self-inflicted. He wouldn't say how he had got the injury, suggesting he was at risk of harm if he did speak to us. The only risk to his well-being was his own stupidity, so we dropped him at the nearest hospital and left it at that.

There were quite a few well-known and well-established traveller camps in my force area, but the travelling community rarely bothered the police, as they in turn didn't want to be bothered by us. They sorted their own shit out and we were pleased to let them do so. It is often the case that the biggest dwelling on a travellers' site is where the head honcho lives. Usually, an older male who has risen through the ranks either due to his blood lineage or his ability to use his fists. One of the only times I was called to a travellers' site was after a shooting. There had been some ongoing dispute between one travelling community and another, and so someone from another site had gone along and shot the lead traveller on a site local to us, point-blank in the head with a .38 revolver.

It wasn't the travelling community who called the police. They had called for an ambulance who had said they wouldn't go onto the site unless it was confirmed as secure, so off we went. Amazingly, the victim was still alive and as there was a clear threat to his life we escorted him to hospital. He went in for emergency surgery and we set up a protective ring around the theatre. Within no more than fifteen minutes at least a hundred of his friends and family had turned up at the hospital wanting to see him. They wanted an update on his status and assumed we were just being awkward when we couldn't give one. It started to get increasingly rowdy, and we had to call for back-up. We needed them out of the way to be able to do our job and moreover, the shooter could be amongst them. For them, it was the equivalent of their president being assassinated, so understandably, tensions were high.

It came as a surprise to me to learn that the surgery went well, and that the victim would likely make a full recovery. I spoke to the surgeon afterwards to understand more about what had happened and how a man can be shot point-blank in the head, and then likely go on to tell the tale. The surgeon suggested that it was a combination of sheer luck and genetics, because his skull was so thick that the bullet had not been able to penetrate the brain. It had entered his head, hit his skull but instead of going through into his brain, it had shifted around and ended up at the back of his head. They had been able to remove the bullet but even without it penetrating directly, the impact had understandably still caused some damage, so they had done some brain surgery. The surgeon went on to explain:

'The initial impact was to the front of the brain, where personality and processing occurs. Quite a portion of his brain there was like mashed potato, so we have taken a small hoover and sucked it out.'

I listened intently.

'He will likely make a full recovery physically, but now has a part of his brain missing, and it's the part that dictates his personality.'

'So, what will he be like when he wakes up?' I queried.

He looked at me, shrugged his shoulders and then walked off.

Amazingly the individual in question had lived after being shot with one of the most powerful handguns available. But his injuries meant that he had lost the ability to regulate his mood, which could be quite dangerous for someone who has spent a lifetime resorting to violence. Or maybe he wouldn't remember that part of himself and would go on instead to develop a love of crochet and kittens.

Shots had been fired outside a pub on the outskirts of quite a large council estate. The pub itself was packed to the rafters at the time, with people whose moral compasses were completely skewed; people who committed crime not only as a way of living but also just for fun. A couple of firearms patrols were dispatched, of which I was one. We screeched up to the scene, blue lights flashing, expecting the worst: a gun wielding thug, potential casualties, and maybe even a hostage situation. We entered the front door and were met with the shocking sight of… absolute normality. Everybody was drinking, dancing, and when some of the women caught sight of us, they started jeering, assuming we were strippers. I couldn't believe it. Shots had been fired, there could have been multiple fatalities, yet nobody seemed remotely phased by the incident. We began to question the customers as potential witnesses, and I was one hundred per cent certain that some, if not all of them, knew exactly who had shot at who, and for what reason.

Sat in a booth I quizzed two middle-aged women who were both blind drunk, and therefore giving incoherent answers. Trying to keep the conversation on track I addressed one of them directly to ask where she was when she heard the shots. Slurring, she began to explain her movements for the entire evening, starting with the fact that she had run out of cigarettes as she was getting ready so had gone to the off licence in her slippers. I couldn't have given less of a shit. As she was speaking, her friend took a swig from one of the two highball glasses on the table. The drink had barely passed her lips when she spat it all out, directly in her friend's face. *'ERGH! That's your rum and coke!'* she screeched, before they both began cackling with laughter. Neither of them were remotely concerned that someone had been shot at, mere yards away, and confident I would not get any further with my questioning I stood up and walked off. Working with individuals who had consumed so much alcohol that their morals had become somewhat loosened was normal for me, but I didn't understand how people could be so blasé about such a potential threat, and I couldn't be arsed with their level of disregard for such a serious situation.

The year 2003 saw the introduction of tasers, which the firearms department received first. There had been some chatter in the press that they were not as safe as the police claimed they were, so, to quash such speculation, our chief constable had offered to be tasered in public and invited several media outlets to attend. One of my sergeants had been given the job of discharging the taser, and one other officer and I were asked to go along to assist: basically, just to be friendly faces in uniform for the cameras. Our chief constable was a very approachable man, but what I had not realised until that day was just how bloody big he was, in size and in stature. Our sergeant gave us a hushed briefing beforehand:

'I am not shitting you now lads, this is probably one of the most important things you will do in your entire career. Don't fuck it up.'

The station car park had been cleared of all armed response vehicles and after the written journalists and TV cameras arrived, my colleague and I stood either side of the chief constable, with a crash mat ready in front of him for when he inevitably went down. He did his thirty seconds to camera before, from behind, our sergeant shouted, *'TASER, TASER!'* and fired the weapon.

The expression on his face whilst his body was being surged with electric is not something I will ever forget. His fifteen-stone body was completely rigid, and we had to take great care not to touch him inbetween the prongs, or risk getting shocked ourselves. Unexpectedly, he had started to fall backwards instead of forwards, and from a forty-five-degree angle we managed to rescue him and guide him gently down onto his face, as everybody watched on.

I knelt beside him on the floor.

'You alright, boss?'

'Yeah, I'm fine' he sighed.

'I'm going to pull the barbs out now, Sir.'

The barbs of a taser are two inches in length, with a small hook on the end. They go into skin very easily, but it takes a little bit of effort to get them out. As I removed them, they brought a bit of flesh with each, and I could see the blood starting to seep through his shirt. We helped the chief constable back up to his feet so he could deliver a closing remark to the cameras, before he retreated swiftly back to his office.

As a police officer, when discharging a taser at a suspect, we were instructed to shout *'TASER, TASER!'* Followed by something along the lines of *'You are now experiencing 50,000 volts surging through your body. Do not resist!'* We took full artistic license and, as a department, developed our own warning for whenever we used our tasers: *'TASER, TASER! It will fucking amaze ya! Light you up with a little red laser!'*

I don't think it really mattered much what we said. I imagine it is very hard to concentrate on anything at all whilst being tasered.

One dreary morning we were called to attend a hostage situation. The circumstances surrounding the incident were that 'Man', recently divorced from 'Woman', was dissatisfied with the access arrangements to his children that had been mandated by the Family Court. His response? To return to the former family home and accost his ex-wife with an eight-inch kitchen knife, before covering them both, and as much of the house as he could, with leaded paint. They were not the actions of a man who would further his custody case anytime soon, but his intentions were clear. He had the potential to kill them both and our arrival had done nothing other than agitate him.

A senior ranking officer was attempting at regular intervals to negotiate with the assailant, suggesting he should step outside and set his wife free. Nobody had to get hurt, but he showed no signs of co-operating. Policing is generally risk-averse in nature, so it really was a stand-off, and we had no real idea how we were going to proceed without significant risk to life. In our attempts to prevent harm coming to anybody we couldn't just go in armed and hope for the best.

The house was a 1980s mews property and every now and again, the suspect climbed from an upstairs window onto the pitched roof of the porch, brandished his knife and shouted hysterically. There was a threat to life, but he seemed to be all talk and no action. He had backed himself into a corner, with only a couple of ways out. I expect he didn't want to kill her otherwise he would have just done it, but the whole episode had been going on for almost six hours and we were having to seriously consider what action we could take to draw it to a close. The best option for us was to disable him in some way when he next climbed out onto the roof. Rubber bullets and tasering him were a couple of the options discussed, but after contemplating the potential outcomes, particularly if we missed, both suggestions were dismissed.

As he had threatened to set the house alight, the fire brigade had also been called to the scene quite early on, meaning the whole of the street was occupied by emergency service vehicles, and everybody was pretty fed up with hanging around. Our deliberations were still ongoing when he appeared again on the roof, blaspheming and continuing to make threats. It was at that point that one of the fire officers approached us.

'We can get him down from there if you like...' he explained.

'Yeah, that would be great,' responded my instructing officer *'How?'*

'Well, we could hose him off.'

The only consideration was that he could somehow manage to fall on his own knife, but it was the best plan we had so agreed to proceed. The next time he came out onto the top of the porch I breached the cordon that had been established around the front lawn and walked a few paces down the path to the front door, trying to engage him in conversation.

As I did, the fire brigade rushed to the pavement that ran adjacent to the house and pulled their hose. The suspect was only of slim build, about the size of Mo Farrah, so the hundreds of gallons of water that hit his chest had a significant effect on his body and he was well and truly blasted from the roof. It was quite an impressive spectacle to behold and was the result we all wanted, as I dragged the soaking wet heap of a man up from ground and arrested him.

31

Sometimes, addressing complex problems demands creative and adaptable solutions. In the police we operated under clear rules of engagement, with tactics outlined in our Standard Operating Procedures (SOPs). While we were all familiar with such procedures, the truth is that plans rarely ever unfolded as intended.

We always trained for real-life scenarios as effectively as we could. By applying pressure, creating stress, and inducing discomfort, we sought to understand and better manage our responses in high-stakes situations. Working under pressure can create clouded judgements or delays in decision-making, neither of which are ideal in a firearms setting. Moments of hesitation can be critical windows of opportunity, which means getting it right is essential.

The most unpredictable factor which usually derailed our plans in any situation was always the public, as they didn't adhere to any handbook rules. This reality compelled us to know our tactics so well that we could adapt them on the fly, making intuitive decisions whilst also maintaining a high level of safety as we worked towards our objectives. Most of the time, this approach proved effective, and when it didn't, we would analyse the outcome afterwards and engage in further training to improve. Justifying our choices, action or lack of action afterwards was necessary. I never made a decision which felt to be the wrong one, at the time of making it at least. However, the fullness of time occasionally demonstrated that the actions I had taken were sometimes less than optimal. But nobody can change an outcome after the fact, and we must all be satisfied that experience gives us more data, which assists in future decisions. The police often work with a great deal of unknown, under huge amounts of pressure, with the knowledge that the choices they make have real impact: on other people, on themselves, on their family and on the public's perception of the police.

32

By the time the year 2004 came around I was approaching thirty and had become slightly disillusioned with life. Time spent at home was mundane in comparison to the job, but even the job was not entirely living up to my initial expectations. There wasn't always a call to attend, and I couldn't sit idle in the break room watching television, so as much as possible I volunteered to assist other teams. Wherever there was any action, I wanted to get involved.

As varied and exiting it was when the jobs did come in, firearms didn't require excessive amounts of brain work, which is what I had enjoyed most during my time training as a detective. Not to mention there were still a handful of old sweats on the team whose values didn't chime with my own. Again, I found myself not completely convinced that I was where I belonged.

After the successful execution of Operation Cool, it was suggested that I had displayed enough aptitude that I could, if I wanted, be considered for the Local Intelligence Office. Every senior officer I encountered during my detective training had nothing but positive things to say about my capabilities and potential.

My initial drive to pursue the path of a firearms officer was only by impulse, so I began to question my future. The wheels of life were turning around me, and I was looking for the right direction of travel for my own personal fulfilment. My life was lacking, and I decided something most definitely needed to change. I paid one of my sergeants a visit and expressing my concerns, I explained how

I wasn't sure if I had taken a wrong turn and that I would like to consider a different role. My detective qualification was still valid, and whilst he was visibly disappointed to hear I wanted to leave the team, he agreed to put in a request for me to transfer to the Criminal Investigation Department (CID), back on my home division. It was there that, coincidentally, his wife was the superintendent, and what would usually take months was expedited. I was moved within the week.

Jane didn't understand what I was doing, or why I was doing it, but she wasn't overly concerned as long as the money kept coming in each month. Any opinion she might have had didn't matter much to me anyway. Home life had become rather inconsequential; it was just the malaise of existence. I lived to work.

Whilst I was at work I had wings, but as soon as I returned home, Jane clipped them, leaving me feeling unable to move. I was stifled by the four walls she had been keen to put around us. We weren't happy in the way she liked to portray to our family and friends, but we weren't obviously unhappy either. I made my mandated appearance at meals with friends and family occasions whenever I was told to, but it is safe to say that behind closed doors there was nothing more than a general tolerance of each other. Although I did my best to say and do the right things, as was expected of me, my veneer slipped more often than hers. It was disappointing, but the assumption I was under was that it was as good as marriage could be.

My work demanded a great deal of my time over the weekends, which meant we rarely spent much time together as a family, but I can't say I really minded. During the available pockets of time I had, I applied myself as much as I could to being a good father to Alice, but as far as my relationship with Jane went, it was satisfactory at best. It seemed devoid of any real connection. We never laughed together. In fact, we barely spoke, and when we did it was only about practical things, outside of which she showed no real interest in what I was doing. She never asked me how my day had been when I returned home from work, and if she ever did, it was never anything more than a false courtesy. It was always a vehicle to move the conversation to something which was more important to her: dinner with friends or new electricals for the home, which all felt unnecessarily prissy, and formulaic.

She regularly vocalised that I was antisocial, positioned as though it was an incredibly negative attribute of my personality. The reality was that I just preferred to spend as much time as possible on my own, or in limited company. Even after six or seven years together she had not yet grasped that doing things in large groups just wasn't me. On top of that, the perspective my job had given me meant that superficial conversations with neighbours about which brand of vacuum was the best or where we were all holidaying that year, were so incredibly hollow that I couldn't stand to play a part in them. Her labelling me as antisocial led me at times to play the part of grumpy hermit on purpose, just to end the discussion or scenario.

Being in her company was mostly quite tedious so some humour and impertinence was a release of the pressure valve for me, but it only ever fuelled her hostility.

There was never any acknowledgement that I could have had a hard day at work, and it always felt like there was a degree of judgement attached to our conversations, which made it difficult for me to feel as though I could approach her with certain topics. Because I didn't feel as though I could trust her to be open and receptive, I didn't talk to her, and she at some point must have decided that she would stop trying to talk to me as well, but I came to decide I didn't mind. Anything outside of work was wholly unimportant to me and as soon as I finished each working day, I was already thinking about what the next one would hold.

Back at my local station there were a few faces that I still recognised from earlier in my career, and within minutes of entering the CID floor it was clear that my role as a detective there would not be anything like it was during my training. This was not only due to the location, and the lesser likelihood of getting straight into it with rough-handed, seasoned criminals. But fortunately, there had been a significant shift in policing standards. The world was changing, and attitudes were slowly catching up. There were no whisky bottles in each desk drawer, and no porn rental service at the end of a dusty corridor. Everything had been formalised and was more process-driven, which of course meant more paperwork, but I didn't mind the work, if I was otherwise satisfied. I wasn't wholly confident about my transition to CID, but I approached it with complete commitment, determined I would do a good job.

My first crime scene was a shocking one, and as the only detective on the night shift, when a call came into the station to advise that an assault had occurred, I was wholly responsible for beginning the investigation. It was a relief to step out into the cold night air after spending several hours cooped up in the office. My dinner for the evening had been a disappointing microwaveable curry, which I ate from someone else's desk to avoid dirtying up my own.

Whilst the victim of the attack was taken to hospital for immediate treatment, I headed to the crime scene; a ground-floor council flat. There was a large and visible footprint on the front door where it had been kicked in, and inside resembled the sort of crime scene that would be mocked up for a television drama. Nothing in the flat had been left untouched, everything had been turned over and smashed up in what looked like an enormous fit of rage. A large mirror which had been hung above the gas fire was smashed on the floor and there was blood splattered all over the walls of the lounge, and on the ceiling too. After photographing the scene, Scene of Crimes Officers (SOCO) came to collect and bag any evidence, to be further examined back at the station.

When the end of my shift came around, I handed over to the detective who was on the day shift to progress further. By the time I returned to work later that same day, the victim was only just in a suitable state to be interviewed so I headed straight to the hospital to understand the circumstances of the attack.

The victim was a drug addict, regularly indulging on Class A substances such as heroin and crack cocaine. By mistake, after getting the wrong address, a local drug dealer had posted around five hundred pounds worth of drugs through the victim's door. Assuming all his Christmases had come early, over the course of the subsequent few days the victim consumed all the illegal wares. After realising his mistake, the dealer, who unsurprisingly was a nasty, aggressive bastard, turned up at the victim's door and demanded the drugs back. The victim explained that they were no longer in his possession, but an agreement was reached that he would get the money to cover the cost of the drugs, and that the dealer could return on a specified date to collect the cash. When the dealer returned to collect the money as agreed, nobody answered the door, so he kicked it in. Once inside he found the victim passed out on the sofa, off his face on drugs without the cash, which meant he was unable to deliver on his end of the bargain. The victim's account was that the dealer then set about beating him up, punching and kicking him before throwing him to the floor. What came next was nothing short of torture. The aggrieved proceeded to make dozens of tiny stab wounds to the victim's arms and legs, and cuts to his scrotum and penis. He cut around the skin of each big toe, so deeply that the bone underneath was revealed and, to complete the assault, he took a wooden drumstick he found lying around and shoved it up the victim's anus.

During the investigation we had asked the Home Office to send a blood pattern specialist to the scene. It cost the division around three thousand pounds, but we hoped it would go some way to better understanding what had happened outside of the victim's statement, which due to the fact he was an incoherent drug addict, was surely riddled with inaccuracies. When we received the report back, under the 'Summary' heading, the specialist had written *There was a frenzied attack*. No shit. The report didn't help us further the case at all and we never found out who carried out the attack. The victim surely knew exactly who it was but would have undoubtedly and understandably been in fear for his life.

My arrival to CID had coincided with a spate of suicide by forceful decapitation. On my first week I attended a local council-run car park, where a young man had tied a rope, approximately ten metres in length, around the parking meter, with the other end tied around his neck. He had then driven his car to the other end of the car park at speed, which resulted in his head being ripped completely off his body. Instant death was ensured, and it was nothing short of horrific.

The following week the deceased, another young man, used the same modus operandi to aid his demise, tied to a lamppost on a residential street.

In comparison to suicide attempts made by females, male suicide attempts are generally more violent in nature, meaning less chance of intervention and subsequent preservation of life. The most common form of suicide for men previously had been to gas themselves in the car, which offered a painless and efficient way for someone to end their own life if they felt compelled to do so, but the introduction of unleaded petrol and catalytic converters removed this as a viable option.

The men were of a similar demographic to myself, and I felt great sorrow at their despair. A part of me understood their desire to escape life, but it was tragic that they saw no other option to alter their circumstances than to kill themselves, and in such a brutal fashion.

Whilst working any crime scene, SOCO and CID always work very closely together. There were only a handful of SOCOs dedicated to our division and over the course of my first month on the job, I had spent quite a bit of time with one in particular, Katie. We crossed paths on several crime scenes and then during the process of photographing, bagging and tagging evidence back at the station, we soon became quite familiar with one another.

Katie began to take an interest in me, and I was interested in her too. She was attractive, intelligent, and there were obvious commonalities between us. Our respective job roles offered a level of understanding that was not present for me at home. We had topical things to share and discuss with one another and it felt good to be seen and heard by someone, to be able to share my thoughts and feelings without any fear of judgement or dismissal. We seemed to share a genuine connection, and it was the warmth that came with that connection which was completely lacking for me at home. During our conversations I had intimated that I was increasingly unhappy in my marriage to Jane, and whilst we only ever saw each other at work, or on either side of a job, before I knew it, my relationship with Katie progressed to one of a more physical nature. An affair was not what I had planned, but the opportunity presented itself to me and with no real thought, selfishly I took it.

Unsurprisingly, given the conflicting nature of the roles, police officers and defence solicitors don't always get along well with one another. Representatives from the firm who often tipped up to defend the prisoners whilst I was working CID were notorious for being nothing more than an awkward bunch of pricks, who were dead-set on releasing criminal scum back out onto the streets.

Solicitors will always look for loopholes, it is their job, and any mistakes in the chain of evidence make it completely inadmissible. The owner of the firm was a real sleazeball, whose practice thrived on opportunities presented by numpty cops who made sloppy mistakes, but I did not fall within that bracket. Any evidence I presented was wholly accurate, and my disclosures were always watertight. Everything was detailed to within an inch of its life, so I never presented him with even an inch of wiggle room. I think he was surprised to see such an attitude and diligence from someone of my age.

During a handful of face-to-face interviews, I served him nothing other than hard facts and cold stares, leaving him futile and unable to help his clients. One morning I was stopped by one of the custody staff, who handed me a piece of paper. On it was a scribbled message from the aforementioned sleazeball, asking me to visit him at his office. To my surprise, when I arrived to meet his request and demanded what on earth he wanted, he offered me a job, right there and then on the spot. He expressed his willingness to qualify me as a legal representative and offered me a comparable amount of money to what my police salary was at that time.

For probably the first time in my life I stopped to think, clearly, about what the consequences of my actions might have been, and it was a firm no.

At the time there was a huge amount of internal confusion about my professional direction. I had even been questioning whether I should leave the police entirely, but to join the opposition would have been the equivalent of signing my own death warrant and was not the solution to my problem.

For a while it had made me happy, but my relationship with Katie was not the solution to my problem either. Although I didn't know what was, as I wasn't aware at the time what exactly was causing me grief. What I did know was that I was increasingly depressed at home, and it was getting harder and harder to conceal my emotions. Despite her lack of interest in my thoughts or feelings, even Jane soon realised that something was amiss.

'Are you going to tell me what the hell is wrong with you?' she demanded one evening, as we sat in silence and watched the television.

'Nothing,' I insisted, *'I'm just tired.'* I was tired. Tired of her. Tired of her judgement and tired of her absolute disregard for anybody's agenda other than her own.

'No. It is more than that, you have been acting funny for weeks now.'

I am surprised she had noticed. With little enthusiasm or energy to continue the discussion, I capitulated.

'I'm not happy, Jane.'

'Okay.' She replied flatly, with no indication she was interested in hearing any more of my woes.

'With you,' I continued, *'I'm not happy here with you anymore.'*

Her expression turned to one of serious concern and borderline contempt. *'Have you met someone else?'*

I saw no point in trying to deny it. By that point I barely cared what she thought anyway.

'Yes. Someone from work.'

The conversation concluded and she gave no visible reaction

as you might expect a wife to give upon hearing of her husband's infidelity. She didn't appear angry or upset and there was no request for me to disclose any further information. The following morning, I packed my stuff into the boot of my car and left, and there was no request for me to stay. For a few days I stayed with my parents, to try and get a handle on my life, and work out what was the best thing to do moving forward. Neither of them offered an opinion on the predicament I had found myself in and were notably passive as I moped around, questioning my entire existence.

After a few days, Jane's brother called and invited me out for a pint. Clearly there was a fixed agenda, and one hot topic of discussion.

'*So, is it definitely over between you both then?*' he queried, after only one mouthful of his drink and barely any introductory pleasantries.

'*I don't know...*' I replied, not wanting to say too much. I had been the best man at his wedding a year previous, but I didn't really consider him my friend and given the circumstances, he had a clear allegiance.

Without realising, I had become trapped in a relationship that wasn't meeting my needs, with someone who I was largely incompatible with. But we had a child, and whilst I wanted it to be over, to not have to return to share a house and life with Jane, I felt a huge amount of pressure to just suck it up and get on with it. It was that sort of pressure, to conform, that saw me married at just twenty-five, when I should have remained a bachelor for several more years at the least. I wasn't remotely mature enough to consider what marriage really meant, and nor did I have any desire to be.

One of the lads at the station had been in a similar position, and by the time I reached the peak of my turmoil, he was living blissfully with his new girlfriend after having left his family home the year before. He suggested I should go and stay with him for a week, to really clear my head. I didn't take him up on the offer, and I regret that. Instead of giving myself the space I clearly needed, to work out what I really wanted and what I didn't, I picked up the phone to seek counsel from my sergeant in firearms, the same one who had facilitated my transfer.

He was fifteen years older than me, and had always acted like a surrogate father figure, so much that I trusted his judgement completely. Explaining everything that had happened, how my head was firmly up my arse and how I had potentially created a problematic situation by shagging one of my new colleagues, I told him I didn't know where to go or what to do.

'So do you want to be with this new woman?'

'No, it was a flash in the pan.' To leave my marriage and settle down with someone else was not what I wanted to do. I didn't want a relationship with Katie, as much as I didn't want one with Jane.

'Then get yourself back here,' he said to me. And with that, I felt a wave of relief, as a great deal of my problems were released.

He told me not to worry about anything. All I had to do was turn up back to my firearms team the following week. It was a Thursday that we spoke over the phone, and on the Friday, I was called to see the detective chief inspector to discuss my leaving. The same day I explained what was happening to Katie and whilst I felt a pang of sadness at the loss of a friend and romantic connection, there were no hard feelings. It had been exciting, but only briefly, and I think she felt that too.

My biggest concern about the whole situation was how fickle and unprofessional my conduct had made me look at work, but I couldn't ignore the fact that being away from Alice was distressing for me too. After leaving the station I called Jane and apologised. I told her that I was going back to my old role and that I wanted to be back at home. Without much discussion at all she agreed, and after I returned we never spoke of it again. The only discussion we had around anything vaguely related was a request from her that I make more of an effort to be involved in family life, so I set about playing my part, ensuring I didn't give off any warning signs that I wasn't necessarily happy to be back in the relationship. Fortunately, due to my work I was not at risk of falling into a regular routine that would see us sipping coffee and sharing the broadsheets on a Sunday morning. It was by no means a shiny new relationship; it just seemed convenient for us both at the time to carry on.

The switch to CID had given me a fresh perspective, and the chance to understand more about what I did and didn't want from my work. It was a complete juxtaposition to what I had experienced previously as a detective, and during firearms. There was a distinct lack in team spirit amongst the detectives, and no gung-ho attitude. They seemed to be nothing more than a dreary bunch of cops in suits who all thought they were Sherlock Holmes, only none of them had any real enthusiasm to get their hands dirty and get out on the streets to catch the bad guy.

I wish now that I had transferred back to the station where I did my training. It might have been stuck in the dark ages, but I would have gone into a team I knew and understood, with an already-established reputation. Things undoubtedly would have turned out much differently. The starkest difference would have been the sorts of offences that required investigating. Had I gone back to where I had trained, I would have worked on a vast variety of high-profile crime, from murder to serious fraud and everything in between. In contrast, there were only handful of decent cases that I handled on my home division. It was mostly assaults and street robberies. Not only that but it seemed as though there were hardly any innocent victims. Most of the people being robbed on the street were being robbed of the drugs they were trying to sell, and most of the assaults were amongst similarly matched, low-level criminals. It was at times, completely soul destroying.

There were no words that could express the gratitude I had to my sergeant for getting me back on the firearms squad. I felt so foolish that I had jumped ship, on nothing more than a whim, after working so hard to be there in the first place.

None of my colleagues knew of the affair, or what had gone on, but they were all surprisingly understanding of my wavering commitment and I was readily accepted back into the fold. My return was a blessed relief, and I was keen to hit the ground running, putting my personal mistakes behind me and prioritising my professional integrity. There was a marked shift in my attitude as I recognised just how lucky I was to have been afforded a fresh start, an amazing second chance to do something truly worthwhile and exciting. The job became even more important to me than ever before. If it hadn't consumed my entire life previously, it did following my return. I couldn't have been any more committed to anything or anyone than I was to being a firearms officer. Being completely prepared and ready to die in the line of duty made me more effective. I began to operate without any fear, or hesitation; both of which could possibly have gotten me killed.

33

Whilst I expressed an understanding into why some people may want to end their own life, I do not agree with suicide. Those who consider it a necessary measure may even think it is a dignified way to go, but for those left behind, it leaves a tremendous mess of destruction and heartache, and often an extremely awful scene. For many individuals grappling with mental health issues, suicide may seem like the only escape from an overwhelming sense of hopelessness and despair. Whatever the cause, be it financial hardship or a relationship breakdown, or simply feelings of inadequacy, the underlying pain must be incredibly severe to drive an individual to such drastic measures. Suicide is a complex and tragic phenomenon, which often carries with it an enduring stigma. It cannot be disputed that women are subject to most of society's downfalls, but out of the numerous suicides I attended throughout my career, only one was a female; the rest were all men. In fact, men are around four times more likely to die by suicide than women. It is a stark disparity largely fuelled by traditional gender roles that discourage men from talking about their problems and seeking help, on any matter.

Men have been socialised to embody strength, independence and stoicism, leading to a reluctance to express vulnerability. Failing to share their issues, many consequently endure suffering and isolation. For two decades I regularly confronted the devastation of suicide first-hand. I witnessed its far-reaching impacts, all those left to navigate the aftermath. It is vital to acknowledge the sombre reality of suicide, and strip away the misconceptions of glamour which sometime surrounds the notion. Instances of suicide are not remotely glamourous; rather, they reveal a narrative punctuated by profound suffering, and I feel in the case of men, tragic misinterpretations of what constitutes strength.

We all carry trauma in one form or another, and it's imperative that if the scales start to tip, and the days become too dark to bear, that we find a way to unwrap that which is causing us trouble. And maybe that is with the help of some professional assistance, which I can personally vouch for. For some, even being able to raise their head above the parapet and see clearly would remedy the despair and confusion about life. Perhaps given the opportunity, people would see that even when circumstances are tough, the world is not as terrible as they might think. Anybody who is struggling must try to give themselves grace, afford themselves the space to understand their issues, then allow necessary time to heal. There is no shame in having problems, we all do, but it is up to us to take steps to remedy them for the sake of our future happiness. Each present moment is a doorway to the next. No matter how bad things seem on any day, week, or month, they are just drops of time in the ocean of life. Persevere. It *will* get better.

34

Along with the fact I was again playing football once or twice a month, the physicality of being back in firearms training several times a week was incredibly beneficial for me. Our mantra in firearms was to train hard, then everything else was easy, and I loved being pushed to my limits. It was important that we were able to practise our tactics as often as possible. Not just on our police base, but in real life buildings that were unfamiliar to us. Each month we would visit a different building to train in. Ideally something with lots of rooms, so the venues varied from abandoned warehouses to disused hospitals. Not knowing where an endless corridor in a rabbit warren of a building would come out made it more challenging for us, as we could unknowingly appear in the face of danger at any moment.

We trained in our full kit including body armour, and used our usual weapons, which in those scenarios were loaded with paint rounds. We were typically given a script and then a few minutes to pull together a plan before getting started. Each exercise lasted no more than thirty minutes, ending either with the baddies being caught or the instructors calling time. What followed was a hot debrief in which any errors made were addressed, before we were issued a new situation and sent back in to practise a different tactic. Every minute of it was brilliant and for every minute of it I was trying my absolute hardest not to fuck it up. Scouring the venue slowly and methodically, I wanted to get it completely right, all the time. We chucked glow sticks ahead of us to light any dark areas that we had to pass through, and several of us used door wedges bought from a local hardware store to put in the doors, so we knew where we had previously been. It wasn't all paintballing war games in dirty derelict buildings however, and whilst it may seem excessively risky, it was also vital that sometimes we trained with live rounds and used dummies as targets to shoot at. Everybody on each exercise had a role to play, and for some that meant having a shotgun fired directly next to them. We needed to understand the reality of the situations we might find ourselves in; how it would sound and how it would feel. The stakes were high, which meant nobody could afford to treat it like a stag do activity, because it was far from it. It was incredibly high-risk and downright dangerous, but the idea was that training with real-life equipment made us so familiar with it that its use became an instinctive reaction, which is what was required on a real job.

Our shotguns could be loaded a couple of different ways. Either with regular cartridges called skeets, or alternatively Round Irritant Personnel (RIP) cartridges. The RIP rounds contained crystallised CS gas and were mostly used if we apprehended a vehicle. From standing at the rear quarter of the car I would fire one or two rounds inside the car, aiming for the parcel shelf. Doing this caused the car to fill with CS gas, making the suspects far more subdued and therefore compliant during their arrest. We trained with CS gas pellets, in a small building on a remote shooting range less than an hour away from our base. We had to learn how to work through the gas, so we knew what to expect when we were exposed to it. We were instructed to run around the perimeter of the building for at least ten minutes, to make sure we were nice and sweaty, then sent into one of the rooms of the building to put gas masks on.

The trainers lit solid pebbles of the CS gas which were much higher in concentration than the cannisters, and the smoke would be allowed to accumulate for a minute or two before they would point at us in turn to remove our mask and tell them our full name and warrant number. It was almost impossible on the first try as the pain of the CS gas entering open pores was excruciating. The most unpleasant reaction to CS gas is the excessive moisture it creates which streams from the eyes and nose, often creating a string of snot so long that it reached the floor from standing. When we were released back out into the fresh air our eyes would be stinging so much that it took a few minutes for full vision to return. As tempting as it was, the key was to not touch your face or eyes at all, rather just stand and let the wind carry the particles away, splashing our faces with cold water if possible.

Being up on that range, situated in miles of moorland, was one of my favourite things to do, in all elements. Some days it was so cold that only after we finished shooting and the feeling started to return to my hands, did all the tiny cuts I had gotten from handling my weapon start to bleed. It sounds a bit of a cliché, but it made me feel alive. We earnt our stripes during those exercises, so much that if we were training in the warmer weather, our sergeant would get a BBQ going for us whilst we practised our drills. We would then spend the rest of the afternoon whacking golf balls into the nearby reservoir, taking the much-needed opportunity to relax, and bond as a team. It offered a small piece of respite from continually putting our life on the line. It was those little instances of feeling at home with a family of comrades, who would all stand in the line of fire for one another, that were the best part of the job for me. And it was not unusual for us after a full day's training to run the ten miles back to the station. The job was not just about strength but also about resilience and perseverance. Not to mention it was a point of pride, with none of us ever wanting to be outrun by another.

In addition to the physicality of it all, I enjoyed the mental agility just as much; always being completely aware and on guard kept me sharp and focussed. We trained to increase our chances of making the correct choice during difficult decisions, as should anybody incur an injury whilst on a job, either colleague or civilian, we would have had to justify our actions to a judge, jury, or a group of investigators after the fact. One of our shooting ranges at the station had large drop-down fabric screens, which had real-life scenarios projected onto them in moving picture. It was a completely interactive, one-hundred-and-eighty-degree wraparound simulator, where we would in effect play video games; responding appropriately using live rounds and scored by the computer which registered our accuracy. The scenarios were designed to make us feel like we had to act, and to test our perception. To give you an example:

Scenario 1: Forty metres away, and behind a large metal fence, a man comes out of building dragging a woman. He fires two rounds from a double-barrelled shotgun in the air, before aiming it towards her. As an armed officer you could shoot him. Do you?

Scenario 2: The exact same scenario but the man has a knife instead of a shotgun. Shoot him?

Answer 1: No. Do not shoot. Risk of imprisonment for improper conduct and unlawful killing. The suspect had a double-barrelled shotgun and, in the scenario, discharged both rounds, so would have been unable to shoot the victim or anybody else immediately without reloading. We would have been hung, drawn and quartered by prosecution upon ever facing that scenario in the real world. Even if it could be argued that he could have beaten her to death with the shotgun.

Answer 2: Yes. Shoot him, no problem. Much easier to justify as he could cause immediate fatality.

We would sometimes be asked to complete the training after going on a run, so our hearts were already pumping. Within the team we would rotate, and occasionally the instructors would throw a flash grenade into the area when a new scenario began. It was essential to put us under excessive pressure, which I loved and hated in equal measure. The challenge and adrenaline was addictive.

We were taught to do something once and do it with meaning.

Essentially, commit to the action. If you had taken the decision to use your baton on someone, don't tickle them with it, hit them hard enough with one blow so they stop doing what they are doing. If you saw it necessary whilst in pursuit of a suspect to knock them down with the car door, don't roll up at five miles per hour, gently nudge them and then have to get out and engage in a physical altercation. Hit them at fifteen and see to it the desired outcome is achieved.

Most of the time, the actions we took didn't cause a great deal of pain, more shock, and then by the time the suspect had wondered what had just happened they were already cuffed and being placed into the back of a police van. To do things properly first time ultimately saves a lot of trouble. And, if ever summoned to court to discuss someone's arrest, I would rather justify hitting someone with a baton once and causing their leg to break, than have to explain why I hit them eight, nine or even ten times. The appropriate use of force is a contentious issue, and I think police officers today are fearful of the potential ramifications of issuing a blow properly, especially given the use of smartphone cameras and social media.

We were able to use whatever force we deemed appropriate, as long as it wasn't disproportionate to the threat. Reflecting on my own time in police training, inadvertently I think being used as the guinea pig paid off as it taught me how to do things correctly. Watching how to do something is one thing but experiencing it is another. Over the course of my career, I saw so many get simple things wrong but during my training I could feel the technique, I knew exactly what to do, and it stuck with me till the end.

Night shifts were still my favourite as the bouts of peace and quiet offered the perfect opportunity for my brain to dial down and my head to tune out. Typically, they would start at nine in the evening and finish at seven the following morning. I would be back home by eight, asleep by nine, and invariably awake again by one or two in the afternoon. Beyond that point, I would just want to relax and conserve my energy so that I could function effectively when back at work. It is difficult for anybody who has never worked shifts to understand the disruption they have on the system, and Jane seemed to consider the time between my being at work as days off. Night shifts were also a great chance for us to wind down and bond together as a team, usually over a takeaway and a knock-off movie someone had brought in to play on the DVD player. Whilst there wasn't anything ongoing that demanded our attention, we could also get our heads down for a bit and get some rest. We worked on a rota. Who could go to the gym at what time, and who could go and get some kip for a couple of hours.

We had two locker rooms. The larger one was attached to the main building and as it was the only one that had showers it was relatively busy, not to mention it backed onto the car park so there was always the sound of cars coming and going. The other was a portacabin near the compound's helipad. It was much quieter and my choice location for getting a couple of hours rest whenever I could.

Using my bergen rucksack as a pillow I would lay flat on my back like a corpse on the benches; fully dressed and ready to go in my boots and body armour, my handgun still in its holster. My radio was always turned down to the minimum but amongst the constant chatter, I had become attuned to listening for our team's call sign, or for my own collar number. As soon as I heard either I was straight to my feet, wide awake again and ready to get to work.

Since my second chance on the team, I wanted to be the best I could be and operate at the highest level possible. What that meant was I sort out risk, by patrolling the roughest areas and never shying away from any difficult jobs.

Quite the opposite, in fact; I took as many calls as possible and turned out to try and prevent as much dangerous crime as I could. Playing on the periphery was not what I wanted. I wanted to be driving from the front, never in the middle or lagging behind, and was completely prepared and ready to die in the line of my duty. My underlying preference was that I would rather have gone out in a blaze of glory, when the only other option seemed to be that I was to end up shuffling around a bungalow in my slippers, with only Jane for company. Where others flinched, I didn't, and I was so incredibly confident in my abilities as an officer that subconsciously I think I had started to consider myself bullet-proof. Stupid I know, because nobody is immune to danger.

One evening we had loaded up one of the squad's ballistic-plated Range Rovers, and I was behind the wheel as we headed across town in the middle of the night to attend a call about some nasty bastard doing something unlawful.

Packed to the rafters with our kit I would estimate the car weighed around three tonnes, and due to the size of Range Rovers, they aren't particularly good at any great speed but rather wallow about the road, meaning it was necessary to allow plenty of time for turning or any alteration to direction. Fortunately, it was the dead of night, so the roads were incredibly quiet, which allowed me to travel at speeds of around eighty miles per hour. I was intent on reaching our destination and getting stuck in to tackling the problem.

Our lights and sirens were on and there was another one of our armed response vehicles only ten feet behind me. The road was wide enough for four lanes of traffic across both sides, and a few hundred yards ahead of me I noticed there was a double-decker bus. It was parked up in a bus stop, so I didn't have to alter my course at all to accommodate it but as we got closer, I saw that someone had appeared off the bus and started to walk across the road. To allow the pedestrian some room I started to veer towards the right-hand side of the road and changed the tone of the siren, to make sure the lone wanderer knew we were hurtling down the road at great speed and that he was stepping out into our path.

It was inconceivable that he wouldn't have been able to see or hear us, yet he failed to alter his course and continued crossing the road, squeezing me further and further onto the opposite side. I couldn't believe what he was doing. At fifty yards away I was doing ninety miles per hour.

I hadn't let off the accelerator at all and I really should have.

My only option was to mount the pavement.

The team behind had slowed down and backed off but it was too late for me, I had committed to my action. With the car mostly on the right-hand pavement, the passenger-side tyres in the gutter, I passed him at ninety miles per hour, and the wing mirror just brushed his jacket. Another half a second, or half a foot from either of us and he would have been killed, and I would have gone to prison.

We arrived at the job, and I practically fell out of the car in relief, as did my passenger. I couldn't believe just how lucky I had been. We composed ourselves quickly ready for action only to find that we were being stood down. The job had been a hoax call, and I had risked it all for nothing.

On 7th July 2005, four co-ordinated suicide bombs were activated in London. The attacks occurred on the city's public transport system during rush hour causing the tragic deaths of fifty-two commuters, and injuries to over seven hundred more civilians. Following the devastating attack on a British mainland target, tensions in the policing and security communities were high, and the collective mindset had changed to one of amplified hyper-vigilance. It was suspected there would be further terrorist activity so to prepare for what was seen as inevitable, a few officers on our team, including myself, began training to qualify as Counter Terrorist Specialist Firearms Officers (CTSFO). The greater need for more specialist officers aligned perfectly with my desire to head in the direction of more intensive work and felt like an ideal opportunity for me to do something of more value.

There are two main methods typically used during a terrorist attack: a person borne improvised explosive device (IED), or a vehicle borne IED. We trained to counter both.

A vehicle borne IED was considered a far less dangerous prospect when it came to taking out the assailant, as it was unlikely that they would trigger the device before reaching the intended destination and therefore we had more time to intercept.

To be able to tackle a person borne IED, we had to be much closer to the assailant to act. Such individuals would be less concerned with their exact location before detonating the device, therefore we were at greater risk ourselves of being immediately blown to pieces.

The ideology behind the training we received was completely different to what I had experienced before. In an ordinary firearms operation, we would typically fire one shot, then assess whether that shot had been effective in disabling the target, before firing another. During our CTSFO training nobody explicitly said it was 'shoot to kill', but when the instruction was that we were to discharge our weapon continuously at the suspect's head from mere feet away, death was inevitable.

The pons medulla is what we were told to aim for, which is the part of the brain that connects to the spinal cord. Its main responsibilities are to regulate breathing and circulation of blood from the heart. If we were able to hit it directly it would shut down the assailant's body immediately. Suicide bombers sometimes choose to use a 'dead man's switch' on their IED; a device designed to be activated in the case of the human operator becoming incapacitated. It meant no positive action would necessarily be required to set the explosive off and it could simply be triggered by their hand opening, say if they were shot. By shooting the pons medulla the aim was to stop every single part of the brain's functioning, meaning they would continue to remain exactly as they were, doing whatever they were doing at the time of death, including clutching a detonator.

To approach a person borne IED we trained to approach on foot and on motorbikes, with a trained police rider on the front, and an armed officer standing on the pegs at the back. We practised standing up on a moving bike and shooting at a target, usually approaching from behind. On the back of a bike, we would never have been able to get close enough to accurately hit the pons medulla, so our instruction was instead to shoot to stop and subdue.

For a suspect entering a town or city in what was expected to be a vehicle borne IED, there were several tactics we could employ, but ultimately someone would be tasked with the job of riding alongside a moving target and shooting through the window. We had the ability to control the traffic light system, to create gridlock and prevent the suspected bomb from entering more built-up areas. My favourite scenario we practised, which would have allowed us to take out the terrorist or terrorists efficiently, was using road works to introduce a contraflow and control the traffic.

The target would be surveyed by a force plane, which was far less obvious than a helicopter, could fly higher and had better camera equipment. We would then receive intelligence as to their whereabouts, and the roadworks would be used to create a situation whereby the target vehicle was stopped at the front of the queue of traffic. One hundred metres straight ahead was an armed officer, lying in the top of a Highway Maintenance van supported by a false roof, ready to shoot the driver in the head. Every single officer manning the roadworks was armed, dressed in workmen's high visibility uniform, and had a specific role in the operation.

During the practise manoeuvre I held the Stop/Go board, to control the traffic. As soon as I heard the rifle shot being fired by my colleague in the van, I had the more active role of coup de grâce, to administer the final and fatal shot. Regardless of where the rifle had hit, I had to drop the board, run up to the driver's side, and empty my handgun into the back of the driver's head as close to the pons medulla as possible; even if they were dead already.

In a real-life eventuality, it was the most dangerous role in the procedure. Should an explosive go off at any point during my movements I would have ended up as toast, but I didn't mind. In fact, I hardly cared. The adrenaline of being so close to death propelled me, further driving my desire to excel in my role.

During a briefing early on, it was explained that should any of our efforts to disarm and disable a person or vehicle borne IED be unsuccessful, there was only a four per cent chance of survival. We were encouraged to make a living will, although were not supported at all with this process.

One day during training we were handed an envelope each, and a blank piece of paper to go away and write on. Before we left for the day, we handed them back to the instructor for them to be filed, only to reappear should the worst happen.

Most of us were in our twenties and thirties, and whilst every day on the job had the increased potential for harm or death, I had never seriously considered a scenario where I met my untimely demise. This is largely in part to the fact that there was no room for any self-doubt when wielding a submachine gun. Any second guessing would have surely impacted my ability to do the job to the best of my ability. The decisions we took had to be made in complete confidence.

No doubt it would have been quite difficult for some to consider they may not return home to their families, but the police service offered no guidance whatsoever, and retrospect allows me to see they were nothing short of neglectful during what was quite a sensitive time, but this could have been purely due to inexperience.

Life at home had showed no signs of turbulence whatsoever since my affair, and Jane and I returned to a semblance of normality. It had been convenient for us both to just sweep it under the carpet and carry on with our life as though nothing had ever happened. My work increasingly kept me out of the house at all hours of the day, so I had the perfect excuse to keep her firmly at arm's length. She had no idea what I was doing during that time when I was leaving for work, even when sometimes I was gone for days at a time. Regardless, she was my wife and therefore my legal next of kin, so it felt as though the right thing to do was to address mine to her. I knew that if the time came, I wouldn't fail, so not feeling the need to say anything more, my letter simply read, *Sorry. I missed.* She likely would not have appreciated my humour had she ever needed to read that letter, but fortunately she did not.

When I returned to active duty beyond the completion of my training, public reassurance was the focus of my daily role for a while. It felt as though another attack was imminent and, understandably, the public were shaken by the events that had occurred in the country's capital. It was a pretty shitty gig, but we all had to take our turn acting as nothing more than a police presence at major landmarks and train stations. There was a sense of general anxiety, so we were instructed not to get out of the car and wander around, as the sight of armed police had the potential to cause more panic than reassurance.

By my second shift, the novelty and sense of nobility had mostly worn off, and to make it worse I was paired with Graham. The same Graham who couldn't navigate his way around his own local area on the way to stop a shotgun brandishing thug.

As if his complete incompetence wasn't enough, he was the sort of bloke who adopted catchphrases off the television and repeated them a dozen times a day. Winding the car windows down was not possible due to the ballistic plating of the glass, so whilst on our shift, outside of comfort breaks it was just the two of us, trapped in our own little bubble.

There was a greasy spoon café on the corner across from where we were positioned, and they had expressed they would gladly feed us free of charge.

Now, it is not beyond the realms of anybody's imagination to consider what they might have done to our food if they didn't like the police, so I was dubious and opted instead to get packaged sandwiches from the nearby shop. Graham on the other hand was more than happy to accept everything they gave him, and he was just so grating, that I was hopeful that they had indeed spat in his lunch.

My experience from the first shift was that it had the potential to be soul-crushingly boring, particularly as police cars don't have a car radio to listen to, so I decided to pick up a cheap portable from the local Argos on my way into work ahead of the second shift. Once we were parked up in position I ducked out of the car and went and bought some batteries from the WHSmith within the station. Soon enough, my partner had taken it upon himself to assume the role of DJ, changing the channel constantly and giving his opinion on every topic of conversation the radio presenters discussed. After three hours of him mucking about with it, like a child with a new toy, the batteries ran out and all I was left with to listen to was his incessant chatter. *'Morning Guvnor!'* he shouted for the fifteenth time that day, at a passerby who could not hear him through the glass of the windscreen. Tosser.

I have never had a natural propensity for violence, but it took every ounce of my will power to get through my twelve-hour shift without taking a pen out of my pocket and poking him straight in the eye. In amongst everything he had to say there was not a single glimmer of adult conversation. It was intolerable and I had no capacity for it whatsoever. Our twelve hours together passed, painfully slowly, but eventually we returned to base to hand over our kit.

'*Same time tomorrow then?*' he gleamed at me from the passenger seat.

Completely saturated and fatigued with his idiocy, I did not want to consider at that point that I was to be working with him again the following day.

'*Graham. If you say one word to me during the entire shift tomorrow, I will punch you so hard that you have to pick your teeth up from the floor. Okay?*' As much as I couldn't stand him, I wasn't being serious, but my tone suggested I was. There was a lot of process involved for us to unload live weapons and pack away our kit which meant it could take quite a bit of time, during which he didn't say another word to me. The following day he tried once or twice to strike up a bit of conversation, but I quickly nipped it in the bud. I had not had the opportunity to fully wring myself out from the day before and couldn't have taken another word from him. He was the perfect example of an officer only in it for the kit and the kudos, but none of the real responsibility, evidenced by his intentional delay to a shooting. Unfortunately for him, in such a high-performing team as ours, there was no room to hide. Anyone who identified themselves as unreliable was untrustworthy, and anyone deemed untrustworthy had little space to exist in our world. He didn't last too long, and went on I think, to be a postman – another uniformed job.

Thankfully the public reassurance exercise finally dwindled, and I was glad to return to business as usual, whatever that really meant.

35

The irony is not lost on me that I previously expressed how I could relate to why someone may want to end their life, and that I just have stated how ready I was to die on the job. I didn't want to die, but I didn't care if I did, which was both stupid, and risky. The intoxication that living on the edge brought me fuelled my life. And I needed that fuel because everything in my life outside work was so empty.

Throughout the story so far, you will have read a brief narrative about a relationship which was wholly disconnected and unsupportive. In fact, the relationship lacked complete purpose. I had been an observer to it all rather than a participant; it had just happened around me, over such a long period of time.

Even the first home we shared was at times like a prison in my mind, but increasingly the entire situation had felt like an overbearing constraint on me.

Unknowingly, I had given up and resigned myself to a life of unhappiness when I returned to my marriage after the affair with Katie. And I was unhappy still, for all the reasons that had driven me to the affair in the first place, with many more layered on top.

Everything for Jane was about materialistic upgrade, and from the beginning I think she saw me as just another accessory to her life. One which promised a police pension.

It was as though when I was at home I lived under a weighted blanket, made up of her expectations and judgements of me. She often criticised me for being miserable, so I further acted it. But when

I was at work, I could be myself, and I was happy as the uninhibited version of myself.

The atmosphere that had been created at home pushed me to be so focussed and dedicated to what I was doing, it meant I never feared losing anything.

It was as though I didn't recognise that the life I had on some plummy cul-de-sac was worth living for. In part due to my constant absence, even my daughter was almost an abstract concept. I loved her dearly of course, but at the time she was just other possession Jane and I had acquired, along with everything else that made up our life.

Whilst not at work, I would find excuses to be on my own, to retreat from life with her. With my headphones in I often took myself to the kitchen, to become fully absorbed cooking a complex recipe. It allowed me to immerse myself in something else other than that life, which I suppose I didn't really associate with being my own.

It wasn't created by me, so it didn't meet my needs or align with my values.

In reflecting on my past, I recognise that I mentally isolated myself in my relationship, and that is because the relationship wasn't supportive. Rather than serving as a sanctuary, my home often felt more hostile and combative than the very streets I was policing. This disconnect created a barrier that pushed me further into emotional isolation. The absence of a supportive relationship left me feeling like I had to retreat into my own mind, navigating the complexities of my work without the emotional support I truly needed at home.

Ultimately, it did serve me to be disconnected, as my job placed me in highly dangerous situations where full focus and presence were essential for success.

With the weight of that responsibility on my shoulders, my home became little more than a place to sleep and eat, before diving back into the chaos of the streets I patrolled. I disengaged and distanced myself emotionally as a protective measure, which, in some ways, made my job easier to manage. I deeply regret not being fully available on an emotional level as a father. Although I was physically present, my mind was often elsewhere, lost in the demands of my job or working through various situations in my head. This emotional absence has left me to wonder what the impact has been.

But, if I had been more attuned to my family life, it might have clouded my judgement and created indecision on the job. The intense focus required in my role meant I had to compartmentalise my feelings and responsibilities. Still, I wish I had found a better balance; a way to remain connected in my role as a father, whilst also performing to the best of my ability at work.

In addition to household appliances and other shit we didn't need, Jane and I continued to accumulate resentment between us, but with no desire from any party to learn how to discuss our issues and manage or resolve the conflict between us.

36

Quite often, major UK airports have a dedicated firearms team. Whilst I am sure they get plenty of requests to have their photograph taken with rowdy groups of women flying abroad on hen dos, there are rarely any major incidents for them to deal with, so they don't tend to get a great deal of exposure to any real firearms jobs. They spend most of their time on the lookout for anything suspicious and are on hand ready to receive a passenger that has been reported as problematic on an incoming flight. As such, being a firearms officer at the airport is the sort of job that many took as a wind-down before retirement. It was a fitting role for the older officer, so when our unit received a secondee from the airport team, Toby, I was surprised that he was younger than I was. It had been the only role available at the time of his application and having swiftly concluded that the job at the airport was nothing short of dull, he had asked for the opportunity to be involved in some more active work. He was as fresh-faced as I had once been. Incredibly well-presented and softly spoken, he seemed more fitting for a role as a latter-day saint than a firearms officer. Up to that point he had not experienced any real crime or conflict, so when I was asked to be his mentor, I was only too happy to oblige. Not wanting to leave him uninspired in the way I had been after my time with Mike, I agreed with my superiors that he and I would go on the night shift, which would undoubtedly offer him some variety and action.

One of the best places to find any trouble was back on the division where I had trained as a detective, which was still well within my county bounds, so when we began our first shift together, we headed in that direction and set our car radio to their channel. A few low priority jobs came and went, and as two in the morning approached, a report of a burglary came through. Someone had unlawfully entered a property, taken a set of car keys and then the car off the drive.

It was a local joyrider. Right up my street and certain potential for a high-speed chase which would be sure to get my ride-along's blood pumping.

Our response car was much better than any of the regular patrol cars that would be tipping out onto the roads to try and find the suspect, but not wanting to necessarily be the first on the scene to investigate, I took my time moseying over in the general direction of the original crime scene. The ideal scenario was that we would turn up, catch the bad guy, and then ride off into the distance, leaving in our wake all the other formalities.

A few streets away from the address where the theft had been reported, I pulled our car over to the side of the road, turned off all the lights and opened my door slightly to listen. And we sat, waiting, which may seem counter-intuitive, but there is not usually a great deal of movement in the early hours of the morning and after a brief pause to observe our surroundings, it was not too long before I heard a car in the distance. It was easy to discern by sound alone that the vehicle was driving well above the thirty-mile-per-hour speed limit, and sure enough, when the car came closer, it matched the description of the stolen vehicle. It sped past the end of the street where we were positioned, and I could see it was full of young people; more in the car than there were seats for.

As I started up the engine and pulled away, we got a message over the radio giving information of the suspect vehicle's anticipated direction of travel. We rejoined the main road and then the dual carriageway which headed towards the city, the stolen car not yet in our view. They had been driving so erratically that it was hardly a surprise when we rounded a bend and saw that they had veered off course and ploughed straight into the concrete barrier of the central reservation. It was upturned in the road with parts of it strewn across both lanes. Before approaching the vehicle, I briefed Toby quickly as to what we might find, as I retrieved our trauma kit and oxygen from the boot.

We proceeded towards the wreck and to my surprise it was completely empty. It was an improbable likelihood that they had all managed to somehow come away from such a collision unscathed, especially as I doubted that any of them had been wearing their seatbelts, but with not one of the passengers in sight it seemed as though somehow, they had managed to scarper.

Two other patrol cars had rounded the corner a minute after us and after a quick assessment and discussion between us all we began to preserve the scene and cordon off the road. Behind the wreck, a few cars had started to back up, mostly taxis on their way back towards town. Toby assumed the role of traffic management and headed towards the small line of cars and knocked on the window of the first one in the queue.

'Good evening,' he began, *'we will try to get you moving again as soon as possible. As you can see there has been a bit of an accident, but fortunately it doesn't appear that anybody has been hurt.'*

'What, apart from him?' the driver responded, as he gestured down to the aggressively severed head of a teenage boy lying on the tarmac, just several feet from where Toby was standing. He rushed to the side of the carriageway, and I heard the unmistakable sound of vomit hitting the ground from over my shoulder, at which point the rest of us realised that there was, in fact, at least one casualty.

So desensitised was I by that point, the scene was barely difficult for me, but for Toby it was a shock. Such an event puts incredible amounts of stress on the body; physical, mental and emotional. It is a test of someone's potential, and of their limits.

The job was innately difficult. Many days were spent dealing with tragedy and the rest were spent dealing with the underbelly of society, which the general public seldom see but is far bigger than they might think.

There was one area on the outskirts of the city which was infamous for being rife with drugs, gangs, and violence. Gang warfare is really nothing more than a game, and we were in effect just another gang, but one with a view to relieve society of unnecessary and fatal crime rather than committing it. We were the elite with the ability to use additional force. Bigger numbers with more guns.

On the odd occasion, if there was nothing better to do during the early hours of the morning, we would drive around the hot spot areas; blue lights on and music blaring over the vehicle tannoid. It almost felt like a part of our duty, to ruffle a few feathers and make our presence known.

Shootings were almost a daily occurrence at the time, and due to the high levels of dangerous offences in that location, and the fact we were the only team that could deal with a lot of the issues that occurred there, we were incredibly busy.

It was around seven in the evening when a colleague, Connor, and I were dispatched to a takeaway food restaurant, after shots had been reportedly fired.

We were there within minutes and with both our MP5s and handguns ready, we entered, each behind a short, handheld shield. A young man lay bleeding profusely on the floor and another jumped to his feet upon our entry. The woman working the counter was visibly, and understandably, panicked.

Connor was the ideal colleague to have on the job alongside me during a crisis. He was ex-army, wise, and practical as hell. He got his hands on the unwounded of the two young men, conducted a search of his person and established him as a friend of the victim, whilst I attended the wounded lad on the floor. He was around five feet and eight inches tall, thick set and didn't look to be older than fifteen years of age. There were three obvious entrance wounds to his upper body and an additional one close to his left hip. I unpacked my trauma kit and began administering first aid.

Turning my attention to the most visibly concerning of the wounds to his torso, I applied an Asherman chest seal, which is a large sterile sticker with an internal gauze to dry the wound. Asherman chest seals are good for penetrative traumas such as a gunshot wounds, and have a one-way air valve, to let air out but not in, which reduces risk caused by any air trapped. As he had been shot in the chest, I was concerned his lung could be at risk of collapse caused by the pressure of air going into the cavity the bullets had each created.

My attention then turned to the other bullet holes in this body, all of which were bleeding heavily. The victim had been shot front-on from several feet away, and it appeared that of the four bullets fired into his body, only two had then exited.

By the nature of their injury, entrance wounds and exit wounds caused by a bullet are a totally different prospect. Everything the bullet collects as it rips through the body at speed, increases its surface area, therefore whilst a bullet hole upon entry is typically small, the exit wound has the potential to be larger. It is because of this, and the fact that entrance wounds are sometimes slightly cauterised by the heat from the bullet, that exit wounds usually bleed the most heavily.

I didn't mind being knelt in the pools of his blood and tissue or plugging the holes with my fingers; I had the opportunity to save the life of a young man and I worked ferociously to do so.

Not too long had passed before the on-duty sergeant arrived, and another couple of firearms officers. The ambulance was next on the scene and the victim was taken to hospital. It was a relief to see him packed off with the paramedics, and there was no doubt in my mind that I had done the absolute best that I could in that moment.

There was a quick round up between us all on the scene before we headed back to the station and, ditching my blood-sodden kit, I had a quick shower and changed. Shootings were so common that, other than the fact I had to deal with a severe casualty, the situation was barely remarkable. After making a brief written statement we continued with the remainder of the shift.

The victim was taken straight into surgery upon his arrival at the hospital, where his condition was stabilised. Once he had regained consciousness following the procedure, he was advised to remain on bedrest in the hospital for a minimum of two weeks. Had he observed the medical advice given to him he would have survived. But, unbeknownst to the doctors at the time, the bullet that had gone into his hip had just nicked his femoral artery. It was not so significant that it had caused the artery to burst but had weakened its outer wall. It would have repaired itself, given the chance, but during the victim's insistence to get up and try and leave the hospital just a day after the attack, the weakened artery burst and in no more than two minutes he was dead.

The shooting was obviously gang related, but during the time we were on the scene, I had no idea who the victim was. He was not carrying any form of identification, and his acquaintance wouldn't disclose a single thing. The only details I had of him were what I could surmise from my observations.

Tragically when it comes to gang violence, there are plenty of innocent casualties; kids caught in crossfire or cases of mistaken identity. But in this case, it transpired that the victim in this shooting was, in fact, an active and known gang member. Despite the press reports that typically follow such shootings, stating how the victim was an upstanding member of the community and surely had a promising life ahead, most of them were just nasty, violent thugs. It turned out that the individual in question on this occasion was a suspect under investigation for another shooting, and that I had met him before, just several weeks earlier when we had executed a firearms warrant at a flat and arrested him.

At the time, the two incidents were not remotely connected for me, but soon after his death, they started to rotate around each other behind the scenes.

To say that he had not been compliant in the arrest would be an understatement. And to further that, after he had been released from our custody his mother had made a formal complaint stating that during his apprehension, the arresting officer had pushed him to the floor and stamped on his head.

I was the arresting officer, and the allegation was that the arrest most certainly constituted the use of excessive force.

It was commonplace for us to use high levels of physicality to subdue someone.

The law authorised us to and the job mandated it. The objective was to overwhelm and overpower dangerous perpetrators, so they had no choice but to give in. The consequences of us not using a greater degree of force could be severe, and we couldn't afford to rely on the fact that we had guns, nor did we ever want to.

He was an aggressive and violent young man, which was further evidenced by his behaviour towards us. At the time of his arrest, he had been reaching inside his coat for what we suspected was a firearm and we had to apply a reasonable amount of force to detain him. My sergeant had tasered him during the arrest and when quizzed by the superintendent as to why he had chosen that action, he responded dryly, *'because I couldn't get to my gun quick enough.'* The lad was a nasty piece of work, and we wanted him banged up. There had certainly been some action during the arrest, but his mother's account was completely falsified. We were proficiently trained to be able to not act in such a manner as the suspect described, and I certainly did not consider myself above the law. He didn't have any injuries to support his story and had been arrested in a very small galley kitchen of the flat, in which there was barely any room to swing a cat once myself and my sergeant were in there with the suspect and our shields.

There would have been no room to carry out an assault as had been described. But there was due process to follow, and after the allegation, I was issued legal documents by the complaints and discipline department. It was expected to be a lengthy process, and I was told to await further details of what would happen next. Until then I was nothing more than a sitting duck, waiting to be called to force headquarters to give a statement addressing the alleged misconduct.

But my conscience was completely clear, so I just carried on with my job.

The complaints and discipline department soon became aware that the complainant had been involved in a shooting and unfortunately died, and that I was the first on the scene to treat him. Then there were questions around my actions following his shooting, as an officer under investigation based on an allegation made by the deceased.

To say I felt uneasy would be an understatement. The original complaint was of little concern to me. It was wholly fabricated and very easy to disprove, but the suggestion soon became that I may have acted in such a way that caused his death, and his mother wanted blood. The CCTV footage from the takeaway restaurant was reviewed, which would quickly establish whether my conduct had been appropriate or if I had done anything untoward. I was allowed to view it and sure enough it showed me in the thick of a crisis, soaked in the victim's blood trying desperately to patch him up and keep him alive, whilst Connor passed me supplies from the trauma kit.

It also showed my sergeant coming onto the scene, who clearly recognised in an instant who the victim was. With an understanding of the ongoing complaint against me the footage showed him begin to pace up and down in panic.

An interview was scheduled to discuss both allegations, the nature of which were so serious that it was advised I had legal representation as I would be under caution when interviewed. I declined. I had unwavering faith in the actions I had taken.

I knew I had done everything correctly, during the original arrest and the subsequent shooting, and even if I had known at the time of him bleeding out who he was, I wouldn't have acted in any way differently.

But as the interview date drew closer, anxiety naturally crept in, and I began to doubt myself. I wondered whether I had done the right things in the right order, whether I had put the Asherman seal on properly and administered oxygen the correct way. Visibly nervous is how I would describe myself when I went into the interview, and it felt as though they were asking unnecessarily pointed questions, which caused me to stumble over my words. It did not go exactly how I had hoped, and I was not as direct as I had wanted to be.

My job was one that many were unable or unwilling to do: stepping through a door, expecting to be met on the other side by bad man with a gun, and being quite prepared to pay the ultimate sacrifice. People don't like to consider death, but it was a potential reality every day that I might die. And my perspective further changed by having the ability to remove someone's life sat at my hip.

We were in an armed battle fighting crime, and it demanded us to be fearless and completely committed to our role and to the decisions we made.

I wasn't conscious of it at the time, but there must have been a large moral driver for me to do the job. I wouldn't ever want anybody to have to walk past a hooded-up gang member with a gun in his pocket, so I wanted them off the streets. There is no place for such people amongst society. During my time as an armed officer there were swarms of them everywhere. They were inherently cruel and worked off intimidation and fear. I saw it as my job to reverse the table, tip the scales, to put them in fear and make them uncomfortable.

The incident in the takeaway taught me a great deal about myself.

Shootings were commonplace but I don't know many other officers who came across someone who had been shot so many times. With multiple entrance and exit wounds there was a great deal for me to contend with. It was a real crisis, and I did a bloody good job. Under fifteen minutes of incredibly intense pressure, I remained calm and professional, and my judgement was bang on.

There was a life in the balance, and I didn't feel the strain. It was an unfortunate case of a young lad who had gotten wrapped up in gang culture, and it cost him his life. But equally, he would have happily pulled a gun and shot someone himself, as we suspected he had previously.

The inquiry, which was a sticky process for me to have gone through, amounted to nothing so I was mostly uninhibited by it. The interviews were marginally stressful, but I knew I was right so maintained my integrity throughout. Afterwards, I was able to reflect on what a self-affirming moment it was. It was the first time I had been forced to fully rely on my sense of self, and if I ever needed, I could revisit that moment in my mind and recognise my own abilities. I had stood up as a leader in an incredibly challenging scenario and it bolstered my confidence.

Jane had no idea what was going on for me at work, during the investigation into my conduct. Our communication had dwindled to a point of non-existence, and we were at opposite ends of the scale in most scenarios, even the foundational everyday stuff. We never rowed but would often spend days in silence following even the smallest of disagreements. It was increasingly easy for me to ignore the distance between us, rather than try and bridge the gap.

My attitude to the job, along with my consistently good performance in training and further CTSFO credential, had made me stand out above my peers, so I had occasionally been asked to act as additional resource on the specialist operations team. Opposed to our more responsive nature of policing as a regular firearms officer, spec ops was much more proactive in that they executed strategically planned operations, based more on pieces of intelligence. The work was super dicey and much higher risk, going after the big-time criminals.

The team had their own office, wore plain clothes and were the next level of cool as far as I was concerned. When one of the permanent members of their team left the police to pursue a career in private security I was offered his space, and I couldn't have said, 'yes', any quicker.

The special operations position removed me further from home, so even more I felt like a visitor in that environment. Sometimes I would start work on a Monday and not return home until Thursday, only to wash my clothes and leave again. I didn't mind at all. The work was exhilarating, and I was satisfied I was doing something worthwhile.

37

The role of a police officer is fraught with high-stress situations that often involve tragedy and suffering. Policing exposed me very early on to the darker aspects of human nature, to the stark inhumanity that exists within society, and to witness some of it was excruciatingly difficult.

Facing grim realities daily understandably takes an immense psychological toll, and whilst the use of dark humour as a coping mechanism was not obviously common across our department, looking back I can see how we would often minimise the impact of trauma by dressing it up with bravado or mild joking.

It was all we could do. The wider police service did nothing to support us in coping with our lived experiences, and it cannot be expected that anybody should absorb great trauma without it seeping out in other ways. I don't know how any of my colleagues coped with the stresses of the job, because we didn't talk about it. Often, we were just so busy moving on to the next thing that we hardly had time to process any of it anyway.

Negative experiences must be processed carefully, to avoid them tainting our view on society as a whole which was a trap that I did eventually fall into, and such experiences began to dominate my world view. I became entrenched in a protective stance, viewing the world through a lens of suspicion and disappointment, which ultimately proved to be profoundly unhelpful.

In a society increasingly saturated with negative narrative, recognising and celebrating the good in people feels more challenging than ever. Our television screens and social media feeds are inundated with distressing stories and images, which create an overwhelming sense of despair. It is essential to take steps to protect your mental well-being, and as such, I find it beneficial to limit my exposure to the news and engage minimally on social media.

The stories we tell ourselves are immensely powerful. They shape our perceptions and the reality we choose to accept. It is crucial to be mindful of the mental diet we are consuming. Reflect on the narratives you engage with, as they will either uplift you or undermine your ability to see the humanity in others. We all have the power to shape our own outlook, despite any past experiences or external dialogues.

38

The special operations team had a plan underway to arrest one of the more notorious criminals in one of the most unsavoury areas on our patch.

During the initial briefing he was painted as the biggest and nastiest man around, I suspect to ensure absolute commitment from our team so we were all adamant going into it that we would get him off the streets. I don't remember exactly what the accused offence was, but feel free to take your pick from a lengthy list of high-level crimes. I do remember, however, that the intelligence stated he had access to firearms, so speed was of the essence to get him locked up and we were the most effective tool within the force that could extract someone of his nature.

We were presented with photographs of our intended target, and it was agreed that we would enter his home address in the early hours, at cock o'clock in the morning, when he would likely be in his deepest sleep. We considered how many people we needed, and which room of the property we would use to detain anybody we happened upon. We discussed what type of locks to expect on the front door, and which way it was likely to open, or whether we should consider entry via a window. We had the kit and had received the training so there really wasn't much that we couldn't do. We had a completely black Land Rover with a ladder fitted to the roof. We were able to set the ladder to an angle and extend it, before driving right up to a property. One of us could then scuttle along the ladder and be right outside the bedroom window.

It was not uncommon to arrive to a property and find bars on the windows, there to protect the residents and their illegal wares from other criminals. It didn't do much good in deterring us, however, as we had access to thermal arc cutting equipment, which was basically a welder's torch that made short work of burning through the metal. We had to take great care whilst using it as it was a potential risk that the glass of the window could also get burnt and on more than one occasion, I saw it causing curtains to be set alight. We also carried a Wham Ram; a heavy piece of cylindrical metal with a handle which is used to smash doors in. Despite ours being a tactical black in colour, they were referred to in passing as the 'big red door key.'

There was not much element of surprise with a Wham Ram, so for this job we agreed the use of a Spreader; a piece of pneumatic equipment that pushed into the edges of a door frame and would ever so slightly stretch it, meaning none of the pins in the locking mechanism were touching their counterpart and the door would simply swing open. It was my preferred piece of entry equipment as it afforded us a silent entry, allowing for more time undisturbed on the inside.

A recce (reconnaissance mission) was done the day before, to gain some additional information about the layout of the property. Sometimes we applied to the council for plans of buildings. Others we would spend an hour or so on the same street pushing takeaway menus through each letterbox, just to get a better understanding of the area. For this operation I went door-to-door with a dog lead, asking if anybody had seen my dog as he was lost. When I arrived at the suspect's address, I was greeted by a woman who I assumed was his girlfriend. To look for my dog, I asked if I could check the back garden, so I could assess any escape routes in case he was quick enough or brave enough to try anything on the night. Unsurprisingly, she refused, but I still caught a brief glimpse inside the house regardless.

The time for the operation came around and we set off to the location, all dressed top-to-toe in black. Not in the Land Rover, but instead in a deep, midnight-blue van. We had taped various parts of our weapons and holsters with black duct tape, so there was no risk of any metal-on-metal sound which could give us away.

Half-way down the street the engine of the van was switched off and we rolled the rest of the way. Once outside the property, we even left the van door open, to not risk making a single sound. Absolute silence was the key to our success on that occasion. We had practised the exact manoeuvre we planned to use, and who would be in what position in the formation. That being said, it was not always possible to conduct an operation exactly as we had planned. To counter this, the department had a mantra, 'one singer, one song,' which we applied to every single job. If it was planned for Officer A to be first at the door, but on the day itself it ended up being Officer B who was first in line, forget the plan. The baton of leadership was passed, and whatever Officer B said was the final ruling, with no dispute. One singer, one song. It did away with any politics that often came along with hierarchy and forced us to think on our feet. It was being so agile which made us successful as a team. We could have all the plans in the world but had to be switched on and alive to other possibilities. The job was always too important, more than anybody's ego, for us to take time to stop and disagree. If something went in a different direction than what had previously been agreed, it was just tough shit. Instead of grumbling or eye-rolling we just got on with it. Once operations had been completed, either still on location or back at the station we would have a hot debrief as a team. During the debrief we would discuss what had happened, why some had gone left when we had planned to go right, what people saw and individual perceptions of the situation. It may have been for example that someone had lingered in a doorway too long, which left others feeling exposed or vulnerable, so they felt they had to act.

It was all completely constructive and always taken on board ahead of the next job. Operating in such a way created an environment in the unit where anybody could speak to anybody about anything, for the good of the job. We never argued or disagreed the day after the fact, we always just spoke openly straight away and that was incredibly empowering.

On arrival at the suspect's front door, we were surprised to find it off the latch, and a couple of inches open. Brilliant. That one inaction of the resident had changed the dynamic of the entire job, and the situation was afforded an even more passive approach.

With someone covering each doorway, and clearing each room as safe, we crept in. There was never any room for error when checking a house for suspects, as such operations saw each one of us putting our life firmly in the hands of our fellow officers. Six of us made it upstairs and into the bedroom, where we found the suspect sleeping in his bed. If he had woken up during those few minutes we were in the house, it would have been because he needed a piss and not because we made any noise, because we didn't. We were deadly silent.

One of the lads gave him a gentle nudge, as we all lit him up with our torches. After the initial shock of being woken abruptly at gunpoint, he almost seemed relieved that the six, armed men in his bedroom were police officers, and not rival criminals. Unsurprising really, as had it been some other thug who had gained entry as easily as we did, there would have been no rules of engagement, and our suspect had been so deep in his slumber that the gun under his pillow would have been no use at all.

That operation was by far one of my more favoured memories, the subtlety of our actions in particular. We were usually more aggressive in our approach and not because there was a violent mentality within the team, far from it in fact, as it is not the sort of profession which suits a destructive personality. But because our handguns operated without a safety catch, and as such, we had to gain immediate and complete compliance from the suspect, as that was vital to ensure weapon retention.

There was an increased number of weapons on the streets which meant that it was becoming even more dangerous for us just to bowl into places as we had done previously. We had to become more sophisticated in our operating methods.

Police forces across Europe were already using police dogs far more intelligently than we were in the UK, so the decision was made that we would take on a couple of Belgian Malinois as passive attack dogs. The Malinois are not dissimilar to a German Shepherd in their appearance, only they are slightly smaller and lighter in weight. An intelligent breed with superb agility and strength, they were traditionally used for herding cattle, which made them suitable for rounding up big nasties on a police operation. They were ideal for covert operations as they didn't bark unless prompted, and not to mention they have truly massive jaws, complete with a terrifying set of teeth.

A member of the dog department had travelled to Belgium to source the dogs and upon return to the UK, began the necessary training before they could be allocated to our department. Our team participated in several of the training exercises to allow the dogs to get used to us, and so that we could be sure of their abilities. On our compound we had a four-bedroom detached house which we used to practise some of our tactics. During their training the dogs were made to wear police issue tac vests, and cameras on their head, as they would be expected to in a real-life scenario. We stood outside the building watching the live footage from the dog camera on a monitor. The dogs were sent into the house to locate an individual based on their scent, and once located they were to back them into a corner and bark for human assistance. If the suspect attempted to move, the dogs were trained to bite. Good dog, job done. It was not uncommon during their first few months for the dogs to focus more on getting their camera off than finding the suspect, which gave us a perfect view of inside their mouths and someone the job of going in and wrestling it off them.

One formation we practised with the dogs was to line outside the house, with our legs spread apart in such a way that I always felt made us look like a shit dance troop. The officer at the front of the line would be ready on aim and would shout from outside, '*You in the house! Show yourself!*' and then the dog would be released through the legs of the officer at the back of the line and make its way through all our legs to get into the house.

There was one dog that was always so excited to be getting on with the task at hand that the last two of us in line would invariably get a nip on the inside of the thigh or even on the bollocks as it passed through.

My first encounter with a police dog was during my early career, and it was just starting to get light when a report was made at around four in the morning. The call to the station had been made from one of our divisional superintendents as a noise had disturbed him in his sleep and upon looking out of his bedroom window, he had seen someone trying to break into a house across the road. The super must have requested a dog as when I arrived onto the street, I spotted the handlers' cars.

I parked up and began pacing quietly on foot, listening for any movement or disturbance. A few hundred metres ahead of me I spotted the super, stood in one of the upper floor windows of his house, gesturing to a parked car on the road down below. I made eye contact with the dog handler and pointed to the car.

He began to approach, his big fluffy German Shepherd colleague only too happy to go along too, its nose to the ground.

Nowadays such an instance would involve a polite request, something like, *'Come on mate, get out from under the car,'* with the dog still firmly on the lead. But things were different in the nineties and from a few paces away, the handler bent down and without a sound unclipped the lead, and the dog rushed to the underneath of the car. Very quickly the suspect decided he wanted to give himself up, and come out voluntarily, but it was too late for that as the dog was already dragging him out. The super had shut his curtains and hadn't seen a thing.

Sure, the dog made a bit of a mess of the fella's jacket sleeve and left him with a few scrapes, but I think it is important that police dogs get a bit of what they are hunting every now and again, otherwise they could risk losing their edge and indeed interest. Good dog, job done.

Being a police officer or a criminal means living a constant game of cat and mouse. The consequences for the mouse being so severe as the absolute restriction of their liberties, that the will and desire of the person trying to get away is usually more than that of whoever is chasing. This usually meant that absconding suspects were willing to take greater risks and put themselves in the path of danger.

Psychologically as humans we are programmed to respond to direct commands, and one of the handlers had explained to me that if someone is running away and you shout, 'stop', they do, in fact, tend to stop. Even if it just for half a second, the act of stalling and having to get the pace going again has the potential to be the difference between catching a perpetrator or them getting away.

He also suggested that even whilst working without a dog it could help to shout, '*Stop! Police officer with a dog!*', as nobody wants to get chewed by a six-stone canine. Particularly more seasoned criminals who may have already encountered a police dog and would not want to repeat the experience again. It was a tactic that tended to work best in the dark, and I once heard a colleague after issuing the verbal warning follow it with a pseudo bark, which did the trick nicely.

The end of our Malinois' training coincided with a spate of armed robberies at a few local post offices, all of which were suspected to have been conducted by the same group of individuals. The use of weapons in the robberies meant our involvement was required. Members of the suspected group were placed under complete surveillance, and it wasn't too long before we received intelligence regarding the expected time and place of the next robbery. Our plan was to stop them during the act itself, and we decided that one of our new canine colleagues was ready to join us on the job.

Our team was split into two groups. The first was stationed in the post office; two officers in the back room and one under the counter, whilst the post office staff continued to work. The remaining six of us, including the dog, were positioned in the street behind the location, in a beat up, old, white transit van.

We sat for ages in the van waiting, as was often the case on those jobs. Inside was pitch black and after a while we became acutely aware, due to the absolute stench, that the dog had quietly taken itself into a corner and done a poo. We didn't have anything on us to bag it up with and couldn't get out of the van as it would have risked blowing our cover. The smell was nauseating but we had no choice other than to sit and wait, trying not to rock the van with each of us retching in turn. For another two hours we sat with the smell as despite the intelligence, the suspects had been a no-show.

A week later we received more information that the same group were planning another robbery, but this time the intelligence was more definitive. We also expected they would be more sophisticated in their method and it was expected to be a more traditional heist; the sort of robbery you would see in a film, where a car laden with baddies pulls up outside a venue, a few get out armed and wearing masks, leaving only the getaway driver in the car as they enter the targeted location and leave with the cash, before driving off into the sunset.

Not on our watch, fuckers.

The target was a bureau de change on a small shopping parade directly off a main road. Since the poo incident we had opted to leave the dog behind but kept a couple of officers positioned in the venue, whilst the rest of us were given various posts on the outside where we were ready and waiting.

It was so far removed from my early years as a PC, where I relished being impeccably presented; the uniform and formality that went along with it. For the week leading up to the operation I had grown my facial hair, and on the day was dressed as a council worker in a high visibility jacket and trousers. My cover was that of a litter picker, and for the three hours we spent on location waiting, I performed my fake role and tidied up the nearby area with my brush and dustpan. The role of refuse collector being quite fitting as I really was there to tidy up the shit of society and put it in the bin where it needed to be.

The dust cart I was pushing had two compartments. One for litter, which a couple of passers-by did use to deposit their waste in. The other contained my MP5, easily concealed as it had a retractable stock which reduced the size of the gun to half its original length but still maintained its firing abilities. The members of the public milling around would have had no idea it was in there, or that I had my handgun under my council jacket, holstered on my waistband. The whole time we were in communication with each other, all using wireless earpieces.

Eventually a red car pulled up and two men got out and headed towards the target, pulling their balaclavas down as they approached the door. The plan was to let them get across the threshold, and begin to execute their plan, as the evidence would then be irrefutable. The officers inside had ushered all customers out of the back and as soon as the suspects entered, I removed the weapon from my dustcart and rushed to the front door, ready to block their exit. Another officer approached the driver of the vehicle, ordering him out of the car and down on the ground.

Before too long, all involved were cuffed and on their way to the next phase of their life. And as was always the case for us, we headed back to the station for tea and biscuits. Belting.

39

Being completely silent as we entered a suspect's house was just one way in which we could have entered. In like a lamb and out like a lion.

On other occasions we wouldn't be concerned with stealth, and instead would make the biggest entrance we could. After making significant noise upon arrival creating an immediate presence, we would then 'have a soak'. By intentionally creating a period of stillness we were granted the ability to discern the echoes of what our entrance had disturbed. Whilst waiting patiently for the dust to settle we would do nothing but observe. What do we hear? What do we see? We could then identify what required immediate attention and move with intelligence. We knew where the biggest problem was and where we needed to focus our resources.

During training we would often practise going in like a lion and out like a lamb, as it is always easier to escalate than to de-escalate. To have your foot on the accelerator is intoxicating and powerful, whereas to step back down from that is difficult.

In both my firearms unit and special operations team, I truly learnt the concept of team trust. We all shared a common goal, and there was simply no room for ego. We took care of each other, held each other accountable, and provided constructive feedback without letting it affect our relationships. Our commitment to the team and to our shared mission fostered an atmosphere of mutual respect and support. The brotherhood we cultivated is something I have found impossible to replicate in any other context.

My team were my family. We trained together, ate together, and slept together. The success of our team was built on the bond which we all shared through doing the job. We had each other's backs and without a shadow of a doubt I trusted each of them with my life, and I know they trusted me with theirs.

As a team we disagreed regularly, but whenever we had fallen out, we would soon enough fall back together again. At times, our disputes could be settled physically, and we wrestled out our concerns in the gym, with grievances being soon forgotten. Often such events were interpreted as necessary acts of constructive feedback, on how much of a prick someone might have been acting at the time.

No other group has ever resonated with me in the same way. The profound level of trust we achieved, trusting one another with our lives in high-stake and dynamic situations, created a unique bond, and I miss it dearly. Trust isn't just a fleeting notion; it is the bedrock of effective teamwork which is cultivated through vulnerability, accountability and a shared vision.

40

Towards the end of 2008 I qualified as a firearms trainer, which was a very natural progression given the amount of experience I had amassed, and I was glad to further my impact and become a part of the Tactical Weapons and Training department[1].

My own learning experience during each stage of my police career with the police had been indifferent, and I wanted to have a go at delivering a better service to my colleagues. The transition didn't mean I was no longer a part of the special operations unit as my specialist skillset was often warranted on active jobs, but I had additional responsibilities, and my working days became a little more within the bounds of normal working hours, with fewer shift commitments.

Work was good, and home life was satisfactory, even if I begrudged the additional time spent with Jane that my more regular shifts incurred. It was around the same time that the decision was made for us to have a second baby. We had not long since moved house, which to me didn't feel remotely necessary and the increased mortgage payments left us uncomfortably tight financially, but my input mattered very little in comparison to Jane's agenda of constantly seeking to upgrade everything we had. It was as though an accumulation of things made us appear to the outside that we were happy, and in many ways it did just that. But our marriage was so greatly lacking in every other aspect that

---

[1] Special Weapons and Tactics were referred to as the SWAT team, which made us the TWAT team, and we had a sign made up for our office door.

I think Jane viewed having another baby as a sticking plaster. Being a father was something I enjoyed so I was contented with the prospect of another child. Even more than before then, our intimate relations became nothing more than a transactional exchange and after a few months of trying, the desired outcome was reached, and the baby was due in the late winter of 2009.

Up until that point I had only ever witnessed the standards of my own team during training, but when I became an instructor, I was tasked with teaching all the firearms teams on our force. Some were okay, but some were not great. Soon enough I found my teaching style, and whilst I wasn't nasty, I wasn't a particularly pleasant trainer either, but all with good intention. I wanted to push people to be better, and as much as possible tried to strip away the veneer of the learning environment to really test their threat perception.

During one exercise someone had managed to pin me to the floor and detain me, and instead of putting a set of handcuffs straight on me, he simply said, '*cuff, cuff.*' Clearly, I was not 'cuff cuffed', so as he knelt beside me, I reached out and drew the handgun from the holster on his leg and shouted at the other six officers to put their weapons on the floor, before I ran away waving the gun in the air.

It wasn't good enough. We were such an elite team, that for anybody in training to not act as though the threat was real, concerns were raised regarding performance and suitability for the role. We couldn't afford to drop the ball when the stakes were so high as life and death. You may consider that such a small oversight in a training situation would not impact performance when executing an arrest in real life, surely, but I had known a firearms officer who whilst arresting someone had said, '*cuff, cuff,*' instead of handcuffing the suspect. No doubt after doing a double take to check if the arresting officer had taken a bump to the head or was just taking the piss, the suspect then stood up and punched him square in the face before attempting to abscond.

Fortunately, there were another couple of officers on hand to properly arrest the suspect, who was then further pumped with adrenaline after smacking a bobby across the chops, but quite easily the situation could have turned out differently.

During scenario-based training exercises it was vital that we made everything as realistic as possible. 'Baddies' were dressed accordingly and behaved in the same volatile way we would expect from a real-life situation.

Playing the baddy was a role that suited me well. I liked to really test my trainees and would be as aggressive and awful as possible.

One of the pinch points for us in any building was a doorway: a fatal funnel, where people often appeared silhouetted. But you don't have to be brilliant shot to just aim for the door. In my role as the baddy, I would wait in the dark and listen as my group of trainees entered each room, shouting, 'Armed police!' I lay quietly, before seeing my trainees look quickly around the door, before ducking back out.

Nine times out of ten they would reappear again in the exact same spot, only to be hit in the middle of their helmet with a paint round.

I enjoyed making people more tactically aware because some really weren't, and if they didn't buck up, they could be a danger to themselves and therefore a liability to their team. I wanted every single officer I trained to be able to go home to their families at the end of each shift. There were some that took the piss, and I was quick to diminish any attitudes that were less than serious, impressing on them all that they were afforded the opportunity to train for a brilliant job. My job was to make sure they were not a weak link; to make sure that the day, week, or month after, when they had to act out a similar scenario for real, they did it right.

Even though I knew it was a boyhood dream for many, to the outside world who didn't understand what we shared as a team, the sell for becoming a firearms officer wasn't particularly strong. The department was struggling to find people who were willing to bear the responsibility of potentially having to shoot someone, and an increased likelihood of being shot themselves, for no more money than they would receive as a regular PC. A recruitment drive was carried out and the result was several transfers into firearms from the Tactical Aid Group. It was convenient as they were already from a similar environment in that they had to be exceedingly disciplined during their work, which was often carried in often hostile environments.

That being said, their previous job had only required them to be physically bigger and stronger than your average criminal, but when using a weapon, it wasn't all about who could lift the most weight. There was a certain degree of intelligence involved, and upon first impressions it didn't seem as though our potential new colleagues had a great deal of the mental agility required.

Those that had applied to transfer were invited on a training day, to allow us to ascertain whether the job was a good fit for each of them. It was designed to be a collection of taster sessions, covering most of what we did in the firearms team, finishing with a brief scenario-based activity which I expected would be enjoyable for most. We began with an hour of classroom learning, covering the basics of the weapons we used; how they worked and general dos and don'ts. The theory session seemed to go well, and nobody raised their hand to say they weren't interested in continuing, so we kitted them up in protective gear and headed across the car park to the shooting range, for the first practical element of the day.

With an instructor by their side, we directed each hopeful recruit towards one of the eight firing stations on the range, where they stood seven metres away from the targets. After I had given them a demonstration of what they would be doing whilst there, I ran them through the principles of aimed shooting; what a good stance was, how they should pace their breathing, and how whilst on a shooting range the weapon should always be pointed away from them and towards the target, even when not specifically on aim. Then for the first time they were each issued a live weapon, and most of them were so big in size that they made our handguns look like tiny pea shooters. 'Futile' is how I would describe my initial psychological assessment upon joining firearms, as it was really nothing more than a multiple-choice questionnaire and an interview conducted by members of the force as opposed to qualified psychologists. So, I did stop and consider that none of them had been psychologically assessed at all, and as such, there was the potential that any one of them could have been dangerous. But at least I was aware of the possibility, and armed.

'Pick up your weapons!' I shouted; their cue to load their weapons by inserting the magazine of live bullets into the handle, as we had discussed, and I demonstrated during the morning's theory session.

Issuing further instruction I shouted, *'Slide forward!'*

It was also explained to them that after loading the magazine into the gun, they would have to push a small button on the side of the weapon, which would then slide the top of the gun forward, closing it. This action loaded a bullet into the breach, which would then discharge once the trigger was pulled. I watched and heard as seven of the eight of them did the correct action. The one who didn't instead took a massive stride forward. The length of his legs meant he was then stood one metre in front of all the others, who were all holding loaded weapons pointing in his direction.

'For fuck's sake, Tony! No!!! Slide forward!'

Again, not stopping to question why everybody else was still stood at their stations, he took another giant step forward and we had to order everybody to put their guns down immediately and stop the exercise. It was both scary and funny in equal measure and he was taken off the range, not to progress any further.

With one man down we continued with the day.

After they had done some shooting, I started to introduce stoppage drills, which is how to deal with a stoppage or jam in a firearm. On occasion, a gun may not go off when the trigger is pulled, which could be caused by a fault with the weapon or more likely, a faulty bullet. Instead of the usual 'bang,' which would indicate a live bullet had been discharged, a faulty bullet would make a 'click' sound. We were taught not to freeze, but to clear the faulty bullet and continue shooting.

We issued our hopeful recruits with new magazines. Each loaded with normal bullets, but each containing a dud round. If a stoppage occurred, marked by a 'click,' they were instructed to rotate the weapon ninety degrees to the left, so it was on its side, then pull the top slide of the gun back and let it go. This action would strip away the top bullet from the magazine, eject it onto the floor, and load the next bullet into the barrel of the gun. They were then told to put their weapons straight and continue shooting.

It always took a bit of time for anybody new to handling a firearm to complete this task, but once more accustomed it shouldn't take any longer than two seconds.

I watched as one of the students discharged his weapon and got a 'click,' instead of a 'bang' and instead of doing as they had been instructed, he turned the gun around and, to see what had caused the stoppage, looked directly down the barrel. It was in that moment I saw my career flash before my eyes.

Another immediate failure. Do not pass go. Do not collect your firearms permit.

When I went into training, I was a stickler for doing everything properly, and I felt that here were some issues with training standards and complacency. Sloppy mistakes were being made because people lacked commitment, and there was general laziness and ineptitude. As much as I could, I wanted to encourage a higher standard of operating.

But it was, of course, impossible to ever fully prepare anyone for the various and nuanced situations they would inevitably face. The rules of engagement were completely different out in the real world.

It was in the summer of 2009 when, due to a fatal gunshot injury, I suffered the loss of a close friend. He was shot on a job I was scheduled to be part of, but with dozens of training plans to refresh, I had sought a substitute for my position.

Kindly, Alex, offered to take my place.

The firearms team was so tight knit, which was even further solidified within the smaller special operations sphere, and Alex was someone I had always enjoyed working alongside. He was constantly smiling, a real happy-go-lucky type of guy. I considered him a good friend, having joined spec ops just a few months after he did, and our kinship flowed both ways. He was a couple of years older than I was and referred to me never by my name but only as 'Spunker,' as a term of endearment.

One job we worked together really sticks out in my mind. It was just the two of us undercover, and it would have been impossible not to have felt like a real super sleuth.

A new apartment building had gone up on the outskirts of town, in an area that was a hotspot for low-level and truly volatile criminals alike. We had received intelligence that one of the top-floor apartments was being used by a gang of particularly nasty lads as a headquarters for their drug dealing operation. The expectation was that if we were able to gain access to the apartment and execute a raid, we were sure to happen upon thousands of pounds worth of drugs and money and shut down their operation. They were violent criminals involved in serious organised crime, and with access to firearms. We had to be careful.

The management company of the building knew criminal activity was bad for business, so when we approached them to explain we needed evidence to apply for a warrant, they agreed to co-operate with us.

We were granted access to the vacant apartment directly next door and set to task.

Our cover was that of two building surveyors, so along we went one afternoon, both in suits with high visibility tabards over the top and a hard hat each. Alex fancied himself as a bit of a techy and had created us some false identification cards, which were completely shit, but he was chuffed with them.

We were there to install some audio surveillance equipment, which would hopefully offer up some credible evidence against the gang and intelligence to further assist our efforts to shut them down and get them off the streets. By drilling into the wall between the two apartments and installing directional microphones, we could record audio and listen back to the conversations that were had. Obviously, we had to carry tools with us to conduct the installation so if anybody were to ask who we were or what we were doing, we were there to measure damp.

After successfully setting up the equipment and leaving the apartment, we headed down a corridor towards the lift. Coming in the opposite direction were two of the shitpot crew. To maintain their intimidating persona, they glared at us as we passed, but we couldn't give off any suggestion that we knew who they were, or what they might be doing there. Or indeed that we *were* intimidated, because why would we be? We were just surveyors after all. Had they suspected we were police officers, they were vicious enough to have tried to attack us.

We got out with no trouble, assured that our work was sure to help put some nasty fuckers behind bars.

To have been partnered with him that day was a great relief to me. His general demeanour was always one of optimism and light, which countered the otherwise ominous atmosphere. He made my days on the job more enjoyable, and I am certain that many other colleagues would say the exact same.

On the day of the incident, I was in the office when I heard communications over the radio. A distress call. The team had gone in, shots had been fired, and Alex had been shot. Amidst the panic and shock, a couple of the lads began to work to save his life on the scene before an ambulance arrived to take him to the hospital, but he didn't make it there alive. He had a family at home.

Total devastation and immediate grief swept the team. Those on the job with him were processing the incident, as we were back at the station. Then the reality set in. He shouldn't have even been there in the first place. It should have been me.

As I rushed to find somewhere private, I couldn't hear anything other than my heart pounding in my head. Dripping with sweat I practically fell into a toilet cubicle to be sick. Sat on the floor of the men's bathroom, my thoughts began to spiral as I wept with despair. He had been killed and I felt responsible, I felt that I had sentenced my friend to his death, and I was completely powerless to change what had happened.

The deep sensation of loss I was feeling became rivalled with deep regret and hatred for myself. Above anything else I wanted to be able to reverse time, to go back and retract my plea for a substitute, to take his place in the morgue, but I couldn't.

Before too long the press had gotten hold of the story, and a circus began in the outside world. After a couple of hours, I managed to compose myself enough to call Jane and my parents to let them know I was okay, that it wasn't me who had been involved in the incident that was being reported on. What I couldn't find the words to tell them was that it should have been, and that I wished it was.

During the immediate aftermath of his death, I spent even more time at work.

An eight-hour shift regularly turned into a twelve-hour shift. There was no compassion at home, so I chose to surround myself with those who understood how I was feeling.

We were family. We felt safe together and I needed to further immerse myself in that environment.

We never spoke about Alex or the incident itself, but we were all going through our own cycle of grief, and it was a comfort simply to have each other. The force offered no support or aftercare to those who were there on the day, or to those who were closely associated with him. There was no offer of counselling or a supportive pat on the back. Nobody even stopped to ask if we were okay.

One of his best friends of many years was on the TAG unit and we used to meet once every few weeks for a brew in the canteen, only to ever sit and exchange idle chatter. The loss of Alex had hit him like a tonne of bricks, and he was never again the same man I had known previously.

A few months after his funeral, Jane and I were heading out one morning to do some shopping in preparation for the baby arriving. Without any obvious reason as to what prompted it, as we drove down a busy dual carriageway I couldn't in that moment carry on, and I brought the car to a halt, tears streaming down my face.

Sadness had suddenly overwhelmed me.

'*What the hell are you doing?!*' Jane said, her voice shrill and impatient as cars overtook us, beeping their horns.

I couldn't answer her, so I didn't, and without saying a word I composed myself and we were soon back on our way. I can't help but think that such an incident would have been a good opportunity for my wife to start a conversation about what I may have been feeling and dealing with, but we continued with our shopping trip as though nothing had happened, and she didn't think to ask beyond that point either.

We welcomed our second child later that year. Another little girl, Mabel, and I fell in love with her just as much as I had with Alice. Her arrival coincided with my Christmas leave which meant the festive season was fraught, but my new baby girl was a wonderful end to an otherwise horrendous year.

She was a flicker of light in an otherwise dark tunnel, even if having a newborn meant that I returned to work not remotely rejuvenated.

The dangers of the job had finally hit home, and I was forced to acknowledge that none of us were immortal. We were angry and we were upset, but the world didn't stop turning. We had to continue with our jobs and our lives, and I did the best I could to push all my feelings surrounding the tragedy deep down within.

During my first week back off leave, I planned to deliver training to the spec ops unit on one of our more dynamic tactics – a Mobile Armed Support to Surveillance Strike. The specific logistics and technicalities of it were complex, but it was something we had done countless times before. As far as our manoeuvres went, it really was like a scene in an action movie. Fast, dangerous, and bloody good fun.

It involved four vehicles: Police Car 1, Police Car 2, Police Car 3, and Bandit Car. During the drill, Bandit Car was facing north, carrying two officers dressed in plain clothes, playing the role of armed criminals trying to abscond. Police Car 1 contained four armed officers, and their instruction was to approach Bandit Car on the driver's side, stopping at an angle, blocking its direction of travel. The role of Police Car 2, also carrying four armed officers, was to pull up as close as possible to the back of Bandit Car, with Police Car 3 remaining directly behind.

Once all the vehicles were in position, the tactic became incredibly fast-paced and dynamic, and each officer had a set of extremely specific movements to make.

The driver of Police Car 1 slid across his own bonnet, before pointing his weapon directly through the windscreen of Bandit Car, before issuing a warning:

'Oi! Fuck nuggets! Armed police! Get out of your vehicle!'

At the same time, the front passenger from Police Car 1 climbed out of the driver side door, (their own door unable to open as it was providing an obstruction to the driver of Bandit Car), and ran around the front of Bandit Car, to stand on aim with their weapon at the passenger side door. The rear two passengers of Police Car 1, along with the driver of Police Car 2, were to assist with covering the doors of Bandit Car.

Officers on all doors of Bandit Car were holding it shut with their bodyweight and kept their handguns on aim against the windows, which allowed us to control the suspect's exit out of the car. We said when they got out, and in what order.

Again, it was vital that we practised with live weapons. The passenger in Police Car 2 was always armed with a shotgun, and their job was to deactivate the tyres of Bandit Car. Even though it all happened in a matter of seconds, there were two possible actions anybody in that position could use. Either, to shoot the back tyre and spin around, going back-to-back with the officer stationed on the passenger front door, before shooting the front tyre. Alternatively, after the back tyre had been deactivated, we had the option to take a couple of sidesteps, and 'scuttle,' before shooting the front tyre. For anybody who chose to sidestep, and remain front-on to the vehicle, we were always taught to always offer a threat to the car, to be on aim with our weapon. Actions beat reactions and, in any situation, we always had to be ready.

Scuttling always felt dangerous to me. It was more blue-on-blue than necessary.

We were always operating at such great pace that there was always the risk of one of our weapons being discharged by accident, through any pushing or shoving, so my preference was always to spin. It was marginally quicker but felt far more fluid and natural. One spin and I knew I was landing straight on the next tyre, with no concerns for my own safety as there was an officer covering my back. Our shotguns were on bungee cords so once I had discharged my second round into the front tyre I could chuck the cord over my head, swing my weapon over my shoulder and get straight onto my handgun.

We were doing a practise run first, walking the exercise through with no real pace so everybody was clear on their positions before we did it again at the speed it would be done in real life. Everybody had made their first moves, and I was stood next to the shotgunner, Phil, when I asked if he would be spinning or scuttling.

'*Spinning,*' was his response.

When spinning with a shotgun, during the transition it should either be in a high or low carry port. That is, either pointed at the sky or at the floor whilst moving. Phil shot the rear tyre and as he spun around, he didn't aim his weapon up or down. Instead, he swung a loaded shotgun right past my jawline and I lost my shit.

Phil was incredibly blasé about it, which was unsurprising as he had not just looked down the barrel of a loaded shotgun. Calling a stop there and then to the exercise I ordered everybody back to the compound.

Being a firearms instructor was a difficult position to hold, for the one simple reason that I was training my peers, and my friends. At the end of each session, I had to sign-off to say whether an individual was competent, or incompetent.

If I had stated that day that Phil was incompetent, I would have been ostracised, for ending a teammate's career. If I had signed to say that he was competent, and he ended up killing someone either during training or on a live job, during any following inquest, an investigative body would have looked at which trainer had signed him off.

I refused to sign the form either way and it was escalated up to the sergeant.

He quizzed me on the incident, and I expressed my concerns about his suitability for the team. But Phil was a rifleman, and we didn't have many of those at the time, so the incident was swept away without so much as even a formal caution. I was furious. Only six months before the worst had happened, someone had died. If anything were to happen again, I felt as though I would be responsible and subconsciously, I decided I couldn't bear that weight anymore.

41

Up until recently, there is nothing that anybody could ever say that would have diminished the guilt I felt towards Alex's death. I didn't pull the trigger, but in my opinion, I created the situation that led to his death. In the same way that a drug dealer may not open the vein of someone who dies of a heroin overdose, but by law they are liable for their death just for supplying the drugs. Now, I have moved to a place of solace and started to unburden myself of the guilt. In every moment we live, there are thousands of possible outcomes, and a range of variables that impact which one eventually comes to fruition. My actions were just one stepping stone on Alex's life path, which regrettably ended far too soon. It is a small mercy that despite anybody's best attempts he was likely dead within seconds of the bullet entering his body. His death was swift, and there was nothing anybody could have done. Even if he had been shot on the doorstep of a hospital, it was unlikely his life would have been saved. The only other place I can find any comfort is in the fact that he died doing something he truly loved, amongst our band of brothers, who all truly loved him.

42

In the UK, major members of the Royal Family and designated members of the government are given armed protection twenty-four hours a day, seven days a week. A need for candidates to serve as Close Protection Officers (CPOs) created my next opportunity for development.

Given the wealth of experience I had amassed, coupled with my previous counter terrorism training, I stood out as an obvious choice and was grateful to be packed off on another training course. It was for six weeks, and I was to leave each week on a Sunday afternoon and return home each Friday evening; just enough time to see the kids, wash my clothes and pack up my kit ready to leave again.

To qualify as a CPO didn't mean I would no longer be a part of my unit or the training department, but the initial training offered immediate distance from that environment, which I needed. Upon successful qualification the role also promised regular respite, in the form of weeks away at conferences and occasional days interspersed here and there, several times a month. It was an ideal scenario for various reasons.

There were eight of us on the programme, with one other attendee from my force, David, who was someone I had never enjoyed working with. Despite the fact he was blatantly inept, he had somehow managed to pass his sergeant's exam and liked to wield his power a little too much for my liking.

Heading to the venue for week one of the training I passed him on the motorway, his legs hanging out of the bonnet of his

Vauxhall Insignia as it had broken down. I could have stopped to assist, but chose not to, and when he arrived an hour after me, he was visibly flustered and covered in oil. Rather than arrange his own alternative transport to support his travel to and from the course, he manufactured a situation whereby it was agreed he would use one of our squad cars for the subsequent five weeks.

It was a complete abuse of his power, and no doubt a monumental inconvenience to the team as we only had a handful of vehicles available to us. I wasn't the only one on the team who felt some distain towards David and after receiving the instruction, some of the lads back at the station decided they would dedicate some time to making sure the car was all set and ready for him to drive away. Behind the scenes, someone had shared with me just how they were preparing the vehicle.

In a collective effort, they had taken the time to hole punch as much paper as they could and collected the small paper circles from the bottom of the punchers. They had then removed the car air vents and stuffed all the tiny bits of paper inside, before putting the air vents back on. After setting all the dials on the inner ventilation system up to the maximum, they left the keys at the front desk for him to collect on the following Sunday morning.

Eagerly I awaited his arrival at the venue for week two of our training, and when he stepped out of the car it looked as though he had been caught in a blizzard; the squad car resembled a ginormous snow globe. After the initial blast he had assumed it was all over, but I was amused to learn that every so often during the journey another handful of paper spontaneously blew out of the vents and into his face.

Protection training was a vastly different type of environment to the one which I had been operating in for such a long while. It was a great shift from overt hostility (which saw us breaking into houses, shouting a lot, and then making an arrest at gunpoint) to a much more covert and discreet way of operating. It meant making a change from being the loudest and most dominant person in the room, to being practically unseen and unknown by the people around you. It was a substantial mindset shift, and as a self-proclaimed introvert, I was relieved to embody it.

Despite all our previous experience, most of the training was centred around the practical application of firing a gun, because it was a completely different method than any of us were used to. Becoming a firearms officer, I was taught to take aimed shots. Essentially, only shoot what you can positively identify as a threat. If you can't see it, don't shoot it. With either of our usual weapons, we had sights to look down, one at the front and one at the back. Once the sights were lined up, then we could accurately shoot the target. The MP5 rifle was so accurate that using the holographic sights, I could hit a 5p coin from fifty metres away.

Any shooting that had the potential to occur whilst protecting a VIP would be done in incredibly close quarters, and in the event of real threat there would be no time to spend lining up sights, so we were taught sense of direction shooting instead. We practised every day; in various formats and scenarios but always using live rounds. We trained to shoot whilst dragging a limp body away, and to shoot a target whilst walking away backwards, shielding a dummy VIP.

When attending a venue or event VIPs typically arrive in a car, and the car would then be the preferred method of escape during an emergency, so we trained vehicle evacuations on the outdoor shooting range. We practised being driven onto the range, exiting the car, and walking a short distance with the 'VIP,' before a threat would appear. The driver would then bring the car back around at breakneck speed, and I had to get my VIP in the backseat of the car and throw myself on top of them before the car drove off, often with my legs still hanging out of one of the doors.

Because of the significance of the people we would be protecting, we had to be uber accurate. If we discharged one hundred rounds during a shooting exercise, we couldn't afford to miss even two or three. A failure of any one of the shooting exercises meant we would be sent home immediately.

Previously I had worn my handgun on my leg, and even after a decade off the force, I could still draw a weapon from my leg now with my eyes closed. As a protection officer I wouldn't be in a police uniform, but usually in a suit instead, which meant my weapon had to be in a holster on my left hip. As I am right-handed it was easily concealed there whilst I shook hands or opened doors. If I had to shoot, I would draw my gun across my body and shoot from my right hip. It took a great deal of practise to get my muscle-memory accustomed to drawing my weapon from a new place.

We were assessed in our weapon retention skills, to ensure we were not at risk of having our guns taken and used against us. Previously I had learnt to shoot a handgun with my arms straight in front of me, but close protection training taught me to shoot from much closer to the body, with my arms bent and handgun positioned near my hip. Our handguns were without a safety switch, so it was less of a risk to keep our weapons close, instead of readily offering them up in an outstretched arm.

During firearms training we were always pushed to our absolute limits, but the physical training to become a CPO was more intense than anything I had done before. Typically, they were fifteen-hour days, and the instructors kept the pressure on us constantly. At that time, the Israeli secret service used a form of physical combat called Kata, which is what we trained in. It consisted mostly of incredibly ninja-like moves and taught us how to use a weapon in defence, but in a non-lethal way without discharging any rounds. We had to be proficiently trained in combat fighting as not every threat was guaranteed to be armed. Some would have just been physical threats, throwing punches, and there is no justification to shoot any old windmilling idiot.

We used a facility like an old-fashioned school gymnasium, with hard wooden floors and various pieces of apparatus fixed to each wall.

During some of the physical training sessions, the room was divided into six sections with floor-to-ceiling curtains. It looked a bit like it had been set up for dog agility, as in each section a different exercise was being conducted. After we had completed each one, we went straight into a sixty second round of Kata with an instructor, who were all dressed like hockey goalkeepers top-to-toe in padded clothing. They wouldn't have felt a single blow any of us issued. As soon as we heard the whistle blow again it was on to the next exercise, plank crawling from one to the next. Some were physical exercises such as climbing ropes or navigating through tunnels. Others were designed to test our mental agility after the high physical exertion of a round of Kata, such as a large foam piece puzzle. It was gruelling, but also incredibly enjoyable, and as ever, I applied myself completely and put as much effort in as possible.

Whenever we weren't conducting shooting exercises, participating in role-play-based training, or being put through our paces in the gym, the rest of our time and attention went into planning for events. We were given a script which detailed who our VIP was, what sort of function they were due to attend, where it would be held and how many other guests would be present. With this information we each had to design an appropriate plan to get our individual VIPs from A to B. It involved a site visit, a route plan, consideration of any contingencies and an escape plan. Then we travelled to the different venues to practise what we had prepared.

One afternoon I took an acting VIP out for lunch, and his backstory was that he was a local politician who had recently been outed in an infidelity scandal, and all the tabloids wanted a piece of him. We arrived at a pub somewhere in the picturesque landscape of the Cotswolds, and once we were seated, I couldn't ignore that it was a less-than-ideal location as there were more doors than seemed necessary, in and out on all sides of the building. To ease some of my visible tension, my VIP came out of character briefly to assure me that everything was okay; that I could relax and enjoy my meal as there was no interception planned at that point.

Naturally, I assumed it was a lie, so remained sat bolt upright on the edge of my seat, barely looking down at my plate as I pushed the food around nervously.

To qualify and obtain the position was a big deal to me.

Of course, nobody wants to be unsuccessful at anything, but it was more significant than that. Being in firearms had given me so much, but it had never fully met with my need to be in a militarised environment. Close protection had the extra edge, and felt even more aligned with what I should have been doing all along.

There was also an element of my seeking internal validation, particularly after what had happened to Alex and the associated guilt I felt. Being signed off to protect people of such high status as the Royal Family would be confirmation that I was good enough, which was not something that I had ever felt before.

It turned out that my VIP was not trying to trip me up at all rather was just being nice, so eventually I relaxed and began to share an enjoyable conversation with him. After leaving the pub we headed to the local high street, and it was there where we were mobbed by fake press, people impersonating reporters and photographers. Throwing my VIP into the doorway of a shop I made sure that my face was the only one visible to be photographed, and after standing my ground and keeping them away from him, they decided they would not get their interview and left.

During the last week we were assessed on everything we had learnt, and the final exercise was designed to mimic a full day of protecting a member of the Royal Family. We had been required to plan and prepare three events for the day, visiting each venue beforehand.

Collection of my VIP was arranged for eight in the morning from Gloucester airport which at the time was nothing more than a single portacabin, and I was all set and ready to go. I had drawn the layouts of all the places we were scheduled to visit, I knew where every CCTV unit was located, where the first aid rooms were, what potential risks we might expect and, of course, where the most suitable escape routes from each were. My VIP was a charming older lady, who in return for a day trip out running errands, was more than happy to lend her time to the police.

Our first visit of the day was to a garden centre in Ironbridge, Shropshire, which specialised in cultivating bespoke roses. She perused them for a while as I paced beside her. She purchased several plants of different varieties which I loaded into the back of our Mercedes Vito, and we continued with the day.

The second venue was a restaurant for lunch, and the third and final venue of the day was a large manor house in Herefordshire. Throughout the day instructors popped up at various intervals along the way, posing as autograph hunters or members of the press, and it was important that I considered everybody we encountered as a possible threat.

We were reaching the end of the day, and I was confident that up to that point I had done a good job. As the fifteen-foot gates to the impressive sandstone manor house opened, I was expecting an ambush in the form of someone with a gun or an explosive device being activated during the final minutes as we drove up the quarter-mile gravel path to our final destination.

Once we had parked up, I escorted her up the steps to the house, and when we reached the front door a member of the instructing team was waiting. He shook my hand and told me it was over; I didn't need to expect anything further.

I was relieved and contented with my achievement, and we spent the remainder of the afternoon enjoying a barbeque in the grounds of the house.

The following week I received my feedback for the course, in which my instructors referred to my outstanding level of dedication to the programme. They had observed that I had not once tried to take a backseat during any of the exercises and said I had shone through as a distinguished and reliable leader. I had excelled.

Before too long I was issued my first close protection gig, as one of four officers shepherding Prince Edward around on a day trip. I was sent to pick him up from a small airfield where he arrived by helicopter, and after visiting a local charity of which he was a patron, we took him out for lunch.

The next part of the day was to chaperone him to a matinee performance of a Greek tragedy, and we had agreed between us which officers would go in to watch the performance with him, and which two would patrol the inner perimeter of the premises. I fell into the latter category, thankfully, as it appeared that for the entirety of the performance, which had a total running time of three hours, the actors were completely nude. Every now and again I caught a glimpse of them running off and on the stage as we waited. Once the show was over, we returned him back to the airfield, and I was pleased to have successfully conducted my first assignment.

My second assignment was to protect the then Prime Minister, as he attended a party conference, and after receiving the initial brief, it took a few minutes for the magnitude of the task to sink in.

But then it was just a task, one for which I had to be hyper-alert.

Being a CPO was a far more cerebral, cognitive activity, than it was a physical one. Few were picked for the role as it required so much more than simply to be a good shot; it was a thinking man's job. If I thought of every possibility, crossed every box, then nothing was a surprise, and I could be confident that it would all go to plan.

Upon meeting the PM my first impression was that he was an odd character, and I watched him eat a least half a dozen bananas during the first few hours of the morning. He was scheduled to deliver a keynote speech at the event and ahead of that appearance he expressed he wanted to get some fresh air, so we set off in the car and found a large green space on the outskirts of the city. It wasn't particularly tranquil, as when we arrived, we were met with some young lads doing donuts in the car park. But it was a large enough area that we didn't need to be too near anybody else, and it had various points of easy access entry and exit. After a short walk we got back in the car and set in the direction of the conference venue.

The roads were busier than expected and we found ourselves sitting for a while in traffic, which was less than ideal whilst protecting a VIP. We were suspended on an elevated road heading towards the city, with no viable escape route should something happen. To make matters worse and to my disbelief, after a few minutes of sitting in the car the PM opened his door, exited the vehicle, and began jogging down the side of the road, wearing formal shoes and a suit, shadow boxing as he did. Quite an interesting sight for those who were also sitting in the same queue of traffic as us. As his principal protection officer, I had no choice but to get out and follow him, repeatedly insisting politely that he returned to the vehicle, which after a few minutes he fortunately did.

Like never before, I felt in the peak of my career. It was such a great privilege to be charged with the safety and well-being of members of the Royal Family and nominated members of the government, and I was readily prepared to put my body in the way and to die protecting someone else from harm. At the time I considered that in that eventuality, I would have at least had an honourable death.

We were issued body armour, which was designed to be worn under my shirt to be unseen. It was made of Kevlar, a material like carbon fibre, and I was told it was both knife and bullet proof. It was undoubtedly up to the job but was hardly covert. I looked lumpy, as though I was wearing body armour. The whole purpose of the job was to be as invisible as possible, so weighing up my judgement on the seesaw of risk I decided I wouldn't wear it. If I had stood out as someone's defence that could have made me a target myself, thus compromising my ability to fully protect my VIP.

My most noteworthy protection job was when I was asked to look after Prince Charles, the now King of England, as he attended the opening of a revamped nineteenth-century monastery. The day was marked with an event led by an environmental charity, who were promoting a new scheme to encourage waste reduction and reduce energy costs. The focus on sustainability meant that the agenda for the day included a farmer's market to showcase locally produced goods, as well as a fashion show that was to exhibit clothing made from recycled waste.

There was not much polarisation of opinion when it came to the Royal Family, so I was confident that the threat level was low, but still went above and beyond in my due diligence. To prepare for the event I had attended the venue earlier in the day, ahead of Prince

Charles's arrival. Walking the floor numerous times, I identified all the entrances and exits, established where his car would park, and the route we would take to get him from the car and into the building. My role was the listed venue officer, the CPO who would receive him when he arrived. The driver was to remain in the car and there was another armed officer to be under my instruction at the venue, who would arrive with His Royal Highness. I was so proud to be doing the job that I had prepared to the extent that I could have easily walked around the place blindfolded. I knew all the escape routes and each little quirky room that you might expect a two-hundred-year-old monastery to have.

Comfortable in the fact I had done as much research and preparation as possible, I managed to keep on top of any nerves that threatened to surface.

Once inside the monastery I stood next to Prince Charles as he sat to watch the fashion show, which was awful. Environmentalism is something that has become increasingly important to me in more recent years, but I can only be frank and say that it was nothing more than a bunch of college students, wearing bin bags, recycled tin foil and bottle tops. I am not professing that I knew much about fashion then, or indeed now, but everyone who took to the catwalk looked as though they were modelling fat loss sauna suits. It was the worst thing I had been required to sit through, allowing for the fact I did not draw the short straw for the Greek tragedy.

After the parade of boil-in-the-bag sixth-formers was over, we began to walk around the farmer's market. It meant that we would be in the thick of the other attendees and the photographers, but I was confident still that there was very little threat.

The vendors had been briefed beforehand, so much that what they would say was practically scripted. They had each been instructed to pick one of their products to show Prince Charles as he perused and were told to discuss with him its sustainability credentials. We visited a stall that was selling soap, and another that was selling a variety of goods which were all produced from hemp. Then we arrived at a stall which was displaying rather delectable looking, wax-sealed cheeses. The vendor at the cheese stall was in possession of knives so I had spoken to him that morning, specifically about how he should offer Prince Charles a sample of his cheese, so I was fully prepared for what was to happen.

'Would you like a sample of some of cheese your Highness?' the vendor asked. Prince Charles gladly accepted and placed in his mouth a slither of the cheese that had been offered to him on the knife.

Prince Charles responded to say it was delicious, and to ask, *'So, which cheese is that?'*

It was at that point I noticed the label on the cheese was facing the vendor; not me, not the press, and not Prince Charles. The fella knew exactly what he was doing, and his timing was impeccable. Prince Charles had eaten the cheese, and the cameras were snapping away. It was a photographer's dream. As though in slow motion, he turned turn the cheese around, and I read the label.

'That one you are eating there your Royal Highness, is… Bob's Knob Cheese.'

It was at that point I swiftly intervened, and ushered Prince Charles away to the next stall. The cheese vendor had unknowingly just made his way to the top of my shit list.

My role as a firearms trainer and special ops officer continued, interspersed with various close protection jobs, and then when London was awarded the chance to host the 2012 Olympics, a special armed response unit was formed specifically for the occasion. I received notice that I had been selected to work on the team for the event. There were upwards of five hundred armed responders scheduled to work the Olympics across the various venues, all highly skilled and incredibly competent. In smaller cohorts of around fifty we were brought together for a period of familiarisation, which was necessary to refine some specific skills and get used to working as part of a completely new team. There was often variation in ways of working from region to region, so it was important to create commonality in tactics and the language used around them.

Again, I was incredibly glad of any opportunity to get away from home for several weeks, as was required of me to train, and if I had thought that my career couldn't have possibly gotten any more exciting, I was wrong. The training very quickly became the most action-packed thing I had ever done.

We practised abseiling down the side of buildings, timed runs from our base to various locations across the city, and fast roping from a helicopter onto a boat which was moving down the River Thames. Training alongside the SAS I was living out my boyhood dreams, and the hole of regret that had been left by my not joining the military was completely diminished.

After the initial training period we were all allocated specific roles and responsibilities for the event. My role was centred largely around the football, and I was assigned a dignitary to look after which was Lord Sebastian Coe. Usually, he wouldn't have attracted armed protection but, as head of the Olympic movement for the duration of the event he had been given protected status.

He was different to anybody I had protected previously in that there were no airs and graces about him, and it was refreshing for me to work alongside a more 'regular' person.

When entering the football stadium on the day of the first fixture, there was the choice to take Lord Coe in through the service entrance, or through the internal press media suite. The latter option was far more secure, which we discussed the day before. After having given him a detailed brief of our planned movements I politely confirmed that he was happy with them, to which he laughed. He explained that he was not Elton John and therefore there was no need to deny anybody access to him, and that he would prefer to spend time talking with people who were attending opposed to being ushered in secretly. As much as I didn't want to, I had to go along with what he had requested.

We arrived outside the stadium and as soon as the car came to a halt he jumped straight out and began meeting the hordes who were gathered there.

There were thousands of people, each of which posed a potential threat, and only him and I ploughing through them all.

To walk the four hundred yards required to get from point A to point B it took us forty minutes. Lord Coe enjoyed himself and no doubt for some Olympics enthusiasts, meeting him would have created a lasting memory. For me however, after weeks spent becoming increasingly hypervigilant, it was forty minutes of overwhelming anxiety.

Whilst not watching my dignitary I was part of the team tasked with looking after a football stadium, training ground, and two nearby hotels where the Olympic football teams were due to stay. For the entire month leading up to the games, I spent ten or more hours a day walking my venues and mapping them out. I needed to know and understand everything about the layout, so I walked them backwards, and I walked them in the dark.

It was much easier to consider any potential dangers that could occur in the training ground as it was mostly open air. The hotel seemed straightforward too as the teams were going to fully occupy a couple of floors, so would be contained to quite a limited area. Hotels also have their own procedures in place for evacuation, which we didn't need to deviate from so there wasn't much additional planning required in that respect. The football stadium, however, felt as though it posed a real issue.

Not only was it colossal in size, but it was an old structure, with dozens and dozens of corridors and stairwells; not to mention one hundred entrance and exit points.

There were several officers on my team who, unsurprisingly, didn't take the role or the potential of threat as seriously as I did, which was incredibly frustrating and led me to dismiss them very early on as reliable allies. Whilst the football matches were in play I walked the stadium, four or five times, checking the entrances and exits for the sight of anything suspicious. My colleagues were mostly sitting watching the games and taking full advantage of the hospitality that had been made available to us.

43

It is crucial to understand that the standards you choose to overlook, are, in essence, the standards you endorse. And this concept transcends any single role, within any organisation; it applies universally, in all settings. If you observe something that doesn't align with your values, and choose to remain passive, then a precedent is set for what is acceptable. Rallying others to embrace higher standards was and still is, my Achilles heel.

Frequently I encountered resistance, from managers and team members, when my commitment to excellence seemed at odds with complacency. Lowering my own expectations or settling for less than optimum effort was not a notion I could entertain.

Consistently, I proved my commitment to doing the job to the best of my ability in the hopes of setting a good example, and in doing so forced some others to catch up to speed.

One incident on an exposed outdoor range, in bitterly cold and wet weather, we were executing a manoeuvre known as 'pepper potting'. Agility and strategic movement were vital as we traversed terrain in pursuit of our live target.

The conditions were both physically and mentally gruelling, and the instructor was a former army officer, relentless in his expectations. After pushing through my run, I was catching my breath when one of my teammates dropped out of the exercise.

Whether his reason was injury or just lack of will, someone had to make up his slack.

Despite my fatigue, I stepped up, motivated only by a sense of team commitment.

Carrying the extra load and supporting my teammate impacted my own performance, which left me feeling frustrated not only with myself but also towards my comrade, for not holding up the line.

Unexpectedly, after that event I got a write-up from the instructor which noted my commitment, professionalism and dedication to my team, and as an experience it taught me valuable lessons about recognising and fostering high standards.

Setting and maintaining these standards is a continuous challenge for the police, as it requires personal adherence, an ability to inspire others to align with them, and of course, the actual want to improve for the better.

The challenge then lies not only in setting high expectations, but navigating the human behaviour that often resists change. Any leader should seek to cultivate an environment where standards are not just spoken about, but actively lived, ensuring an understanding of the commitment that is required to truly excel. Establishing a culture of excellence, where values are at the centre, leaves a legacy of positive change in its wake.

The police need to do better.

44

As hard as I found it to admit to myself, the physical element of my regular firearms training had gotten increasingly demanding. As much as I felt at the height of my shooting abilities, as I got towards my late thirties, I felt my body slowing down.

Our team trained a different tactic each week, and every few months or so we ran a more formal full day of training which was never anything short of brutal.

We began individually in a cell, with concrete walls of seven feet high, but no roof.

The first thing we had to do was scale the walls of the cell and get out. Beyond that was a series of challenges set out in several other rooms, the door to each was always locked so required knocking off its hinges, and if we were lucky there was sometimes a Wham Ram to hand. Once inside the room, an immediate mindset switch was required, to one of stealth, as opposed to the absolute aggression which had been required to get the door down. Everything was carried out in the pitch black whilst we were wearing a gas mask and body armour, so upon entry to each room we used the torch on our weapons to assess whether there were any threats, or victims that needed assistance. After a couple of minutes someone would come along and manhandle us to a different part of the complex, and another room to gain entry to.

The exercise all took place in the wider context of a mock-up village which was staged in a police-owned warehouse. Once we were done with all the rooms, we had to collect a ladder and run up to a 'house' at the end of the 'street.' Then climb up the ladder multiple times, carrying various bits of equipment all increasing in weight, into the top floor of the building. Then back out and down again in decreasing weight order. Once complete, we were then directed out of the warehouse into the fresh air, across to the firearms building and onto the range for a live shoot. We would then trade our dummy weapons for live ones and load them ready to shoot.

By that point we would be pissing with sweat so our visors would be steamed up, and to make visibility even worse someone would throw a smoke cannister or flash grenade into the mix. Once the smoke had cleared and our sense of orientation returned it was time for Five Alive. Five Alive was a game which involved a dozen or so human shaped, paper targets; a black figure on a white background, about three feet in height. Each target would turn around individually and on each black figure there was a tiny number printed in white. If it was the number five, they were innocent. The decisions we made had to be made quickly, and they had to be the right decision every time. Anybody who was too slow to act, missed a shot on an appropriate target, or consistently misfired at a number five, would likely soon after be encouraged off the squad. The demands of my work required both mental resilience and significant physical capabilities, and my body began to protest.

It was all incredibly tough. So tough that the last time I participated I struggled to even get out of the cell at the beginning of the exercise.

Over my eleven years carrying a weapon I had ridden my luck long enough. But more than that, it would have crucified me to have ever been the slowest on the team, holding others up. I have never been comfortable with the notion of finishing in second place or holding anybody back, after all, who wants to be seen as a liability? I had encountered enough of those throughout my career and was adamant that I would not be perceived as one. I had to go out on top.

After painfully deliberating for several months whether I was still young enough to do the job anymore, I expressed to my superiors back on my home turf that beyond the Olympics, I didn't want to go back to firearms. It was the toughest decision I have made, but as hard as it was for me to swallow, after over a decade of truly excelling in a job that I loved, I needed another career, and hoped I could find another way to do some good elsewhere.

After hanging up my gun and giving up my spot as a firearms trainer, I was given the lead on a short project around modernisation of the police force. It focussed on how to get the best from our officers through the appropriate allocation of resource, and the incorporation of modern technologies. My main role was managing ongoing change within the institution, of which I had experienced so much personally up to that point.

When the project was a few months from ending I was struggling to see where I might fit, what role might suit me next. Propelled by the prospect of being sent back to work as a PC on the beat, I applied for the role of Police Crime Trainer, and thankfully was successful.

On the first day of my new job, I turned up still wearing my dark blue firearms polo shirt and cargo trousers and straight away my manager pointed out that I should be wearing a more regular police uniform of white shirt, and black trousers. I didn't give a whisper of a fuck about what he thought I should be wearing. It was a uniform I had worked so hard for and was so proud to wear; I wasn't remotely ready to give it up. Regardless, it hardly mattered what I was wearing as for the first couple of weeks I did nothing other than observe the lead trainer, who was inducting onto the force twenty, fresh-faced and enthusiastic, police constable probationers.

Whilst I had some concerns regarding the pace at which my new job would keep me ticking over, it was clear that the instructors tried to make the training as interesting as classroom learning could be, and immediately they created some tension in the atmosphere to ensure the new recruits sat up straight and understood they were there to learn. During the first session I observed a member of the training faculty burst through the door and engage in quite an aggressive verbal dispute with the trainer leading the session, before storming out and slamming the door behind him. Clearly it was all staged, designed to see who out of the recruits had really been paying attention to what was going on, and not just blinded by an outburst of conflict. Afterwards they were quizzed on the exact words that were said, what colour hair our unexpected visitor had, and whether he had a particular accent or any distinguishing features.

Later that week there was a police dog and handler demonstration scheduled, which was a clear highlight for all in attendance. Most people think of German Shepherds when they consider police dogs but often Springer Spaniels are the best breed for drug detection, and that is what was brought along for session.

'Good morning, everyone. I'm John and this is Molly. Molly is three years old and works alongside me as a drugs detection dog.' Molly sat eagerly at John's feet, eyes wide, her tail twitching rapidly as she struggled to contain her excitement. John continued, *'Molly operates using this ball...'*

Molly was nothing short of manic, and intensely ball motivated. To not keep her waiting too long, the handler threw the ball for her, and she darted after it, retrieving it straight back to him from underneath one of the student's chairs. She then sat waiting for it to be thrown again. After a few queries regarding where Molly lived, and what would happen if she needed the toilet whilst on a job (to which I shared my anecdotal tale of the Malinois that shit in the back of the van), one student asked the more sensible question of *'How do you know when the dog has found drugs?'*.

'She will give me a clear indication by sitting in front of the person or package, and pointing with her nose... If she doesn't think I am paying her enough attention quickly enough she will also bark to make sure I get the message, and then she gets her ball.' The handler said in response, throwing the ball for Molly again.

On her way to retrieve it, she passed several of the seated students along her way, before stopping dead in her tracks. Forgetting her ball completely she sat at the feet of one of the male students and stared up at him. A few moments of silence passed as the recruits looked nervously at one another.

'*Right mate,*' John addressed the individual in question, '*just grab your bag, you will have to come with me now.*'

They stopped bringing the dogs into training after that, I only assume to avoid any tricky situations politically. If the student had been carrying drugs, the instance would have had to have been reported, and it wouldn't have looked good for a police recruit in the final stage of the process to have been dismissed in relation to drugs. Nor would it have been in the favour of the institution to have kept making similar discoveries as they needed the resource.

Molly's actions were a clear indicator that the recruit in question was in possession of or had been in recent contact with drugs. He returned to training later that day which meant that either he got a measly slap on the wrist, or the drugs detection dog was mistaken. I know which of the two likelihoods my money is on.

With all the action behind me I struggled to adjust, but after several months I had my feet firmly under the table. Eventually, after a few more reminders, I did put my firearms uniform behind me and realised it didn't matter what I was wearing. My attire was irrelevant. It was my attitude and experience that allowed me to bring the value into my work and I was satisfied with the impact I was having, even if it was just from behind a desk.

Working in crime training was my first real glimpse of 'normality,' in terms of the type of job I was doing and the hours I kept. Even though I was still firmly planted within the institution of the police, it was a different pace, with different people who had different values. One of the most unusual characters I met was Charles. A fellow instructor and an incredibly interesting, if not complex, individual. He resembled a dishevelled Albert Einstein, with wild, white hair and a large moustache. He could read any book and retain its entire contents in his mind and was a walking encyclopaedia of the law, often citing cases or acts of parliament, even in passing conversation. If I ever needed to know anything, Charles was the man I would seek out.

As wonderfully brainy as he was, like everyone, he did have some limitations. Primarily the fact that he had not actively policed in the public domain for at least fifteen years, so although he knew the law inside and out, he was out of touch in terms of its practical application. He was also not always the cleanest of individuals, and often wore ill-fitting uniform. One day his trousers would be two inches too short, then the next they would be six inches too long. Eventually I worked out it was because they were never even his trousers. Whenever he needed a clean pair, he would just take whatever was available in the lost property box, or what had been left in someone else's locker. Then at the end of his shift he would dump them in the internal laundry. He never wore a belt but instead tied a length of rope around his waist, then covered it with an oversized police issue jumper.

He would often share with us details of what he had been cooking at home, which involved throwing ingredients into a dodgy old Russian crock-pot and waiting for it to be ready. Amusingly the theme soon emerged that everything he cooked took exactly one hour.

During conversation he would often chirp up with, '*Ah yes! That reminds me of...*' then begin a conversation about something completely detached from the original discussion. During training he would wander off mentally into a completely different space and bombard the students with anecdotes, so much that I questioned how much of the set curriculum he ended up imparting on them. Nevertheless, the students always seemed to really enjoy their time with him. Whenever I approached him to seek his counsel he would always say, '*Go ahead, my friend!*' – a testament to his good nature.

The only thing I didn't appreciate about Charles were his eating habits.

They were so bad that people often left the room when he ate.

And whilst at work he only ate one of two things for lunch: soup or fish. Our office was right above the kitchen, and it was only a minute or so after hearing the microwave going that we would begin to smell the kippers or mackerel that he was warming through. Whenever he ate soup, chunks of vegetables would get embedded in his large Dick Strawbridge moustache, and it was a stomach-churning sight.

The single most disgusting thing I ever saw him do was produce a black dog waste bag, roll the top over, and without the aid of cutlery, put his face in the bag and lap up his porridge for breakfast. I put my own breakfast down on the table as I gawped in disbelief, *'Charles!'* I addressed him in dismay, *'What the hell are you doing?!'*

'Well, my friend, I am just having some porridge, which I made at home.' Was his response, as though it were the most normal thing in the entire world. I suspect if I had pressed him on it, he would have told me that it took exactly one hour to cook in his crock-pot.

'Yes, okay,' I dismissed, *'but why are you eating it out of a bag???'*

'Well, how else would I transport it?' he replied innocently.

'A Tupperware? A bowl?'

'No, no. This is the easiest way,' he assured me, *'if I eat it like this then there are no bowls or spoons to wash!'*

He ate his breakfast like that on most mornings.

His peculiarities were rife, and I got the distinct sense that management felt he had served his purpose. They were undoubtedly trying to get rid of him but as with any institution, it was a little more complex than just giving him his marching orders. He was approaching his late fifties and had thirty-three years' service under his belt so could have retired at any point on a full pension but showed absolutely no signs of wanting to go anytime soon.

Many people, perhaps understandably, didn't like to engage him very much in conversation, but I did. He was unconventional, but nice enough and I was glad to have him around as a friend.

'How do you get into work, Charles?' I enquired one morning across my desk.

'Ah, my friend, I get the train.'

'That's handy,' I replied politely. *'I expect it is quite a busy service?'*

'Yes, usually. I always get a seat to myself though!' he spoke enthusiastically.

'Why's that then, Charles? Is it because of the porridge?' I laughed.

'No, no. I never eat my porridge on the train,' he explained, *'I always keep that in my bag... this bag.'* And with a large grin on his face, he pulled out a plastic bag which said on it in large print, 'HOSPITAL PSYCHIATRIC UNIT.'

It was what people were issued with for their personal possessions when they were discharged from the local psychiatric ward. Charles sat with it on his knee every morning on his commute to work, and because he resembled someone who could have the propensity to be a little mentally unstable, nobody bothered to sit near him. No doubt it was an accidental turn of fortune the first time it happened, but beyond that he knew exactly what he was doing, and it was genius.

The police aren't allowed to have a union but there is instead the Police Federation, and as my new role gave me some additional capacity, I decided I wanted to become a representative. It was just something else to fill my time with; an excuse to stay longer at work. Needless to say, I was struggling to adjust to the additional time spent at home because of the more regular office hours.

Previously I had seen how useful the federation had been supporting colleagues who had shot and killed people in the line of duty, and the level of support they offered when an officer was facing a disciplinary. But they also worked to assist the people who were issuing the discipline. It is incredibly difficult to get sacked from the police and bad eggs often stayed around longer than they should, so I was keen to see if I could make a difference and assist in ridding the system of those who had no place there.

After a short campaign, I was voted in and after attending a few meetings, regrettably it seemed to be nothing more than a Boys' Club. There wasn't a single female representative, and it was clear that there was a Masonic connection. I felt uncomfortable, but once I had signed up, I had committed myself to a few years in the position.

The Annual General Meeting came around about six months into my time as a representative. The president held the rank of inspector, but his only responsibility was the running of the federation. During the AGM, it was down to all representatives to cast a vote on what we thought his salary should be.

It came to the point of the meeting where his salary review was scheduled and he stood up and addressed the room, *'Right, I will leave now whilst you have a discussion amongst yourselves.'*

Waiting until his footsteps could no longer be heard in the corridor one of the more seasoned members of the federation looked around the room, *'Can someone just check he hasn't done it again please?'*

And with that, someone else stood up and went over to his desk, where he had left his phone to record our conversation. It was from that point I decided I couldn't do it. Even though I was committed to a three-year position, it was a voluntary one, so whilst it didn't go down well, I resigned the day after the meeting.

It was completely bent, and incredibly disheartening to learn that some of the members were there only to protect their own interests, not primarily to serve and look after the officers that needed them. But I don't suppose I should have been surprised.

Of course, the police are drowning in issues of corruption and misconduct, but during all my time on the force I had hardly been exposed to any of those things. Nine out of every ten I worked with good people who were trying their hardest to do the right thing.

Unsurprisingly, I was ultimately unfulfilled in my role in crime training, and frustration and disillusion crept in. My mindset was still an active one and I felt as though I was not achieving anything, therefore my sense of personal value was low. It was moderately satisfying to see the impact I was having on the new recruits, as they frantically scribbled away as I spoke and listened attentively as I relayed some of my own experiences on the job, but in comparison to the technicolour spectrum of everything I had done previously, it was completely beige.

Crime training was the same to normal policing as the airport gig was to firearms, and I found most of my new colleagues were nothing more than pen-pushers. There was no collective aim or drive to instigate change. The staff there viewed their jobs simply as a place to hide, away from the streets and the potential of meeting an angry man. They were happy to just wear the uniform and stay out of the way; a comfortable place to sit under the radar until their pensions kicked in.

The contrast for me was stark, as I had worked for so long next to people who would never have compromised on doing the right thing. People who would have done literally anything, including step into the line of fire, to alter a shitty status quo. The people who held the top positions especially didn't appear to be in them for the right reasons and I couldn't identify anybody in management who had done anything I considered to be a proper role in the police. I found myself questioning what possible right they had to lead me, and almost began to deny them permission to do so.

My rank was still that of a police constable and I began to investigate what other opportunities may be available to me, to progress to something more significant.

There were so many essential qualities lacking amongst those in positions of leadership in the back-office departments. Qualities such as courage, transparency, authenticity, and trustworthiness; all of which I recognised within myself. So, when in the new year of 2014 I was one of a handful of applicants nationwide who was accepted on an accelerated promotion programme, I was confident of my chances.

Whilst it wouldn't guarantee me the position, successful completion of the programme would have afforded me the ability to apply for an inspector's role when one next became available. It had the potential to be quite demoralising, and I had seen people be put through the sergeant's exam in the past, only to have to wait until someone either left or died to be able to apply for the position. Not to mention that the system had a way of giving the roles to people who couldn't think on their feet; the sorts of senior officers who come onto our televisions in the time of a crisis and deliver an incredibly wooden speech, when the public need and want something more from their police.

There seemed to be two distinct camps when it came to policing: those who understand the theory and concept, and those who could actually do the job. Problematically, most of the senior positions were people who fell into the first of those two categories. People simply were not being led, and I wanted a shot at stepping up to take the lead. Becoming an inspector would have given me a large geographical area of responsibility to set the strategy for, and authority over dozens of officers. I wanted to steer away from weak-willed leadership, and direct people in the way that would have been more productive and beneficial.

The programme didn't mean I stepped away from my role as a trainer, just that I had extra duties. I attended strategy meetings, carried out project work, was given management responsibilities for people who were ranked above me and for parts, it felt I played the role of the superintendent's bag man. There was no transparency whatsoever in the process and it seemed as though I was just issued unspecified qualifying tasks, to see if I would fuck up or if I could bear the weight that being inspector would carry. The only thing that was certain is that it would culminate in an individual review and a set of qualifying exams. In my mind it was the final push at being able to achieve something great, so I went at it with complete dedication.

During the time I was on the programme, British police fostered a relationship with the Qatari Ministry of the Interior, who had already visited the training school. It was an affiliation designed to assist with Qatar's bid to host the FIFA 2022 World Cup. To win could have given Qatar some much-needed positive standing on the international stage, and securing the contract meant good money for the British police; around five million pounds. As a nation, we have some of the world's most successful football clubs, but we also have a reputation for football hooliganism, which made us the ideal partner for their training.

For them to win the bid they would need to be able to operationally plan for large-scale events and demonstrate knowledge of how to handle riot situations and general crowd control measures.

My superintendent at the time was female, and my chief inspector a homosexual male. Neither of which, due to the beliefs of the Qataris, would have been considered as holding the same position of authority as our UK policing system did. It was a tricky situation to politically navigate, but when it was asked that someone from our force would go out to Qatar for five weeks to deliver some training, they were both already out of the running.

It was a Friday when an email came round the department.

Does anybody want to go to Qatar for between five and six weeks to deliver training to the Ministry of the Interior? This will be to start next Sunday. Apologies for the short notice. Expressions of interest by 5pm today.

Immediately I responded. It was an opportunity I couldn't afford to turn down as it aligned so perfectly with my desire to progress to inspector. And the other obvious benefit was a prolonged break away from home. My relationships in-house were solid, and I had been in the welcome delegation for the Qataris visit to the UK. It seemed I was a safe bet, a no brainer, and I like to think a trusted pair of hands. Later that same day I received a response, asking for details of my passport to arrange a visa. The following day after arrangements were firmed up, I dropped the bombshell at home.

'I have to go away for work in a few days,' I explained, *'to Qatar, for five weeks.'*

My fortieth birthday was imminent. It was to fall on the Thursday, and I was going to fly on the Friday.

'What are you on about?!' Jane blew up. *'I have a surprise party planned for your birthday on Saturday night!!!'*

I told her I wouldn't be there and that she would have to have it without me, before heading off to find my suitcase. Instead of celebrating that I had been given an amazing opportunity, her concerns were that her party-planning efforts were to be ignored or wasted. I had no idea a party had been planned, but what Jane was most definitely aware of was that I hated surprise parties, or anything remotely similar in nature. By the time my fortieth birthday was approaching we had been married for almost fifteen years, during which I had always expressed my reluctance to ever be the centre of attention. She knew I would not have appreciated the party one bit, so I concluded it was not designed really to be about me, it was completely for her. And no doubt I would have been left to clear up the mess after it was all over.

We didn't discuss my trip or her party again and after some false pleasantries in front of the children, a few days later I took a taxi to the airport.

She did indeed decide to carry on and have the party in my absence. Good for her, but on the day of the event she video called me so I could explain how to work the gas BBQ. It was at that point I realised if I had been at home I would have ended up doing the catering, for a party that I certainly never wanted.

45

In my work I always found it difficult to remain in restrictive environments for too long. Fortunately, I had experienced so much flexibility throughout my police career which allowed me to explore diverse avenues and spaces that sparked my interest, where I found I could contribute meaningfully.

New challenges were precisely what I needed to thrive, and such opportunities are rare in many professions, so I am exceedingly thankful to have experienced such variety.

It was a pivotal moment, when I recognised that I had hit my ceiling in firearms and was on the brink of decline, and it led me to seek a new direction.

I resented having to leave the team as the excitement of being a firearms officer is something that I could never replace or replicate. If I was younger, I would return to that lifestyle in a heartbeat, with the wonderful added benefit of hindsight.

In challenging moments, sometimes the only way to navigate through a tough situation is by harnessing the power of positive thinking. It's essential to take our present circumstances at face value and actively seek out the silver linings, as they often exist, even in adversity.

If you want to go somewhere or do something, progress forwards, you cannot do it by standing still, and so the inevitable change of life should be embraced.

It is that sort of advice I would have liked to have received at any point, in relation to my marriage. I also wish someone had reminded me to stay true to myself, no matter the circumstances, and not to let anyone, (Jane), extinguish my flame. The truth is, I had become someone I barely recognised. I complied and remained silent when I should have defended my beliefs and values. The result was a profound loss of my sense of self, a version of me that felt like a distant memory, obscured by layers of compromise and conformity. Choose your company wisely. I found myself shaped by my ex-wife's narrative and ideology, which stripped me of my confidence and led me to internalise a deep-seated self-loathing. It served her purpose for me to adopt a limited, narrow worldview, as this made it easier for me to meet her needs without question. I often reflected contrasting identities: the person I was at work, where I could express my true self, versus the individual I became at home.

46

Despite being given a short brief by my chief inspectors of what to be mindful of whilst working out in the Middle East, I really had no idea what to expect when I headed for Qatar. The budget was not such that I was flown first class, but the aircraft was immaculate. The leather seats were practically armchairs, the movies that were on demand were all recent releases, and the food was basically gourmet.

It was a far cry from grabbing a kebab whilst on the night shift.

Upon arrival there was a driver awaiting with my name on a board, and after a short drive, we reached my hotel. The flight had arrived quite late in the evening and as it was dark, I couldn't see much of my surroundings on the journey over, or indeed from the floor-to-ceiling glass windows in my substantial corner room. But when I woke early the following morning, the sun was already blazing, and from my window I could see the ocean. The change of scenery was a breath of fresh air, and I couldn't have been more grateful to have been away.

There were other representatives from the UK who formed the training faculty, and when I went down for breakfast on the first morning I was shown to a table where the rest of them were already seated. Having arrived in Qatar a couple of days before me, they were already an established group and as I sat down at the table and introduced myself, I felt uneasy, but soon enough felt able to relax. They were all incredibly welcoming and interested to learn about my background. I was at least fifteen years younger than most of them and the only current serving police officer. The rest were a mixture of former servicemen and consultant trainers, all hired by the same company and supplied to the Qatari government.

After breakfast we paired off, to begin preparation for the week ahead. My delivery partner for the duration was called Chris, a former chief superintendent and divisional commander for the London Metropolitan Police. We shared a bit of personal history with each other and to my relief we very quickly established a good rapport. He had been out there a couple of times already over the six months previous, so was able to give me some advice on what to expect. He explained that most of the attendees were relatively senior in terms of their position within the MOI, and that in additional to their policing roles they also doubled up as the country's fire department. During training he said that they seemed collectively to have quite a short attention span, so engagement at times was tough. He also suspected that as many of the delegates came from phenomenal family wealth, it was their financial status that seemed to have created a muffling effect on anything said by anybody not perceived to be of the same social position.

Due to the staggering heat, we began work early at six in the morning.

I will never forget the first time I walked into the room at the training facility, where thirty men sat regimented: completely still, straight-backed and facing directly ahead. Due to their identical uniform and the fact that they all appeared to be around six feet tall with dark hair, dark eyes and either a moustache or a beard, at first glance it would have been hard to distinguish between any of them.

We conducted a few short exercises designed to break the ice and familiarise ourselves with them. Chris delivered the first session of the day whilst I sat and observed, and from there on in, we alternated with delivery of the sessions.

There was not a single English speaker in the room so for the full duration everything had to be communicated through a translator, which from a training perspective was quite a unique experience. It meant everything was fragmented, but I soon got used to it. We took regular breaks throughout the morning and finished at twelve noon. By the end of the first day, I was content that it got off to a good start, although all I had been given was a crappy laptop, and instructions to deliver the material was on it, all of which was also pretty crappy. It felt as though it had not been designed by anybody with any training experience, but rather copied and pasted from a manual.

After having a bite to eat I returned to my hotel room and began to review the material for the following day, before rewriting the whole thing to better suit our delegates. Given what I had learnt about their culture, and Chris's advice about short attention spans, I considered that they would benefit from a more practical learning style, testing techniques rather than hearing about them. And as the days went on, the odd individual began to ask as I was explaining something, *'Mr Robert, can we try it?'* So, we did, and every day after the session, heading back to my room and rewriting the following session became the norm.

I am grateful for my entire policing career and none least the transformative experience I had in Qatar. Being immersed in a completely new culture, away from my usual environment, sparked innovation and creativity. Armed with nothing but a folder of papers I realised I had the opportunity to shape something meaningful.

As the weeks rattled on my confidence grew, and I felt comfortable enough with my group that I thought it might be worthwhile to offer some gentle challenge around gender diversity within their police force. There were some female officers within the MOI, but they were viewed as wholly inferior to the men and given no great responsibilities at all.

To mark the end of their training, each cohort was split into two groups, and to demonstrate their learning they were asked to plan and execute a real-life operation. They were tasked with designing the basis for their operation and delivering a presentation to their trainers on what they would be doing. We were assessing how they planned for an event, what contingencies they would consider, how they planned to communicate with each other during the event itself and what strategy they had for dealing with any arrests. One of our groups had outlined their plan to tackle pickpockets in one of the more tourist-centric souks. During their presentation they produced a map of the souk, showing all the entrances and exits, and disclosed some intelligence they had which was a good indicator of what times of the day they could expect that an offence was more likely to be committed. Once the operation had been carried out, one of the officers approached me ahead of our next session together.

'Mr Robert!' he exclaimed gleefully, with a beaming smile from ear to ear. *'I did it!'*

The interpreter soon stepped in to further facilitate the conversation. *'He says that he involved a female police officer in his operation.'*

'Brilliant!' I responded, before probing a little more into my new friend's attempt at inclusivity. *'And what role did you give her?'*

The interpreter relayed my student's response: *'He put her on car park duty.'*

Whilst I wasn't sure what form of car park duty was really warranted on their operation, I was pleased my efforts had gone some way to making a difference, even if just a drop in the ocean.

'And why did you see fit to give her that particular task?'

His smile widened after he finished sharing his reasoning with the interpreter, who then communicated the message to me. *'Because she was the best man for the job!'*

It was a small but well-meaning step in the right direction and rightly so, he was pleased with himself for getting his female colleague involved. Since we have now arrived in the future, I understand that, regrettably, not much has changed with regards to equality in Qatar, but at the time I hoped that beyond our departure there would at least be increased female involvement in real policing work.

On our final weekend there, we were taken out to the desert to camp overnight. Chris was completely comfortable with it, but I had some reservations as had been warned before leaving the UK that I should be wary of such invitations. It was not lost on me that we were prize assets should we be taken hostage, but despite my scepticism we left in a convoy of jeeps straight from work on the final Thursday.

My feelings of unease were not helped when we negated any sort of formal passport checkpoint and crossed the border into Saudi Arabia. Not long after I clapped eyes on the pre-established camp, and as we hopped down from the vehicles and were greeted by several of the officers from our cohort, I was able to put my anxieties behind me.

Facilitated by a couple of interpreters we sat around for hours into the evening, sharing a large array of food which had been prepared by the wives of some of the men. Lamb, which had been cooked traditionally underground, and then dozens of bowls full of fresh salad, fruit, couscous and flatbreads, amongst other things.

It was a true Arabian feast and the most delicious meal I have ever had.

It had gotten dark very quickly after our arrival, but we sat out in the warm air until very late at night. In the middle of the desert all around was pitch black, until I looked up and saw tens of thousands of stars. I almost pinched myself to see if I was dreaming as had never seen a sky like it before.

The day before our scheduled departure there was an awards ceremony for those who had passed the course. Everybody was scored objectively, and some did fail. Logically, that is the correct way to run a training course, but not what I was used to back home.

The ceremony was held in a staggeringly large room, where the rows of immaculately presented and near-identical officers were seated. The other trainers and I, along with senior members of the MOI were up on a stage in front of them, all behind a long table, seated in grand marble and leather thrones. It was surreal.

Each participant's name was called in turn, and they joined us on the stage and made their way along the line, shaking each of our hands. A scripture was then passed along the table for us all to sign, before being handed over to the delegate in a rather decadent presentation box. I had no idea what I was signing as it was all written completely in Arabic, but I was still glad to play my part.

At some point over the course of my time in Qatar, it had come out in discussion amongst myself and the rest of the training faculty that I only held the rank of police constable. They were all surprised as had all themselves held very senior positions, and Chris remarked how he assumed I must have been an inspector. Not only because of my obvious capabilities and expertise, but because that would have been an acceptable rank in the eyes of the Qataris. I can only assume they considered me acceptable without such a status due to my backstory, and therefore breadth of knowledge and experience. On the day of our departure, I shared with Chris that I was on the accelerated promotion programme. He gladly agreed to provide some written feedback to my chief superintendent, which I hoped would further my chances of successful completion.

Unsurprisingly, there was no welcome for me at the airport and I returned home alone on the train to arrive at an empty house. At the time I appreciated the peace, quiet, and time to settle in and unpack, but looking back, it makes me a little sad. Whatever engagements Jane had with the children, she could have surely altered them for such an occasion as my returning home, so I could have been greeted by my children after so long apart. Naïvely I had expected that the time away and space would have created a better atmosphere between my wife and me. It never had before, but I was always hopeful it would hit the reset button and improve our situation. Unfortunately, everything went straight back to how it had been before. Anywhere there was the possibility to misconstrue communication, or create tension or difficultly, the opportunity was taken, by both of us. She was still dismissive of me, and rude, and I was more than happy to continue being insolent and awkward in response. Whilst I had missed my children terribly, within twenty-four hours of being home I wished that I could go back. I had been so relaxed and happy in my surroundings in Qatar, that without consciously trying I had stopped biting my nails whilst I was away; a habit which had always bothered me. My hands looked freshly manicured upon my return, but after just a day of being back home I had bitten them all right back down to the skin.

There was no praise issued for all the good work I had done when I returned to work on the Monday, not even a debrief, I was just thrust straight back into mundanity. The five weeks I had been away were some of the best weeks of my life, and it only amplified that everything either side of it was pretty shit.

The institution that is British policing is a highly politicised environment, something which I had not seen a great deal of until I left firearms. It was a game I was not very good at, and for a while, my thoughts had been wandering to what I would do if I left the police. The accelerated promotion was the only thing that would have kept me there, so the eventual output of all my hard work was the proverbial straw that broke the camel's back.

Amongst my peers and superiors, I was well thought of, and I was firmly under the wing of both the chief inspector and chief superintendent, both of whom I assumed regarded me highly. I was operating at the level of inspector, assuming way more responsibility than my rank would usually permit and doing incredibly valuable work.

Chris's feedback had arrived electronically with myself and my chief superintendent before I had crossed the threshold back into the training building after my return, and it was a glowing review of my contribution. He had stated how he and all the other trainers had been incredibly impressed with my dedication to, and delivery of my work, and how as a collective we had proven the UK police force was up to the task and secured the contract to keep the working alliance ongoing.

The feedback had arrived just in time for my appraisal so when I was informed that I had not been successful in obtaining the chance of promotion, I realised that I had been used as nothing more than the acceptable face of British policing.

The comments were that I was not quite what they were looking for at that time, there was room for improvement and maybe in a couple more years.

I left the meeting absolutely seething inside, with a lump in my throat that I couldn't swallow. I read through the appraisal document I had been given and saw that whilst my name was listed on the top, there was another officer's name in the main body of the text. It had been copied and pasted. Without saying a word to anybody I left the building, got in my car and drove straight to the force headquarters, where I had it out with the chief superintendent. She gave me no straight answers, suggesting that it was a tough decision, but that they sometimes had to be made.

Professionally it was a massive blow, but even more so on a personal level.

As far as my superiors were concerned, I didn't even deserve individualised feedback. For the best part of two decades, I had given everything to the job, and at the end of it all I felt as though I had no value whatsoever.

In the eyes of the institution, I really was just a number, despite all the great impact I had made over the years.

With a bitter taste in my mouth, I immediately became resentful towards what I was doing at the training school. The cracks in the system which were always present became even more obvious to me. Many of my colleagues were lazy and borderline incompetent, there were no standards, no degree of accountability, and the organisation and its management were shambolic. Figuratively I downed tools, which was such a stark attitude change within me, having always taken so much pride in my work.

The tides turned and from there on in I just didn't care.

My apathy was further fuelled by the government's announcement regarding a change of conditions to police contracts and as I was approaching my twentieth year on the force, I had missed the cut off by just a couple of months. Instead of being able to retire at fifty-one, the new forecast would have been that I had to wait until sixty to retire. My goal had always been to retire at a reasonably young age and then pursue something else, whereas the new arrangement would have seen me paying more into my pension yet receiving less at the end. It was beyond ridiculous. Not to mention the fact that policing is a young person's game, so it is beyond me as to why any government would encourage loads of doddery old farts to remain in uniform; some of them still on the beat.

My obvious disappointment with the entire situation was barely acknowledged at home, so I made no attempt to broach any conversations about my future. Instead, I wrestled with it all in my head whilst inadvertently becoming a bit of a nuisance at work. I didn't know what to do.

I considered going back to being a detective, which would mean I was still within the police, but away from the training department and all the pencil-necked pricks who worked there. Even if that meant I had to suck it up and accept the insulting changes to my pension. I had maintained some good contacts so decided to query whether my qualification would still be valid and if there was a future for me anywhere as a detective. During the conversation I had asked for complete confidentiality, so naturally, it got back to my inspector straight away and he called me into his office for a chat.

He expressed that if I wanted to leave my job in crime training, he would gladly post me back onto D division, which was the city centre.

My response, I imagine, was quite trite, as I expressed that I had absolutely no desire to go back on the beat in Shitsville, Tennessee, to which he concluded that perhaps then I would be better off not remaining within the organisation at all.

His approach couldn't have been any less supportive, or any more spiteful.

It felt as though he was pushing me to leave, after all my years of dedicated service.

People around me, all of whom were lacking any degree of courage or common sense, were being promoted left, right and centre, all for the wrong reasons. I had given my life to the force, worked so hard throughout my whole career and knew that I was the best at what I did, across all the roles I had performed, and that was simply because I had dedicated so much of myself to them. The lump returned to my throat and as I walked out of the building that day I felt as though I could cry.

It was a feeling that I was quick to stuff away before arriving home.

The conversation with my inspector fell just before Christmas leave, so I spent the whole of the festive period brooding and mulling everything over. I shouldn't have let it, but it ruined the festive period for me, and once the new year came, I decided to eat some humble pie. When I returned to work, I took my head out of my arse and applied myself again to my work, until I could figure out what to do next.

What I did know was that I had come to detest what I was doing and the institution I was within. The only real consideration for me was what I would possibly be suited for outside of the police, where I had been for most of my adult life up to that point. After some light digging on recruitment websites, I happened upon a couple of jobs that seemed suitable, in the private sector. When I was invited for an interview to be a Learning and Development Manager at a national law firm, the engrained urge to do a reccy of the premises got the better of me, so I arrived early and stood across the road for thirty minutes, watching people going in and coming out. It offered a snapshot into who the sorts of people were that worked there, and if I could work there too.

For almost an entire lifetime I had been a police officer. Outside of being a father, it made up my entire identity. The private sector was a round hole, and I was most definitely a square peg, but I needed to get out and I had a chance to do so. It was a Friday morning when I received the call to say I had been successful in obtaining the position.

The police offered a job for life, and even though it felt as though there was a significant amount of risk attached to the move, I was humbled that the hiring firm had shown faith in me, and gratefully I accepted the job.

The following Monday morning I headed straight to the inspector's office to resign.

It was a conversation that I couldn't wait to have and had been looking forward to for the entire weekend. Once he permitted me entry into his office, I said I had been reflecting a great deal on our conversation from before the Christmas leave, '*and well, I have actually come to hand my notice in.*'

He was visibly shocked and was quick to explain that I still had one month to work, as per my notice period.

Cutting him short I explained, '*Actually, I have looked at my remaining annual leave entitlement and taking into account my notice period I think Wednesday will be my last day.*'

Stunned, I left him in his office and returned to my desk to email HR.

The total expression of gratitude for nearly twenty years' service was a balloon, a bottle of wine, a shitty crime novel and a free lunch. I would never have wanted any razzamatazz but would have appreciated an authentic thank you, from someone I liked and respected. As it happened, I looked around and there weren't many of those people about. I was happy to be leaving, but disappointed that my extraordinary career seemed to have ended on somewhat of a sour note.

No doubt I could have handled the situation and my exit differently, but any negative attitude I had over my final few months was one born out of frustration with the system, and self-preservation. I had given all of myself to the police, and I couldn't keep giving with nothing fruitful in return.

47

There were several senior officers I worked under whose positive influence left a lasting impression on me. They inspired trust, loyalty, and I would gladly put myself in the line of fire for them, both then and now. Beyond my firearms team, I didn't encounter many genuine leaders, and as a result, I became difficult to manage. Instead of rising to the occasion, most resorted to power plays, hierarchical dominance, or attempts to undermine colleagues to elevate their own status within the organisation. It is a leader's ability to uplift and empower those around them which sets them apart.

To have been passed over for the promotion left me distressed, but more recently I see it as a blessing in disguise. It is likely that, whilst I would have had an impact, it would not have been on the scale I desired, and I would have become further disheartened and bitter. It didn't matter what rank I held; I was not cut from the same cloth as those at the top of the tree. To 'fit in' meant conforming to a prevailing mindset, and those who didn't were often marginalised, ostracised, or compelled to leave. Such an environment fostered a force that largely resembled itself: homogenous in thought, action, and outlook.

To have been ever further integrated within such an institution would have ruined me.

It was, and still is, a system that tends to favour academic ability. What that means is those people viewed as future leaders are not instinctive or agile enough. Being led by people who are all theory and concept is problematic.

The lack of diversity within the organisation is a critique that can be levied at many institutions, but in addressing recurring problems, varied perspectives and approaches can be invaluable assets. Diversity transcends mere metrics of race or gender, and whilst staggeringly important, those things alone form only a simplistic checklist for the shortsighted. True diversity encompasses a rich tapestry of experiences, backgrounds, and ideas. It is this depth of diversity that can drive meaningful change, enrich discussions, and strengthen an organisation's capacity to tackle the complex challenges it faces.

As my career in the police ended, I identified one of the most significant challenges facing the force was the misallocation of human capital. It was astonishing to me that a considerable number of warranted police officers were relegated to back-office roles that could have been and should have been filled by other personnel. I was one of them, and it raises serious questions about the efficiency of resource allocation.

The work I was doing in crime training was largely theoretical and could have easily been conducted by a civilian member of staff. In my crime training team alone, we had around thirty warranted officers, some holding significant rank and all earning decent salaries. And there were many other teams in the wider training school.

I am not criticising these individuals. Many of them performed well in their roles. However, whilst a small number of warranted officers are advisable for contextualising theoretical knowledge, the reality is that reassigning those officers to front-line duties could have made a substantial difference to my home force.

Visibility and accessibility are paramount in police. They are the principles that form the bedrock of public expectation. Yet today there is a concerning rhetoric of un-investigated crimes, extensive delays for victims, and a concerning lack of focus on local issues.

I recognise that for many officers in training school the thought of returning to the front line could have been daunting; it was for me, but I was not overweight, out of touch and lacking necessary street sense like many of my colleagues. Many of whom indeed would have been more of a liability than an asset. This raises a critical question: if officers cannot perform the core duties for which they were originally employed, duties that are foundational to their purpose, should they remain in the service at all?

Many join the police as it offers 'a job for life', and this is perhaps problematic, as we already know that many are permitted to continue wearing the uniform longer than they rightly should.

48

My official last day fell in the mid-May of 2015. The sun was shining, and many people had taken to the grass and benches in the grounds of the training school. As I sat and had lunch my colleagues around me made small talk, and I watched the comings and goings outside. Sitting down over that final lunch felt strange, like I had spent two decades out in space and had finally returned to earth.

Suddenly, my journey was over.

All of the trauma, the people I had helped imprison, the lives I had touched, the bits of bodies I had collected, and my own personal accomplishments, all came down to a complimentary ham sandwich, a packet of crisps and a can of lemonade.

When I had first been at the training school as a recruit, the canteen offered a tiered system of a full English breakfast. Three different variations, all for a different price, and all of them self-serve. I would never have considered being so dishonest back then, or at any point in my career, but cops being cops, some of them wanted something for nothing, and would try to conceal extra breakfast items under a pile of beans or a slice of toast. At the till they would then declare they had a number two breakfast, when, in fact, they had a number three.

There was one woman who worked in the canteen who I only knew as Till Monster. She was a large and intimidating woman, who from behind the till on her high stool, would peer over her glasses at the plates of food presented to her, before rooting one of her rather large fingers around in people's breakfast to find any hidden bacon or sausages. Rightfully with experience, she had learnt not to trust anybody.

She was one of the first people I had encountered during my first week of training as she poked her grubby fingers, (that had spent the morning handling petty cash), through my breakfast to try and expose me as a thief. It was an attempt that amounted to nothing. She never made any formal reports of dishonesty as I think she was just satisfied with her own informal investigations, and safe in the knowledge that her actions reminded those who needed it that they were not exempt from following the rules, just because they wore the uniform.

As I watched people busying around on that final day, I saw her again; her hands were full of catering equipment when she tripped and fell in the forecourt. The place was teeming with budding new bobbies and trainee detectives, but it felt like a minute passed and still nobody had gone to her, so I rushed out to help. After taking her inside I administered some basic first aid. She was mostly fine, just a few cuts and grazes to her knees and elbows.

To spend my final moments in the police with someone who had been there, unknowingly, from the beginning, seemed liked a fitting end. I never fully understood what had driven me to join the police, but through the course of my time the most satisfaction and enjoyment I got was from helping people. The fact that nobody else rushed to help Till Monster still sticks in my throat, but, selfishly, I am glad. It allowed me one final opportunity to help someone who needed it. To step up and act when nobody else was. I didn't realise until now, but that incident was the full stop at the end of the sentence, and I really needed it.

On the first day of my new job, I was taken to an Italian restaurant in the city centre for lunch; the sort where a portion of pasta is eighteen quid and would barely sustain a small child for half a day, never mind a grown adult.

Both my line manager, Ashley, and one of my own direct reports, Katherine, were impeccably made up, and it was clear that my new workplace was destined to be the complete opposite from the male dominated environment I had left behind. Criminal law was far behind me, and I had swapped it for Pinot Grigio and Prada handbags.

As we were chatting away at a table by the window, I noticed a couple of people I recognised outside. A surveillance operation was in progress and within seconds I spotted the individual who was being followed. After a minute or two of watching the watchers, my attention was brought back to the conversation with my new colleagues.

'*Sorry,*' I apologised for my distraction, '*I just noticed a police surveillance operation happening outside.*'

'*Oh, really?*' Ashley chirped up, crooning her head and neck to see, so indiscreetly it made me cringe. '*It really is going to be so interesting working with you.*'

If only I could have said the same, but it didn't take me too long to conclude that the work I was doing, that they were doing, really didn't matter. No longer a literal case of life or death, it was completely inconsequential.

Being ready to leave the force made the transition much easier for me, but I still found the adjustment to 'normal' civilian challenging. I was wired differently. Being a police officer was not just a job, but my entire identity, and I understood how many ex-service personnel struggle when they are expected to return to society and hold down a more conventional role. After living day in, day out in a war zone, everything outside of what they had previously known must be alien, and completely devoid of any real meaning.

To some extent I did start to enjoy my new role. During my first few months I was tasked with designing a leadership programme from scratch, before being sent to all four corners of the British Isles to deliver it. Everything I had done in the police had to be well within a set of guidelines, and whilst I always added my own flavour it was the first time, aside from what I had done in Qatar, that I had written, designed, and delivered something that was completely my own. Throughout the process I was observed and closely monitored, but at the end of it my manager and those who received the training all seemed to be very pleased. The firm had never had a dedicated Learning and Development team before, or any real strategy, and I was getting good results, so from that point I was given free rein do what I saw fit.

One thing I had hardly considered was how stepping into a much more conventional role would mean I was spending so much more time at home. I thought I may get the odd day away in London, but with carte blanche to do whatever I wanted, I began to create opportunities for myself to be away from home on a regular basis for a couple of nights at a time. For so many years I had benefited from the time alone that shift work offered, and even crime training sometimes warranted evening or weekend work, so it was a real shock to the system when it all stopped. Whilst I had been working shifts, when Jane was at work and the kids at nursery or school, I would go out walking up in the hills, where I was certain not to see another soul the entire time I was out. The wind on my face, just roaming in the solitude was idyllic. Not at the behest of anybody else, or a police radio; my time was my own. It was an opportunity to think, or not to think, whichever I preferred at the time. When I did think, my thoughts often drifted to what it would be like if I left Jane, because for as long as I could remember our relationship had been lacking in any care or kindness, love, affection or open communication.

She never sought to understand me or support me through what anybody could identify was a taxing career, and it must have taken her some real concerted effort to not have shown any interest.

We never had any discussions around the things that mattered, such as household finances, but she always spent beyond our means, and it was always me who went without. To this day I do not even know how she chooses to vote.

I cannot say that I was ever truly happy with her, which of course manifested in my affair with Katie. Not too long after our own wedding we attended another and during the speeches I teared up at the beauty of such love and dedication the two people displayed for one another. Jane griped at me as to why I had not cried at our wedding, and I couldn't give her an answer. I didn't know then, but I do now, and it was because we weren't really ever in love. There was a lack of profound feeling and connection in our relationship, which others are so lucky to share and witnessing it had made me emotional. Perhaps I was grieving something I knew deep down that I didn't have, but that each of us need to thrive; to love and to be loved.

Jane always considered herself to be completely above me and tried at every opportunity to belittle what I was saying or doing. She discouraged me from new opportunities, constantly putting me down, as though any signs of my growth or expansion made her uncomfortable. Latterly it became glaringly obvious that everything in our life was designed to suit her and her needs, and I wanted as much as possible not to be in her company.

Eventually I settled it in my own mind that I wouldn't leave until Mabel had turned eighteen. The societal expectation and familial pressures had convinced me that doing so would mean I would have done the right thing and sacrificed myself to provide a stable home for both my children until they were adults.

Until then, a new life for myself without my wife remained a pipe dream, but one that was never too far away from the forefront of my mind, and I had my sights on the eventual ending.

In the legal industry, partners of law firms are issued an inflated position of hierarchy, which is a long-standing sentiment that I didn't agree with. Such an approach, to be in awe of or fearful of someone of a higher employment status would not have served me well in the police, so whilst others viewed themselves as inferior to people with a perceived position of hierarchy, I certainly did not.

Any time I was sent to one of our other offices to speak to the partners I was always told to be mindful of their position, that they were short on time, or notoriously unpleasant. *'Yes sir, no sir, three bags full sir,'* was the attitude I was expected to adopt, but my own previous experience was far more meaningful and important than anything they were doing, so going to speak to someone about their piddly little problem with their team paled into insignificance.

Doing the job I had for so long altered my perspective so greatly, that my tolerance of people with no perspective was low. On numerous occasions I had delivered the news to people that someone they loved was dead, which meant asking people if they could be better at spreadsheets felt entirely unimportant. Being a police officer had also meant that I treated everybody with the same degree of common decency, whether they were a homeless man on the street, or a rich, elderly, housewife. I didn't need to cower in the presence of anybody, and I think the senior members of the firm appreciated my directness and the fact that I didn't stumble to mince my words. My communication style had been sharp and authoritarian for so long, and I had always been dry and quick-witted, none of which I could shake if I tried.

Time is money, particularly in a law firm where fee earners bill their time literally to the minute, so I didn't bother to waste any with unnecessary pleasantries or arse-kissing, and they were glad of it.

Fractures began to show when I started to naturally question the authority of those who were in immediate control of me. The veneer that Ashley had painted, to try and appear as a collaborative and supportive manager, was incredibly thin. I was obviously better at the job than she had expected or indeed wanted me to be, which saw me gaining increased exposure across the firm. As a result, she began to try and undermine me at every opportunity, which created an air of unease for me.

Given her position within Human Resources, she should have been a massive advocate of the feedback and appraisal system I developed, but when I asked her for some feedback on my own performance she wouldn't partake. Instead, she advised that if there was an issue with my performance, she would feed it back to me directly. That, coupled with the atmosphere she had created and the fact she had been ignoring some of my emails completely, made me uncomfortable. On a returning flight from visiting one of the offices in Glasgow, I was contemplating having a conversation with her, to clear the air. She had made me feel so awful that I assumed she was just waiting for the right moment to sack me. Overthinking every interaction that we had shared over the few months previous, I started to feel as though I was struggling to breathe, I was gasping for air and was chilled to the bone, yet sweating profusely, then I started to feel faint. I had never experienced anything like it before, but I suspect it was the beginning of a panic attack, which I fortunately managed to navigate my way out of before anybody really noticed.

Back in the office the following day I did have a conversation with Ashley, but it hardly seemed to serve any purpose at all, and that was the catalyst for my next job hunt to begin. Within the police I had always subconsciously pushed myself into roles that were high-end, and niche, so I always knew I wouldn't stay with that firm forever. It was low-level, which I needed to begin with as I was starting again. It benefited me to be on the shop floor; to understand my role, the sector and then ultimately, how to stand out.

That firm may not have proven to be the right environment for me, but I will always be grateful for the golden ticket out of policing that it offered. When I had first interviewed, they commented on how much external confidence I had, but inside I was terrified of the unknown, and my own ability to adapt to something completely new. But I did. And in the September of 2017, I moved on again, to greener pastures in the form of an international, magic circle firm.

49

Stepping into a politically charged corporate environment never intimidated me. Considering what I had experienced up to that point, the condescending barrage of pin-striped suits was completely inconsequential. And after all, if someone must resort to shouting to get their point across, their message likely lacks substance.

However, even amidst my direct approach, which has earnt me both praise and critique, I still grappled with my inner critic. Such a relentless inner voice can sometimes become so harsh that it drowns out our self-worth and reinforces our self-limiting beliefs.

By acknowledging our inner critic, we can impose ceilings on our own potential, failing to recognise our unique contributions and the value we bring to the table.

The internal narrative we construct influences our reality, and many of us are guilty of repeating detrimental stories that diminish our self-esteem.

To combat this negative self-talk, we need to become more mindful of the stories we tell ourselves. Recognising that the narrative we internalise profoundly impacts our subconscious is the first step. The next steps are to extend kindness to ourselves, and to forgive our past mistakes, as it is those very mistakes that offer us the teaching moments required to take proactive steps forward.

50

My former office was situated right next to a Korean restaurant, which served incredible food, but caused a constant smell of grease in the air. It was a smell that was only ever masked by cigarette smoke originating from colleagues who stood smoking outside, that either seeped through the single-glazed windows or wafted into the building through the main entrance. The ceiling was fitted out with polystyrene tiles, which were mostly stained, the kitchen was often left in a bit of a mess, and at one point the building had rats.

In comparison, my new workplace was a breath of fresh air, with not a poor amenity in sight. It was a brand-new building situated on the waterfront, seven stories high and had floor-to-ceiling windows on each aspect. My previous office had offered a jar of Nescafe in the kitchen cupboard, and when I was in the police, we had pre-packaged plastic cups of coffee that just required water to be added. My new office had barista standard coffee machines in every kitchen and was a complete world apart to everything I had known before.

Within the first week I was flown to Brussels to observe a training course that was running for thirty international delegates, all senior lawyers in their respective specialist field. My role was only to learn the ropes from my German counterpart, but just two hours into the first day he approached me and said how sorry he was but that he would have to leave as wasn't feeling at all well.

I was going to have to run the remainder of the course alone; two and half more days of it, with people I had never spoken to before.

With that he passed me the material, wished me good luck, and left. Whatever he said was the matter with him, I remember thinking that it was such a poor excuse it wouldn't have even gotten me a day off school had I tried it with my mother. It was daunting, but I extended their morning break by another twenty minutes so I could familiarise myself with the rest of the content for that day, and got stuck in. Really, I didn't mind being thrown in at the deep end. In fact, I think it is my preferred method of learning.

My experience in Qatar had been a real baptism of fire which had given me an inner confidence to be spontaneous and creative in my delivery. If I ever find myself low on self-belief I reflect on that time, and how I was a low-ranking officer in a hostile foreign environment with a definitive language barrier, but how I delivered something I had made up pretty much on the spot, and it landed perfectly.

At the end of my scheduled time in Brussels it appeared that, fortunately, I had again managed to have pulled it out of the bag.

Between the course ending and the taxis arriving to take everybody to the airport, there were a few hours spare. The venue was a restored castle on the outskirts of the city, set in some truly remarkable scenery. Using the free time afforded to me I set about on a walk in the grounds, winding up in a forest. It was early September, so the temperature was still relatively warm, and as I wandered through the damp pines, breathing in their unmistakable smell, the sun glistened on everything it touched. I stopped for several minutes to recalibrate myself. I couldn't believe where I was or what I was doing. It seemed no time at all since I was plugging bullet holes with my fingers, or behind a shield being shot at.

It was as though the sun was shining down on me, illuminating my good fortune to have been afforded such a tremendous opportunity to do something else beyond all the violence. It was job that I enjoyed and felt very comfortable doing, that paid well and promised a myriad of opportunities to take me around the world meeting well-educated and often very polite people. After so long working with the complete opposite extreme of the social spectrum,

I wondered how on earth I had wound up where I was and counted my lucky stars for the chance.

A couple more months went by, and I was relishing the challenge of my new position. Again, I found the assumption was that anybody who wasn't a partner, or fee-earning lawyer was viewed as a second-rate citizen with a second-rate contribution. My manager expressly implied that it was unlikely my suggestions would be taken seriously by senior stakeholders within the firm, and as though someone had thrown a gauntlet down at my feet, I seized the challenge and began to implement and embed some successful ideas in our offices around the globe. My work had again become all-consuming because I had encouraged it to be. When I wasn't at work I was thinking about work, and looking forward to leaving the house again, to go to work. And the fact that my schedule saw me away from home once or twice a month was keeping me mostly satisfied, and any feelings of unfulfillment originating from my home life were at bay, for a while.

It didn't fall within the remit of my normal responsibilities, and I only ever did it the once, but in the February of 2018, I had been asked to help deliver some training sessions on a new starter induction in our office.

When I walked into the room on the Monday morning my eyes were immediately drawn to a young woman sat around one of the tables, on what was the first day of her new job. Her name was Chloe, and her beauty was undisputedly captivating. Dark blonde hair fell softly around her face, and down to the middle of her back. Her petite, athletic figure was perfectly showcased in a high-necked, long-sleeved, blue dress, and throughout the morning, I was conscious that my eyes were being constantly drawn to her. As the session progressed, it wasn't just her appearance that caught my attention, but what she said and indeed how she said it.

She was a facilitator's dream; a vocal participant who was not afraid so share her opinion, and in a room full of corporate hopefuls, her wit and charm stood out. I estimated that she was perhaps twenty years my junior, but every time she spoke, she commanded the room.

She had a depth of knowledge to her that I had not before seen many others emulate and I was completely fascinated by her.

Our office accommodated around eight hundred staff, but it wasn't long after that day our paths crossed again, ever so briefly. There was something about her that made me subconsciously or otherwise look out for her whenever I was moving around the building. She was a wonderfully intriguing character, and I was hopeful to see more of her. It had seemed during our first interaction that there had been a connection between us, and it excited me. I wanted more opportunity to see her and speak to her, to feel and explore what I expected was absolute electricity.

It was rare that I visited the restaurant on the top floor of the building. It felt over-priced and pretentious but of course, it seemed that way to me as I had spent years eating in police stations. But my thoughts were somewhat justified by the fact that it was referred to as a restaurant, when it was just a glorified canteen.

One morning in the early May, uncharacteristically, I decided to pop up before a meeting and pay for someone else to make me a coffee. As I entered through the glass double doors, I saw her stood at the till, waiting to pay for her breakfast. As I placed my order, she glanced sidewards at me and smiled.

In that moment, I felt an overwhelming physical attraction to her and had we been better acquainted I would have liked nothing more than to draw her in for an embrace. She was practically a stranger, yet in her presence I felt an indescribable closeness to her, coupled with a feeling of inner peace.

She was the first one of us to speak. She asked me how I was, and what my day entailed. There was some sort of event ongoing that week which meant I had been asked to offer taster sessions of coaching to anybody who wanted one, as opposed to my normal clientele which would have only ever been lawyers or partners. I explained that as a result my day was mostly filled with coaching.

'*Oh yes!*' she exclaimed. '*I saw something about that and actually tried to book on a session with you, but there was no availability.*'

That was my opportunity.

'I have just had a cancellation for one of the afternoon sessions. If you still wanted to, we could get together later?' It wasn't a lie, just an incredibly fortuitous circumstance.

She smiled, with a glint in her eye. *'That would be wonderful,'* she said, *'I will see you this afternoon.'*

For months I had been craving conversation with her, and a chance meeting had afforded me a full hour with her, just to spend talking.

The time that day couldn't pass by quickly enough, and then eventually our slot arose, and she joined me in one of the smaller meeting rooms on the top floor of the building. Coaching within a corporate environment has the potential to be incredibly rewarding, but from time to time has the potential to be quite dull. Everybody seems to say the same thing, and that is they experience a lack of recognition by management, or they don't see any real route to progression within their career: that sort of thing.

Within minutes of being seated, Chloe displayed no signs of presenting me with the usual problems, but instead dove straight into how she had made a mistake taking her job and would soon be looking to leave. I couldn't help but smile in response to her complete transparency, coupled with her somewhat wily demeanour, as she continued to rant about her complete distaste for the world of corporate law, within the wider setting of a capitalist system that seemed to have no morals.

Amidst the wildly illuminating experience of sitting and conversing with her, I felt a tinge of sadness and concern at the prospect of her leaving the firm so soon into our knowing one another. It was even more disappointing for me to learn that she was married, but not a moment passed before she swiftly caveated that information with the fact that her husband didn't treat her particularly well, that she was ending the relationship and had the wheels in motion to find somewhere else to live.

She was an incredibly headstrong, albeit a touch hectic, young woman. And I could see that the fire within her was not going to be approved of, or contained by the figurative four walls of the firm we were in.

As it became increasingly apparent throughout the conversation that she was uncertain of her future path, in all aspects of her life, I was becoming increasingly certain that wherever that path took her, I wanted to follow.

We agreed we would like to meet again in a few weeks' time, and when I left the interaction, I was a little bit shell-shocked. It appeared that one way or another, we had been fated to meet that morning. There was an undeniable connection between us that I couldn't explain, and I felt it from deep within me. I had to stop and consider if I was being slightly, if not completely delusional. I simply couldn't fathom why on earth such a beautiful and intelligent young woman would be remotely interested in spending her time and energy on me.

From that point on we conversed regularly, and I was overwhelmed by the attention she was giving me. She wanted to see me and talk to me as much as was possible. She wanted to listen to what I had to say and each conversation we had was alive with ideas and topical discussion.

The thought of seeing her spurred me out of bed each morning, and each interaction we shared left me with a feeling of warmth and happiness. It was a wonderful reprieve from all the interactions I had previously known with Jane, and I let myself become completely wrapped up in it.

It was a notably hot summer, and we spent every lunchtime together.

We sat, ate and laughed, and I felt revived. Resurrected almost. When I woke up in the mornings I felt a renewed sense of enthusiasm for life, and I looked forward to the future.

Our forbidden and immoral romance had been so quick to blossom, and my only concern was the age difference between us, but I soon resolved it in my own mind as she seemed far older than her age. Her general demeanour, coupled with her unrivalled self-belief and confidence elevated her in terms of her level of maturity, which meant our actual ages quickly became immaterial. In her presence I was completely relaxed and content in a way I never had been before.

After spending time with Chloe and being on a high, whenever I returned home, I felt the monumental lows that were always present for me in that environment. Only they had become significantly amplified. Without her companionship I was nothing short of depressed.

A couple more weeks went by, and I told her I loved her. It came so naturally, whereas I had always been criticised for never making romantic declarations to Jane, and simply saying, *'You too,'* in response when she said she loved me.

Chloe told me that loved me too, although she needn't have said the words as I felt it. I had allowed myself to be open and receptive to her love, which meant being vulnerable; something I hadn't been in so long. She had unknowingly encouraged me to remove some of the layers I had wrapped myself in for protection, and in doing so I had let go of what I thought love was and re-established my expectations of how people in love should treat one another. Everything that had been missing for me before, connection, trust, communication, and support, had somehow all fallen into my lap, in a wonderful golden bundle. I felt different to how I had felt for decades; I felt safe and self-assured.

Chloe herself was completely unwavering in her self-belief, and had a connection to the world around her, spiritually, in a way that I had never understood before. Being around her forced me look at things differently and gave me all the energy and confidence that I had previously lacked. We talked about what the future might look like if we were together and then reality set in. A change of course was what I needed more than anything, and I needed to act.

My marriage was dead in the water, it had been for well over a decade.

For so long I had felt trapped, by a sense of moral obligation that I had created for myself around the children, and looking back, every time I moved job roles, I think it was just to serve as a distraction from how deeply unhappy I was. It was as though I was wearing soiled underwear but kept trying to change only the trousers on top, in the hopes it would remedy the issue, but it never did. It was something else that needed to change. For years I had wanted to leave, but I had been lacking backbone and was without any plan. I had been standing on the edge, waiting, ready to jump, but it was the prospect of a future with Chloe that finally pushed me.

51

All the significant shifts in my life have stemmed from taking risk. Joining the police was a risk; stepping into firearms was a risk; leaving the police and forfeiting my pension was a risk; and leaving my marriage of nearly two decades to start anew was a risk.

In each instance I faced the choice to either stay in familiar but stagnant circumstances, or venture forward into the unknown.

Opting to remain would always have been the easier choice, but it would never have propelled me into new growth. To flourish, we must view challenge as fertile ground for our development. Without moving forward, we inevitably stagnate.

Just Fucking Do It. Embrace change, even if it means navigating difficult paths or starting anew at any point in your life. Resist the urge to conform; do not yield to societal pressures that compel you to fit in or go along with ideas you don't believe in, simply to avoid conflict.

Don't shy away from being the one who chooses a different path when everyone else is following the crowd. No one who achieved anything remarkable ever conformed to societal expectations. We need mavericks, those willing to shine brightly against the dull backdrop of complacency. It's never too late to start again. Don't dwell in regret or wish for what might have been. Be true to yourself; let your authenticity be the light that guides you forward.

52

As a society, we have been conditioned to believe that a relationship which lasts forever is a key variable of success. But the length of a relationship is not an indicator of how healthy it is, and many dysfunctional relationships last decades simply because both parties learn to accept it for what it is.

For me, true success in a relationship has everything to do with how psychologically safe each party feels, how free they are to be themselves and how much they evolve, both together and separately.

Far from a success, my relationship with Jane was my biggest failure.

Only now do I realise that from the very start, deep down I knew it wasn't right for me to be married to her. Perhaps I just considered her a safe bet, a guarantee of a steady relationship, which was a supposed marker of success. Or more likely that I was railroaded into a situation by a woman a few years older than me, who had more experience of long-term relationships and a clear desire to settle down and get married. I was never strong enough to express when I didn't want to do something, and just like that I found myself on the hamster wheel of life.

But I cannot possibly say now that I regret the decision to get married, or even that I regret the decision to remain in the marriage longer than I know I should have. Because the output of my doing so are Alice and Mabel, both of whom I love dearly and couldn't possibly imagine my life without.

The decision to finally leave Jane was an incredibly easy one to make, and it was only the thought of not seeing my daughters every day that added a layer of difficulty and complication for me. My relationship with them was the only real consideration in it all, but I couldn't sacrifice myself any longer. For almost twenty years I had failed to listen to my inner voice which had been informing me I was unhappy, and that I longed to feel wanted, valued, and loved in an equal relationship. I had been underappreciated at home, taken for granted and used for nothing more than a monthly income and domestic duties, receiving nothing in return that went any way to fulfilling my emotional needs. I had to take the risk, because the future possibilities with Chloe promised something far better.

She was my second chance at true happiness, something that not everyone gets, and even those that do get such a shot don't always take it.

For once I had to be selfish and ensure my own happiness.

We do not get the opportunity to live our lives again, but after meeting Chloe, mine had been completely transformed.

My senses had come to life, as though for the first time I was no longer seeing in black and white but in complete technicolour.

Just for a moment I considered reducing it to nothing more than a brief fling and putting an end to it, to continue with my marriage, but that would have been the single most stupid thing I could ever have done.

It was as though Jane constantly sought to put a wet towel on me, to dampen me down, and discourage me from being myself. I never truly lived within the confines of my life with her, I had merely existed. My real life was whilst I was at work.

At work I had purpose, meaning and respect. I was an active leader, in control and it felt good. At home was the exact opposite. I was disengaged, mentally absent and in constant conflict with myself, which made me angry and ultimately passive in everything I did in the confines of that situation.

Being in that relationship had felt like I was contained within a box, with no light or air. Occasionally, in the form of a new job role, new acquaintance or hopes for a new hobby, it would be as though someone had prodded a hole in the top of my container, allowing a thin shaft of bright light in. But Jane was quick to block out the light by figuratively taping over the hole. In those moments of lights, I became more lucid and aware that I didn't want to play a part in the facade anymore. But the moments were fleeting, and my ability to get out had been compromised by the erosion of my foundations. I had lost sight of who I was, and what I wanted, and so I was trafficked into mediocrity because of my inability to stand against a what felt like a riptide of pressure.

Chloe and I had discussed when might be an appropriate time for me to draw a close to that chapter of my life, and I settled in my own mind I should wait until after Christmas, to allow everyone to enjoy the festivities without any distress or upset. But waiting to leave became tedious, and even more I withdrew from Jane. She sensed something was amiss and suggested we sought some relationship counselling, which I flatly refused.

For years I had made a monumental mental effort, to always reset and start again; never being truly honest with myself. I forced myself to look beyond any issues that were present and tried to just be content with my lot. Throughout all those years, to improve our relationship dynamic, she tried the square root of absolutely nothing. In the end there was nothing worth preserving. All that was left behind the painfully thin veneer of posed photos for social media, were short discussions about the children, and pitifully average sexual exchanges. It was simply too late.

Chloe and I were sat one lunchtime in a café above a bookshop, one of our more regular haunts, when I received a text message from Jane.

'We need to talk when you get home.'

As certain I was that I couldn't be remotely arsed with whatever issue she had that day, I took it as my opportunity and told Chloe that I would be putting an end to my marriage that day. I couldn't wait any longer. I couldn't even wait for the working day to be over so whilst Chloe returned to the office, I headed to the station. Getting back earlier meant that I could begin the discussion before Mabel returned from school and Alice from college. Jane was working from home and was surprised to see me when I appeared hours ahead of schedule but was quick to progress her insignificant and snippy agenda.

'I think the real problem here, and what we should be discussing, is our marriage.' I informed her, with more gumption than I had ever brought to a conversation between the two of us.

The school run came around quicker than I would have liked, but we agreed to continue our discussion later, away from the children. After dinner we left Mabel in the care of her sister and set out on a brief stroll.

'I'm sorry, I just don't love you.' I told her.

'How long have you felt like that?' Her reaction was not one of visible surprise.

'A long time...'

'Since the affair?'

'Yes.' Although I knew deep down it was likely before then, if I had ever really loved her at all.

She didn't seem overly distraught and was a little teary at best. Many years before that conversation I had moved on from the relationship in my own mind, whereas she was only just learning of its demise. But such is life. Nobody died and nobody went to prison, which is the threshold I generally apply to gauge the severity of a situation.

Whilst I felt a huge amount of guilt for my wrongdoings, there seemed little point in beating myself up over them. With little else to discuss, our twenty-two-year relationship ended, and I was finally liberated.

Despite the disdain I felt towards her, I did pity Jane for the fact that I was guaranteed a better life after our separation, whilst she would likely live in limbo for a while.

The bubble that was her life popped, and the outward appearance of perfection she had created for herself was soon to alter. The bubble that was my life, on the other hand, was inflating. It had been a difficult message to deliver, but the conversation left me feeling energised and ready to move on to a better future. In that moment I caught a glimpse of the light at the end of the tunnel, the path out of the maze.

There were several practical things to discuss, and without any deliberation I agreed to step away and sign my share of the house to her, which I would have done twice over just to get away.

The rhetoric around the separation was as you would expect. I was painted as a selfish, egotistical man, who had fallen trap to a fling with a younger woman at work; what a cliché. But I hardly cared what my ex-wife or her friends thought.

Within a couple more months I had explained to my children that I didn't love their mother anymore, packed my things and moved out of the family home. And, after a short but wonderfully intense courtship, Chloe and I moved in together.

It was November and the nights were dark and cold, so we spent most of our time hunkered down in the warmth of our new home. It was modest two-up, two-down terraced cottage, with an enclosed back yard and minimal chance of getting a parking space on the street outside, but we couldn't have been happier; apart from my missing the children, which made the first few months painful at times.

I suspected it was worse for me than it was for them, and any discomfort I felt was quickly dispelled by being in my new sanctuary, with a woman I loved and who truly loved me. It was a sacrifice that I had no real choice but to make, and I hoped that one day they would see that I couldn't have forgone my chance at happiness, and in time come to understand and forgive me of my actions.

Alice was of an age where she had her own social agenda, but I was granted access to Mabel every Saturday and one night in the week. We made the best of it, but it was hard. Leaving her was always gut-wrenching, but in the same breath I was glad every time I dropped her off, to drive away from the oppressive place I had once called home.

The first twelve months with Chloe were nothing short of amazing.

Our bond was irrefutably strong, and there was no question of our future together.

It was a real eye-opener for me, to be out in the world, really living my life instead of just existing. We went to Paris, and I watched on as my beautiful girlfriend gleefully flitted round a flea market and acquired an assortment of oddities. I suggested she may not have room to take them home as we only had hand luggage, but I watched as she very smugly managed to pack them all perfectly into her very small rucksack. She had a beautiful way of just getting stuff done. It was an incredible power of hers and enamouring to me. Every moment I was with her, I was completely lost within it.

Like myself, Chloe didn't have a large family, but it really was a case of quality over quantity. She introduced me to her grandmother, who was completely accepting of me right from the beginning despite the obvious age gap between Chloe and myself. At ninety years old she still displayed an astounding amount of fire and wit, and I was humbled and honoured to get to spend time with her in what turned out to be the last few years of her life. She was a warm and loving woman who delighted in the simple things: a cup of tea and a slice of cake, or half a bitter shandy and a cigarette. In the absence of spending any significant amount of time with my own grandmother throughout my early adulthood until her passing, I was grateful to be able to link her arm and escort her around the supermarket or hold her hand from the car to the pub. It was clear to see where Chloe got so many of her best attributes from. It was a privilege to watch them together as the best of friends, and to be invited into the fold of an incredibly precious relationship.

The house we first shared together was great. Chloe had poured her heart and soul into making it a wonderful home for us and a safe retreat for me during the initial upheaval of the separation, but it was always going to be temporary.

We wanted something a little more rural that had an extra bedroom, so that I could accommodate Mabel overnight when her mother finally allowed, and so that Chloe and I could have a baby of our own. Whether I would consider becoming a father again was one of the first things she had asked, before we pursued our relationship more seriously, and it didn't take a moment for me to confirm that I would gladly father a child with her. I had enjoyed being a dad so much to Alice and Mabel that it was a very easy commitment to make.

After another house move, I was finally able to settle into fatherhood in a completely different context than the one I had previously known; in the comfort of my own home, without any sort of agenda being pushed onto me by my vacuous ex-wife.

We had been put into the first lockdown of 2020, when the Covid-19 pandemic began, and from the top of the stairs in our new home Chloe called down to me to tell me that we had successfully conceived our first child.

Our dream of having a baby together had come true and we were blessed with an incredibly special, headstrong and charismatic baby girl, Rose.

Like a duck to water, Chloe settled into her role as a mother and life was more wonderful than I could ever have imagined it being.

Chloe had ripped the figurative lid off the box I had been living in, filling it full of her glorious golden light. The only thing I had not stopped to consider for even one minute was what could be lurking within, ready to be illuminated.

53

Jane and I never had a big bust up row and maybe it would have been better if we had. The alternative was that consistently over a long period of time, she chipped away at me, like the sea eroding a cliff, until eventually the big immovable object fell. I didn't realise the ramifications of that until it was too late.

Aside from the children, I do not know of one other meaningful thing we shared, and of course, I accept my share of responsibility for the collapse of the relationship, but really my only error was staying in it far longer than I should. For years I had imagined freedom, and my brief affair with Katie had showed me a glimpse of light, but then I found my way back down to the bottom of the well. I was unable to see a way out, until someone chucked me a rope and used all their strength to pull me out of my hole.

One of the reasons I had mentally checked out of my marriage so early on was because everything was always about materialistic upgrade, and that just wasn't me. Jane wanted a big house full of things, for the status that came along with it – just so she could say, 'Look what I have got.'

When I first told Jane that I was moving on with someone else, she screamed at me, *'she only wants you for your money!'* – which was laughable. In fact, Chloe and I did laugh about it, because I didn't have any money.

But as far as Jane was concerned, everything was geared towards my retirement. So much so, that I wouldn't be surprised if she sought a police officer husband for that reason alone.

She held onto me like a premium bond, and when we did ultimately divorce, she was disappointed to learn the real value of my pension.

54

Whilst writing this book I was asked to consider what scares me, which was a very easy question to answer. Moths. I simply detest them. Put me on the front line against violent offenders and I will have no problem tackling the problem at hand but shut me in a room with a moth and I will undoubtedly be reduced to a panicked wreck. The reason as to why I loathe them entirely is unknown to me, but I am largely perturbed by their little grubby bodies, which unusually turn to dust. And all the erratic flitting around they do. Due to the unpredictability of a moth, they are largely uncontrollable, which brings me to the only other thing I am afraid of, and that is lack of control.

Early into the year of 2021 I was tired and feeling quite a bit of pressure from work. I had probably sensed that stress was brewing beneath the surface, but for one reason or another I failed or refused to acknowledge it. That was my first mistake.

It was nearing eleven in the evening and Rose had been crying for almost thirty minutes, resisting our attempts to settle her back to sleep. Chloe was exhausted, and I was too. She passed the baton of responsibility to me and left the bedroom to go to the bathroom, and as the relentless noise continued, all I knew was that I had to make it stop.

I don't know exactly what happened and have absolutely no memory of the events of the evening, so it is only through Chloe's account that I am able to share the events of that night. Ultimately, I lost control. As she re-entered the bedroom, Chloe saw me shaking Rose's crib violently and, to stop me posing a threat to our daughter, she was quick to shout and rush towards me. She had approached me from behind and when she got within touching distance, I launched myself at her in a rage.

I was shouting at her, but nothing I was saying was making any sense, as though I was trying to communicate but it was nothing other than strained noise.

She fell to the floor screaming as I stood over her. And then everything went quiet.

My senses started to return. My heart felt as though it was beating out of my chest, and I noticed how cold I was, but that I was sweating.

I looked down to see my partner cowering in fear.

Noting the pause in my outburst she took her opportunity to rush and scoop Rose out of her crib, who amidst the noise had stopped her crusade of wailing.

'*What's happened? Are you okay?*' I asked, trying to put my hand on her shoulder.

'*Get away from me!*' she screamed, backing herself further and further away from me into the corner of the room, cradling our subdued child. '*What have you done?! What is the matter with you?!*'

She demanded answers from me that I couldn't give. And she had to explain the events of the previous few minutes to me, maintaining that if she hadn't appeared at the exact moment she did and diverted my attention, that I would have caused serious harm to our baby girl. I didn't know what to think and I didn't want to believe what I was hearing as it made me feel sick. She ordered me out of the bedroom and once I was on the other side she blocked the door with a wing-backed armchair.

Neither of us slept a wink all night. Chloe out of fear. Me out of shock.

I didn't know what had happened to me and I was terrified. I needed comfort and the only person who could offer me any solace at all had locked herself away from me.

It appeared that the loosening of my shackles had unforeseen consequences, and my newfound freedom of thought had unlocked parts of my brain that I had both purposely and unknowingly kept hidden. It was as though all the emotions and memories associated with the trauma I had witnessed were in a dark room, behind a door. The safety of my new relationship meant I subconsciously let go of the handle, and when I did a flood of dirty water hit my otherwise clean floor.

It was not something I had expected or was remotely ready for.

The following morning, I didn't know what to do with myself. Chloe was emotionally cold, and I was not allowed to handle my daughter. It hurt, but as much as I didn't understand what was happening, I understood her response to it. I had an acquaintance who was a clinical psychologist, and Chloe suggested I place a call to her in the first instance to explain what had happened. It was a good start as I knew I could air it with her without any fear of judgement and when we spoke later that day, she said it was likely I was suffering with post-traumatic stress disorder, and that the episode had been induced by a situation of extreme stress.

Babies' cries have evolved to be stressful for the caregiver, to elicit a response, and being a parent impacts the nervous system, meaning that our fight-or-flight is more easily activated. The stress in my body caused by my daughter's cries had pushed my body into a heightened fight-or-flight response, and my threat perception had gone into overdrive. It was a skill that had served me so well previously when my responsibilities involved trying to protect myself and people around me, but on that night, it had dominated to a point where I was out of control. My other senses had become submerged as my brain interpreted my daughter's defiance as a significant threat. It was as though a dark blanket had been thrown over my head, and I was left to navigate the world only on instinct and muscle memory. My personality had developed in such a way that whenever stress arose, in whatever form, I sought to eliminate that stress by exerting control. In the face of a distraught baby, there was no easy way for me to do that.

For weeks after the incident, I felt, and indeed looked, dreadful. Tensions at home were high and whilst my doting partner did her best to support me, her efforts were overlapped by her obvious fear. It was as though she expected me to blow up or break down at any moment, and I was completely struck off all baby-related duties and not left for a minute unsupervised with Rose. Chloe accused me of brushing the incident off, and tried as much as she could to encourage me to talk about it, and engage in activities that may improve my general well-being.

A lifetime of habit is hard to break, and I admit I was brushing it off as though everything was okay, and supporting my view, after a few months things seemed to have returned to normal. I chopped it down to a one-off event, keen to dispel any notion that I was in anyway 'broken' or 'unwell', and gradually, I was permitted to fulfil more parental responsibilities and for a couple more months, life carried on.

We moved Rose to her own room, where she often still fought Chloe at bedtime. Generally speaking, she was more pliable for me than she was her mother and after feeling as though I had let them both down so terribly, I wanted to prove myself to Chloe as a good father and not just some useless, old, maniac. I wanted to show how much I loved my family. One evening, after I had been allowed the responsibility of bedtime, just as I was struggling to gain co-operation from Rose and settle her off to sleep, Chloe appeared at the bedroom door.

The strength of her mother's instinct was remarkable.

I was more aware on that occasion that something was happening and can only liken it to receiving an injection at the dentist and feeling the cold rush of anaesthetic, but I felt it throughout my entire body. Aggressively I lunged towards Chloe, screaming *'NO!'* as I did, but fortunately that was the end of it.

My senses began to shut down, and I blacked out, collapsing on my daughter's bedroom floor.

The only assumption I could draw was that I was going mad. My actions were so alarming, and not least to Chloe, who had been on the receiving end of both outbursts. I too was terrified of what was happening to me physiologically speaking, but my greatest fear amongst it all was that Chloe would leave me, as much as she promised that she only wanted to love and support me.

The morning after my second episode she ordered me to the local Accident and Emergency department, to ensure there was nothing else causing my behaviour. Then to begin the process of tackling whatever the problem was.

Unprotestingly I went, even though I barely had the energy to turn the key in the ignition. But there was no other choice. To secure my future I needed help, and it wasn't forthcoming, I had to go after it myself.

At the hospital I went through to motions of explaining to several different members of staff why I was there, before receiving an MRI scan. When that showed nothing untoward, I was sent for a consultation with a psychiatrist. Once satisfied that I was not at imminent risk of suicide, she recommended a programme of over-the-phone counselling.

The subsequent few days the entire household was wildly sick due to a bug that had returned from the hospital with me. In a fashion very typical for her, Chloe brought an air of light to the situation, and she laughed at how we were fully purged of everything from inside our bodies, and how it could be a part of my healing process. I knew that with her support I could push through whatever was happening to me and come out the other side.

With regards to the therapy, I was wildly sceptical. Whilst I had never been referred to counselling previously, I am certain that if I ever had, I would never have fully engaged with it. That would have been most definitely due to the stigma attached, and because committing to such a process would have meant acknowledging a weakness within me that I could never have shown in my previous life.

I would have just played the game until it was over, but I knew in my new life I couldn't afford to gamble. I needed to be completely committed and confront the issue, and I was willing to do whatever it took to rid myself of the toxicity that had been poisoning me from within.

Over time, I had accumulated layers upon layers of trauma that needed to be stripped away and released, and I didn't realise how rotten I had felt, for so long, until it started to drip away.

The first session was mostly an introduction of who I was, what had happened, and the obvious mention of my previous occupation. I didn't have the energy to be anything other than completely honest and open, and to my surprise even after just one conversation, I felt the release of weight off my shoulders and out of my mind. The counsellor scored me against a list of markers, and I received a formal diagnosis of PTSD and generalised anxiety disorder, with a further reflection that it was likely I had also suffered with depression intermittently for many years.

It was the most talking I had ever done about how I felt, and about my work.

Despite all the hours we spent together as a firearms team, we never discussed how we might have felt. We were still very much the era of policing who denied and quashed our vulnerabilities. That inability to express my emotions at work also carried over to my home life, as I had never been able to discuss anything there either. Jane never sought to provide me with any emotional support, throughout my entire career, or even acknowledge that my job had the potential to be quite distressing, even after Alex's death. It would not take a genius to conclude that being a police officer could mean having a difficult day at work: telling someone their loved one has died or seeing a mangled body in the wreck of a car, and I don't remember her ever asking once if I was okay. No doubt I would have felt sad, angry and afraid, but I could never have allowed myself to display or acknowledge it.

Due to the absolute lack of support, and constant dismissal within my marriage it had been easier for me to simply retreat into my own silence. And at the time I assumed that to have allowed any intrusive thoughts, or to even stop to examine my own feelings would have impacted my ability to operate effectively as an officer.

It is only now I recognise that I denied myself the necessary time and space to pay attention to, and process emotions which were attached to events. My work was necessary, and I am proud of all of it, but it was difficult, and I had never recognised how affected I had been by it.

People don't ring the police for a chat and most of what I attended was critical.

For someone somewhere, it was their lowest moment.

The new start I had been so lucky to find with Chloe had meant I had allowed myself to experience positive thoughts and feelings, which had opened the door for negative thoughts and feelings to come through too; ones I would have previously repressed. Being in the light after so long in the dark and becoming so rapidly aware of my situation was confusing and I couldn't avoid confronting my past. The exposing of my wounds left the skin underneath raw, and it triggered a process of remembering who I was, and then trying to piece together the last twenty years of my life to understand where that person had gone.

It made me angry and resentful. What had happened to me?

I realised I had wasted my entire life, or at least all the good years, with someone who had no respect for me and nothing but their own interests at heart. My journey was like one of a chunk of limestone, was shaped over the years by my environmental conditions. When I was younger, I was a bit directionless, but ambitious, driven and most importantly, happy. That solid foundation of myself was slowly compromised; so slowly that I didn't notice as the core of who I was washed away. I was left on a flimsy base in need of repair, and I hated Jane for the part that she played, but I hated myself just as much. She had stolen my sense of self. But I had allowed her to. I had lost complete sight of who I was and went along with the joke that was my marriage to her. Laughing along, not realising that the joke was on me.

The need to always be prepared drove an element of perfectionism within me, and it was that perfectionism which Jane had seen and chosen to exploit for her own gain.

Throughout our marriage, she had always implied that things were never quite good enough; what I was providing was never good enough. I had become conditioned to constantly try and deliver, and to subsequently feel inadequate when inevitably I fell short. It was as though everything had to be perfect, and that any mild imperfection in our life was my fault. She made me feel unworthy, and never showed me any real love that would prove otherwise.

I had a further eleven counselling sessions, during which we never spoke about specific events, but instead about my attitudes to risk and threat, potential triggers for my anxiety or another PTSD episode, whether those triggers were real or hypothetical, how to see them coming and how I could manage my reaction to them.

During my second episode it was again the stress caused by my unco-operative daughter that had set the ball rolling, and then it had been Chloe's appearance as a dark figure in a doorway that had cemented it in my brain that I was under threat. I had shouted, 'No!' and fallen in the direction of the door, and that was because I saw Chloe as someone who posed a threat to Rose.

Prior to my therapy I had considered PTSD as being caused by one single traumatic event, and then later triggered by innocuous things such as a certain smell or sound. Instead, what I learnt was that PTSD has the potential to be caused by a series of lesser events. The incident of Alex's death and lack of support we received at the time obviously played a large part in my diagnosis. But aside from that, my PTSD was an accumulation of everything I had been first-hand witness too, which for me was hundreds of unpleasant incidents, all of which had gone completely unprocessed at the time.

My episodes were triggered by feeling out of control, which my brain had come to interpret as meaning I was under significant threat. The areas I had policed were urban, and some of them local to me, which meant that I could be there in uniform one day, then there on my day off the next. But I could never switch off my awareness to the danger and criminality that lurked around every corner. In that respect it made it easier for me to just be on guard the whole time. For so long I had been living in a state of heightened awareness, and I had come to believe that my existence and safety were reliant on such an attitude.

Life is unpredictable, yet I had spent so long trying to control and predict everything in my environment that it was a shock when that changed. I still saw threat and danger everywhere, but was no longer a man with a gun in a position of authority and it made me feel vulnerable.

As I paid more attention to my emotions, they came more readily to the surface, which was no doubt beneficial but not always pleasant.

A notable and overwhelming spike in anxiety came one sunny afternoon, as Chloe and I walked a disused train line with the dog. It was a path that was surrounded by rolling green hills and woodland, but was just a stone's throw away from one of the larger housing estates in the area. It was a picturesque and safe enough setting for children to play and explore, but the sight of two girls of around nine years old, wandering through the long grass, both wearing football tops, took me straight back to the Soham murders of 2002. My heart began racing and I started to sweat profusely as I remembered how two young and innocent girls had been enticed off the streets and murdered by their school caretaker. It was hard to rationalise the feeling that they were in immediate danger. All I wanted to do was escort them back home, and tears filled my eyes as Chloe gently coaxed me away from the spot where I had become rooted. The duty of care I felt so strongly as a police officer was still completely present, and likely always will be.

My therapist encouraged me to journal. Particularly when a problematic thought entered my mind, and then the task was to assess whether it was real or hypothetical. If it was real, what was the anticipated outcome versus the actual eventual outcome?

It soon became apparent that the things which caused me the highest level of worry and concern, that drove me to want to act to control a situation, were approximately ninety-five per cent hypothetical. And it didn't take much to understand the reason why. Whilst on the job I was always preparing for and expecting the worst, and never knowing when I might have to drop everything and go is the reason why I still eat my meals so quickly to this day. I always had to be ready for anything and consider all the potential outcomes of any given situation, many of which were unpleasant.

It exhausted me yet stole my ability to rest without constant hypervigilance.

There were some members of my team who couldn't even read a map, whereas because such a great majority of our serious firearms calls came from the same area, I had taken the time to memorise the map, and all the street names so I could better navigate. It just felt so compellingly important to me to be all over the detail.

If an urgent call came in to get to 45 Smith Street as shots had been fired, and our task was to get from A to B as quickly as possible, (with the potential for a rendezvous point first with another team but avoiding the scene on the way to the rendezvous), it was life or death to get it right.

My therapist also advised that I take care to monitor what I consume in the media and be more mindful of what I watch on the television. I had never really considered it before, but my exposure to extreme trauma had left me mostly desensitised to the sort of stuff that causes other people shock or sadness, but I came away from one session and remembered how I had once been reduced to tears watching the film American Sniper. There is a scene in the film where one of the characters is given a military burial, with a flag draped over the coffin, and that is what we did for Alex. It absolutely floored me, but I left the room where Jane stayed to continue watching, made myself a cup of tea in the kitchen and composed myself. It was as though nothing had happened, and I pushed the emotions back down again.

Nowadays, whenever Alex comes into my mind, I try as much as possible to think about the fun we shared together. The laughs we had as we stood shoulder to shoulder for so many years, doing incredibly dangerous things. He was a remarkable officer and friend.

To our delight, in the October of 2021 Chloe and I found out we were expecting another baby, and in the November of the same year we got married.

Having both been married before and being very similar in our nature, we agreed that neither of us wanted to have a typical wedding, but that our wedding day would be just the two of us and Rose. We arrived at the venue, a remote house on the Western coast of Scotland. The morning of our wedding day we took a leisurely walk down to the nearby beach before returning to get ready separately for the ceremony. We said our vows in a candlelit barn, in the presence of our daughter and our witness (the bagpiper), before returning to the warmth of the house to enjoy a three-course meal, just the three of us.

Nothing was overly scripted or planned, we were just in our own space with nobody else around to bother us. It was a blissfully peaceful experience, one that not many get on their wedding day. I couldn't have been happier to commit the rest of my life to my biggest cheerleader, a wonderfully beautiful, and fearlessly loyal woman, who had been nothing short of my saviour.

After the extreme lows of the two years prior, the new year of 2022 brought about a new sense of self for me. There were moments where I could almost feel the shedding of a layer, leaving behind parts of me that no longer served my highest good. I felt sheer relief. Like removing a layer of clothing when you get too hot and feeling much-needed air on your skin.

That July, during a heatwave, our second child arrived. A boy.

Chloe's unwavering faith in me meant that the following year I quit my job, and to my surprise, the transition from the world of secure, full-time employment to a self-employed consultancy role, was seamless, and changed my entire life.

It was something I always knew was an option for me, promising reduced working hours and a higher level of income, but I had never bothered to mention such a prospect to Jane. Whilst she enjoyed spending the money I earnt; she never encouraged me to progress. Quite the opposite in fact; she had done her best to confine me to a version of myself that she was comfortable with; one that would not outgrow the mediocre life she had carefully curated for us.

I was concerned whether I had the skill and image to truly succeed as an independent entity in the work of big business, but Chloe helped me to see that there were no limits to the level of contribution I could make, and that what I had to offer was of real value. As much as I could, I had suppressed twenty years of experience, but therapy taught me the importance of embracing the past to be able to fully live in the present. I learnt that I had to stop denying myself access to things that are useful. My experience is a tool, which I eventually felt comfortable tapping into.

Gradually, I developed some of the self-confidence that I had lost and put more faith in myself and my abilities to succeed. My view now is that a positive mindset goes a long way; reaching places that other things, such as skill, do not always reach. If we harness our self-belief, we are truly capable of anything.

My definition of success has also altered in more recent years.

Previously, it would have hinged on external validation, but now I understand that success for me centres more around personal satisfaction and being fully present in whatever I am doing. Whether that is in my work, or as a husband and father.

Before, I never took the time to stop and sit on the floor and play with my children and that was mostly because I felt uncomfortable and oppressed at home, so would busy myself with other things that would serve as a distraction in my day. And I feel guilty about that, because I should have been more self-aware and honest with myself about what I needed in my relationship, and ultimately stronger. I wish I had been strong enough to have left sooner and set up my own home, where undoubtedly, I would have had plenty more opportunity to spend quality time with Alice and Mabel as they were growing up. I love both my older girls dearly, and I hope they can forgive me for my mistakes.

PTSD is not something that can be cured to the point of extinction. It is something I must live with, in the same way that former alcoholics are always considered to be in recovery. Regression is completely normal but can be mitigated by certain considerations and lifestyle changes.

Even now, years after checking in my badge, I still look in the reflective surfaces of buildings to see who is around me, and what potential threat they pose. I plan escape routes wherever I go, in case of an emergency. Worrying about the hypothetical tends to take away the enjoyment from life, and it can be incredibly tiring. It is a constant battle to consciously rationalise any negative thoughts and feelings that arise in the moment, before they grow uncontrollable. I had spent so long trying to manage my environment and the people around me, sometimes succeeding and other times not. The reality is that there is only so much that any of us can control, but to curb my anxiety I try as much as possible to avoid places or situations that could be triggering for me. For example, the saturation of people, cars or buildings is not ideal, and as much as possible I prefer to spend my time in open spaces or the comfort of my own home.

During the August of 2023 we took a family trip to Scotland, and the day we stopped in Glasgow just so happened to coincide with the Cycling World Championships, which meant the city was heaving. I wasn't expecting the event itself, and certainly wasn't prepared for my reaction to it. We squeezed through the hordes of people who were lining the streets, trying to find somewhere for lunch, and I could feel the panic starting to rise within me at the sound of the helicopter overhead and the sight of so many uniformed officers and police vehicles.

'*Are you okay?*' Chloe enquired anxiously, having noticed my reddened complexion and the tears I was trying so desperately to fight back.

I wasn't, and she understood. Grabbing my hand, she pulled me along, trying to get away from the main street. My auditory processing was distorted, as I could barely hear the whooping and cheering of the public as the cyclists whizzed past; I could only hear the buzz of the police radios all around me. Time seemed to stand still.

We stopped in the large doorway of a shop where I backed up to a wall and for a few minutes focussed only on my breath. Being able to see in front of me, and not feeling as though I needed to look over my shoulder allowed my anxieties to subside and when I felt ready, my loving wife led me and our children to the train station, where we carried on our journey to our final destination of the trip.

For the remainder of the day I was completely fatigued, that was until the time came for me to go to bed and sleep. Like a movie reel, my brain kept showing me events from my past, and I couldn't make it stop. I crept out of the room I was sharing with Rose and headed downstairs to make myself a cup of tea and some toast.

It was the only remedy I could provide myself with in that moment.

After watching several back-to-back episodes of *QI* reruns, I returned to bed and, holding the hand of my youngest daughter, I drifted off to sleep.

The following morning, I jumped straight into the shower and found the motivation to rid myself of a few days' worth of stubble. The sun was shining so straight after breakfast we headed out for a walk down the promenade; our squabbling infants' side-by-side in their double buggy. Everything was going to be okay.

Had I paid more attention to the way I had been feeling for all those years or had a trustworthy sounding board, maybe I would have seen such a diagnosis on the horizon as an inevitable product of all I had experienced. Or even been able to recognise warning signs and symptoms, and head it off years before. But I didn't, and the beast within me reared its ugly head at the worst possible moment, in the presence of my infant child.

It is only through professional help that I have been able to unburden myself of a lot of things that were causing me problems. And as difficult as it was, I am relieved that the negativity that had been previously trapped within me did eventually surface.

It was like holding onto a fart, which nobody can do for too long.

It is always best just to let it go, and with every therapy session I felt relief as all the bad left me.

The past is something I cannot change. All I can do is be gentle with myself and consciously manage any unpleasant memories or intrusive thoughts that undoubtedly seep in from time to time. When I look back, I find it difficult to say that I am proud of anything I did, as I never considered my individual actions as particularly remarkable. I was simply doing my job. But I know such perspective stems from my own discomfort around being able to admit I have achieved something.

Aside from the circumstances that surrounded Alex's death, I don't think there is much I would want to change anyway. Chloe has encouraged me to be more than just satisfied with the impact I had, to even a handful of people. The exact ripple effect of the work I did whilst I was a police officer will always be unknown to me, but I know now that I undoubtedly made a positive difference in the world.

I did it all. Saved lives, driven at incredible speeds, and driven at snail's pace as part of armed convoy taking the big, nasty bastards to court. I did my best to interrupt the enterprise of dozens of generational crime families and put an abrupt end to many dangerous acts and criminal careers. But it was being of service to people after their death I am the proudest of and that gives me the greatest relief; knowing that as one of the last people they encountered on this planet, I exhibited great care for them all.

When I went into the police, I wasn't aware that a clear driver for me in doing that job was to help people, but I know now it was. My more recent work as an executive coach has reminded me that I am largely driven to help others, and helping people change for the better brings me a great deal of personal satisfaction. The most fulfilling aspect of my job now is working with those whose percentage of success is less than their percentage of failure and helping to push the scales and redress the balance somewhat.

Of course, my recovery wouldn't have been quite as seamless without the support of my vibrant and courageous wife; the most eccentric and erratic woman I have ever met. She turned my world upside down but kept me anchored to a point of stability at the same time. To love and to be loved, to be respected, heard, valued and appreciated, are things that we could easily take for granted, but are essential elements of a healthy relationship.

Chloe has helped me find direction and purpose, whilst simultaneously helping me regain my independence, autonomy, and find my own voice. Neither of us are the same people whose eyes met across a corporate meeting room over five years ago. We have grown as individuals, and together as a couple. Instead of seeking to contain me, she has pushed me to develop and expand, and I am now becoming the person I should have always been, the truest version of myself, which had been under a bushel for so long. I am carefree, light, and humorous, just as I was when I was younger.

Chloe and I are two individuals united by love and respect for one another, pulling in the same direction to create a wonderful life for ourselves and our children. Whenever disagreements arise, we swiftly laugh our way out of them.

It is refreshing and rejuvenating for me to be so settled. I am content with where I am and what I have. There is no void that requires filling, and I am allowed to sit and breathe, no longer constantly being pushed to pursue the next materialistic upgrade. I finally understand what it feels like to be truly content, and optimistic for the future.

There is never any need for me to want to escape my home. It is my sanctuary, and I am always relieved to step through the door and feel the love and warmth of my family. For the first time in decades, I feel like an equal in my relationship. I feel I am allowed a voice and an opinion, and the freedom to do things with my children without the implied permission of someone else.

Chloe has challenged me intellectually which caused me to re-evaluate my values and forced me to look at myself in a different way, to give myself a more compassionate review. I owe so much to her.

We communicate on a level I had never previously known. Rightly so, that is the expectation she has always maintained for our relationship. There is an intimacy of knowledge between us, with no fear or judgement.

It was her curiosity to learn all about my past which encouraged me to write this book, and it is only through the process of doing so have I had the chance to recall my experiences and recognise them as pretty spectacular, when whilst I was in the thick of it the job seemed almost mundane. If I had not joined the police, I am not sure what I would have ended up doing, or the person that I would have ended up being, but I feel more like myself now than I have for the last twenty to thirty years.

My initial PTSD induced episode marked the beginning of was the most difficult period of my life and I struggle to glorify it as a life lesson that I have been blessed with. To acknowledge that I was 'broken' was crippling, and for a time I felt so incredibly low. For so long I had been alone with my hurt, but I learnt that it was possible with the right guidance and support to be happy again and rediscover my true self and my true value. Occasionally I still fail to understand why people consider anything I say as valuable, but I know that is just my struggle with shaking off self-doubt.

My demon will always be there; it requires regular management and whilst at times it can be discouraging, I don't begrudge it the space it holds. It is only through its insistence to surface that I have been able to unpick decades of harrowing experiences, ultimately ridding myself of the bad.

I am mature enough now to own my mistakes and process my hardships. I should have spoken to somebody, anybody, about how I felt in my relationship, but the truth is I never really paused to assess my life or even acknowledge the truth to myself. I wish above anything that I had opened up, because it would have saved years of misery. But better late than never.

I am grateful now for the awareness I have of my feelings, and I am healing from my wounds. I am more mindful, more present, and completely grateful for the life I have. It has taken some effort to shift my perspective to the point that allows me to appreciate all the small joys that life offers us daily, but every day I am learning to find pleasure in the little things and not sweat the small stuff. Achieving absolute perfection is unattainable and attempting to reach that mark had driven me into the ground so long. Now I accept I must be satisfied with achieving ninety per cent perfection, and not crucifying myself for the other ten per cent as I would have done previously.

After living as a shadow of myself, and in the shadow of someone else for so many years, I now feel light, like something that has come out of hibernation. I am rested and ready to go. I am whole and repurposed, like a recycled piece of engineering; set to a new task with a whole new life ahead of it. There are still days that for no reason at all, I feel low and unworthy, and there are days when I am reminded more of the loss of my friend. But as it is for anybody, mental health should be considered as operating on a spectrum, and it is always subject to change. It is a helpful reminder of the fact that I am only human after all.

55

The experience I have of wrestling with mental health challenges, is that they are profoundly consuming, and for anybody navigating the complexities of trauma, or depression, or anxiety; know that you are not alone. The episodes that ultimately compelled me to seek help were undoubtedly the darkest chapters of my life, and I was plagued with feelings of worthlessness. In those bleak moments, where I considered myself a threat to those nearest to me, I thought the world would have been better off without me. It was only with Chloe's love and support that I was able to shed those accumulated experiences and feelings that had held me back.

We each have our own unique experiences, and therefore individual paths towards healing.

If you are struggling with something, seek help. It is there, and it works, if you commit to it. By persevering through the discomfort of formal therapy, I was able to emerge from a dark space, into one significantly lighter.

For so long, I had been perpetually on alert; my senses heightened to the degree that every situation morphed into a potential threat, and I felt an overwhelming compulsion to exert control over every aspect of my environment to protect myself from unseen dangers, but they were really only lurking in my consciousness. It was a state I had been living in for such an extended period, oscillating between moments of terrifying clarity and episodes of blind panic. The duality of my existence made it difficult to discern when to let my guard down. The skills I had developed to keep myself safe at work, had become shackles that hindered me from experiencing any semblance of peace.

We can't always control external circumstances, but we can choose how we respond to them. Whilst you can't stop it from raining, you can choose to wear a coat.

To embark on the journey towards a new life, I had to shed layers of my old existence, which ultimately revealed a healthier core underneath. As I continue to peel back the layers, I have realised that shedding my old self is not the end goal, but a continuous journey to work through the remnants of my past. It involves a conscious effort to embrace vulnerability, recognise my inherent value and a forge a life defined not by fear, but by strength, resilience, and love. Each layer I shed brings me closer to my authentic self, and each step forward is a testament to my commitment to healing.

Reflecting on my past, I wonder how things could have been different had I ever had a safe space for open dialogue, a space free from judgement where I could have expressed my fears and vulnerabilities. But wondering doesn't change the present, and I am satisfied that now I am exactly where I am supposed to be; surrounded by people who love and value me. Life truly doesn't get any better than that.

After years of seeing the worst in people, and looking only for the bad that surrounded me, I am learning to look for and see the good instead. My hope is to truly embrace life, still with caution but without any fear. I take each day as it comes, one at a time, and that is all any of us can ever really do.